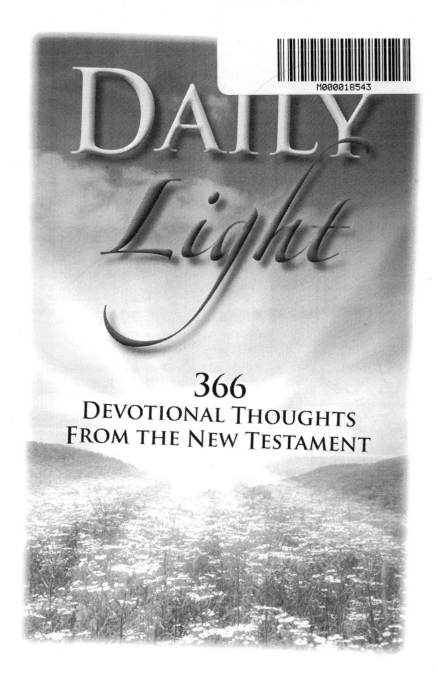

DAILY *Light*

366
DEVOTIONAL THOUGHTS
FROM THE NEW TESTAMENT

PUBLISHED BY
HELP4U PUBLICATIONS
CHESTERTON, IN

HELP4U
PUBLICATIONS

Daily Light: Devotional Thoughts from the New Testament,
Second Edition
by David J. Olson
Copyright©2013, 2018 by David J. Olson

ISBN 978-1-940089-42-3

www.Help4Upublications.com

Credits: Photo from Canstockphoto.com

All Scripture quotations are from the *King James Bible.*

DEDICATION

To our faithful brethren in Zambia–
Thank you for your love, prayers, and friendship.
We miss you immensely but know God's plan is best.
"But continue thou..."

PREFACE

"Sometimes I just don't get anything out of the Bible when I read it," was a comment I overheard a church member make to my wife. This served as confirmation that I should press on with my goal of writing a daily devotional. Not only did I want the people in our ministry to read the Bible, I also wanted them to discover a truth each day that they could apply to their lives. The result of my desire to help our people is *Daily Light*.

This book is designed to provide the reader with a schedule to read through the New Testament in a year's time. Such a goal can be accomplished by reading the passage indicated in each day's heading. Additionally, one thought from the daily reading is included to provide either a challenge or promise for the day.

Used for either personal or family devotions, this book provides practical insight for daily living. Because the book is not necessarily intended to be a commentary, it can be used as a stand-alone devotional even if you follow another Bible reading schedule.

Just remember that a devotional book should never take the place of personal Bible reading. If you seek the Lord, He will give you thoughts and ideas that these pages could never provide. Therefore, the use of any devotional book should simply be a supplement to your own meditation of the Scriptures.

Are you ready to begin a journey through the New Testament? As you read, be sure to look for *Daily Light*!

INTRODUCTION

Light from the sun is amazing—it guides, brightens, warms, and cheers. What the sun does for the body, the Bible does for the soul. God's Word guides our steps, illuminates our path, warms our heart, and cheers our countenance. Although every Christian faces periods of difficulty and darkness, God's Word provides light to dispel the shadows of doubt and fear. The Psalmist exclaimed, *"Thy word is a lamp unto my feet, and a light unto my path."* (Psalm 119:105) Whether on the mountaintop or in the valley, every servant of the Lord needs heavenly sunshine for his journey.

Personally, the Bible has provided hope when discouraged, guidance when uncertain, and peace when troubled. While serving as a missionary in Zambia, Africa, for ten years, my faith was greatly tested. At times, I often wondered if I could meet the challenges. Whether I faced dysentery, African tick-bite fever, near-death experiences, opposition from government officials, threats, false accusations, encounters with poisonous snakes, or mysterious illnesses, God's Word never failed to sustain me. It was in the midst of these struggles that many of the pages of this book were penned. I rejoice that the Lord has used my trials to draw me nearer to Himself and strengthen me through His Word. He has repeatedly reminded me of His goodness, challenged me to persevere, and provided me with promises to cling to just when I needed them most. Though your trials may differ from mine, God's Word provides exactly what you need to get through them.

It is my prayer that the rays of hope that God has graciously bestowed upon me will be a blessing to others. The best thing any believer can do when facing affliction is to get his eyes off of his problems and begin to focus on the promises of God. Knowing that the Lord is *"a very present help in trouble"* is wonderful reassurance. When tempted to quit or complain, the necessary remedy for such a bleak condition is daily light from God's Word.

While I hope that you will glean a blessing from the content of this book, I also desire that you will find many gems of your own while searching the Scriptures. Never underestimate the power of the Bible to transform your life. A consistent, heartfelt devotional time will help prevent disobedience, discouragement, and disappointment. Though you may never take the time to write your discoveries in a book, I hope you will gather life-changing truths from your own study of God's Word.

Dave Olson
December, 2013

For thou wilt light my candle:
the LORD my God will enlighten my darkness.
Psalm 18:28

*...they shall call his name Emmanuel, which being interpreted is,
God with us. Matthew 1:23*

Doctrinally we know that Jesus was God in the flesh. Unfortunately, some religions deny the truth of the Trinity, and many modern Bible versions remove references to Christ's deity from their pages. We are assured that the birth of Jesus was a fulfillment of prophecy. Jehovah had promised to visit His people and did so when Christ was born. What a tremendous truth!

Surely we must stand for the truth of the Trinity, but we must not lose sight of the daily reality that God is truly with us. If Jesus is your Savior, He is with you today amidst all of your trials, turmoil, temptations, and toil. Never allow doctrinal truth to lose its significance in your daily experience. Whatever you face this day, remember that God is with you. What can you fear if that be the case?

Because He is with you, you have all of the wisdom you need for your decisions, all the strength you need for your weaknesses, and all the comfort you need for your heartaches. Whatever obstacle confronts you today, take heart and be courageous—God is with you!

*And when they were come into the house, they saw the young child with
Mary his mother, and fell down, and worshipped him: and when they had
opened their treasures, they presented unto him gifts; gold, and
frankincense, and myrrh. Matthew 2:11*

These wise men had already spent a great deal of time and money to make their long journey. Now, after all the expense and effort, they were thrilled to do more. They sacrificially *"opened their treasures."*

Many of us can say that we have already done something for our Lord, but where is the attitude that wants to continue giving of self and substance? True worship leads to giving gifts voluntarily out of a heart of joy and gratitude. We all have our "sacred cows" that we fear to make available to the Lord, or it may be we think we have done enough already. Whatever the case, we must realize that giving stems from humility and true worship.

Perhaps it is not a material treasure that you have withheld from the Lord but a dream, aspiration, or plan for your life. Don't hoard anything! Open your treasure and give God a worthy sacrifice. After all Christ has given you, what will you offer Him?

And think not to say within yourselves, We have Abraham to our father:
for I say unto you, that God is able of these stones to raise up
children unto Abraham. Matthew 3:9

God had previously brought forth water out of a rock, so why should it be so hard to believe that He could raise up children from stones lying around on the ground? The key phrase to remember is that *"God is able!"*

If cold, lifeless stones could receive life, that should encourage us indeed. It makes it possible for our hard, frosty hearts to also receive new life. As indifferent as you may have become, God is able to change your heart! Possibly you don't have the burden for souls or the desire for prayer that you once had. God is able to warm your soul and renew the fire that kindled in time past.

You may have tried to stir the embers yourself and found your efforts futile. That's because you are lacking something. Man has never had the power to revive himself. Take these words, *"God is able,"* straight to the throne and ask our life-giving Lord to make the promise true. What may seem impossible to you is not only possible with God but promised.

That it might be fulfilled which was spoken by Esaias the prophet...
Matthew 4:14

Jesus had just left Nazareth and moved to Capernaum for the sole reason of fulfilling a prophecy made by Isaiah. Christ provides us with a wonderful example to follow—He repeatedly did things *"that it might be fulfilled."* His life was about fulfilling the Word of God, which was, in fact, fulfilling the will of God.

Our every step and action today must be with a goal to fulfill God's Word. In some way we must strive to do something He wants us to do. Shall we witness to a lost soul or encourage a fellow believer? In Jesus' case He left his hometown to fulfill God's will, and it may be that we will be called upon to leave something dear to us for the same purpose.

Have not many missionaries left their families, friends, and comforts behind with the goal that God's will be fulfilled? Can we not make a similar sacrifice? Perhaps we could give up an evening or Saturday for a ministry that would help fulfill God's will of evangelizing this lost world.

Blessed are they which do hunger and thirst after righteousness:
for they shall be filled. Matthew 5:6

We all want to be happy, but often happiness is preceded by a time of sorrow and sadness. Here is a promise to those who are in such a case today. Perhaps you are not satisfied with your Christian life; you sense an emptiness and dryness that should not be there.

Don't wallow in your misery—claim God's promise! Don't let the hunger pangs leave you feeling weak. It is time to crave the righteousness that will both please God and satisfy your inner man. You can have revival and victory over a hollow life.

When very thirsty, you not only long for a drink but seek one. When your soul is hungry and parched for the right things, God will fill you up if you ask Him. Remember His words to the children of Israel, *"...open thy mouth wide, and I will fill it."* (Psalm 81:10) He likes to satisfy those who want His goodness. Cheer up! Your sorrow shall soon be turned to joy. A man driving his car with the gauge on empty gets desperate for a gas station; but once he fills up with fuel, he is greatly relieved. Will it not be an even grander feeling when God fills you with His righteousness?

But I say unto you, Love your enemies, bless them that curse you, do
good to them that hate you, and pray for them which despitefully
use you, and persecute you... Matthew 5:44

Some commands in the Bible may seem more difficult than others, and to many of us, this is one of them indeed. We are to both love and bless our enemies! It is more natural to retaliate against those who oppose us; and if it does not come out in our actions, it does in our attitude.

We tend to pat ourselves on the back and think we have done well in not cursing them or plotting for their fall. However, we have not kept the Lord's command until we love and bless them! We must do more than simply refrain ourselves from evil. We must do good towards them, speak kind words to them, and pray for them.

Praise God if you have not returned evil for evil, but go the next step and overcome evil with good. This may seem difficult, but if practiced you will experience more of the peace of God in your heart. Try it! If it doesn't change your enemy, it will at least change you.

Take heed that ye do not your alms before men, to be seen of them: otherwise ye have no reward of your Father which is in heaven... That thine alms may be in secret: and thy Father which seeth in secret himself shall reward thee openly... Matthew 6:1, 4

Our text contains both a prod and a promise. We are cautioned not to do our good deeds with the intention of being seen of men. If we try to impress others, God is not impressed! However, doing things for God's audience gains His undivided attention and richest blessings.

Earlier in this Gospel, Jesus commanded us to let our light shine so men may see our good works. There is no contradiction here. We are not to hide everything from man, but we are not to do it for their praise! The motive must be that God gets the glory, not us. Isn't this one of our biggest problems? We want to look good in the eyes of men and gain their praise, but that is shallow and unrewarding.

When we do our good deeds to gain God's attention, He promises to reward us so bountifully that others will notice. However, when we seek to gain favor with men, God withholds His reward. What are you living for? Are you aiming to promote yourself or glorify God? By the way, God's blessings are more enduring than man's short-lived attention.

And the rain descended, and the floods came, and the winds blew, and beat upon that house; and it fell: and great was the fall of it.
Matthew 7:27

This is the fate of all who hear our Lord's commands but refuse to do them. This parable tells of two men who built separate houses. Both homes were tested by the storms of life, and the foolish man's house was destroyed. He was foolish because he had obviously been instructed never to build on sand. However, he thought he knew better than the experts. We often act the same way. Although we know what we ought to do, we think we have a good reason to do otherwise.

What has the Lord told you to do? Failure to obey will surely result in a ruined life. As surely as God can hold one up, He can cause another to fall. However, the Scripture tells us it will be a great fall!

We may be like the builder in the story who, no doubt, built a beautiful structure. Everything may appear wonderful on the outside, but it will all crumble if we have not laid the foundation of complete obedience. Don't live to look good—live to be good.

And he saith unto them, Why are ye fearful, O ye of little faith? Then he arose, and rebuked the winds and the sea; and there was a great calm.
Matthew 8:26

Jesus and His disciples had entered into a ship to sail across the Sea of Galilee, and a fierce storm arose that threatened the ship while the Lord slept calmly. In a panic, the disciples woke up Jesus, thinking they were all going to perish.

Likewise, a great tempest is sure to arise in your life—perhaps even today! Are you ready, or do you timidly walk through life always expecting the next crisis? Don't let your trial find you fearful and faithless like the disciples. Remember that Jesus is still with you even in the storms of life! With Him by your side, you can face anything.

Your faith can rebuke the winds of adversity and bring a great calm. Jesus asked the twelve, *"Why are ye fearful, O ye of little faith?"* The answer was found in His question: they had little faith. Don't quit when things are the most difficult; if ever there was a need for faith, it is at such a time. Though the gales may blast and the tempests rage, we will not fear because our Lord is near!

And as Jesus passed forth from thence, he saw a man, named Matthew, sitting at the receipt of custom: and he saith unto him, Follow me. And he arose, and followed him. Matthew 9:9

The man whom Christ saw was Matthew, the tax collector. When others beheld someone of such a profession, they saw corruption and felt contempt; but Jesus saw something different. He saw a future disciple!

Too often we see things as they are and not as they could be. People did not want to keep company with tax collectors, but Jesus expressed the opposite when He said, *"Follow me."*

Notice that all of this happened *"as Jesus passed forth."* Through life we need to be observant of those we pass on a daily basis. God may have a great plan for some, and we need to be willing to give them an opportunity. I'm glad Jesus did not pass me by!

So often we judge who would and who would not be a good disciple. Most of us would have passed by Matthew and never given him a chance. Let us be careful not to pass so many by without trying to get them to follow the Savior. Perhaps we could be like Andrew and bring a great Simon Peter to the Master's service. Let's try to see as Jesus does.

And when the devil was cast out, the dumb spake: and the multitudes
marvelled, saying, It was never so seen in Israel. Matthew 9:33

The Lord Jesus had just cast a foul demon out of a dumb man, and afterwards that man could speak. This was a true miracle which caused the people to be amazed, and such is the purpose of all miracles— to bring glory to the Lord. It is always a testimony of the power of God when people say, *"It was never so seen."* Don't you long to hear similar words uttered by those around us?

That same God is still able to do things that have never been seen. May this be a motivation to pray that God will do something big to cause people to witness His splendor and glory. As surely as there is a devil to afflict, there is an Almighty God to cast him out. He is the God of the *"never so seen"* and still wants to prove Himself to us today.

You may be in a difficult situation and cannot see the way out, but you must have courage! Faith is the evidence of things not seen; and when we exercise faith, the *"never so seen"* will be manifested. That is the reward of faith! Oh, to be able to believe God enough to bring such blessings down from heaven!

And when he had called unto him his twelve disciples, he gave them
power against unclean spirits, to cast them out, and to heal all manner of
sickness and all manner of disease. Matthew 10:1

What a blessing to see that when God calls people to a task, He also gives them power to accomplish it! What has the Lord called you to do? Fear not to undertake your duty even if it seems too difficult for you. How would you like to have been one of the disciples and told to go cast out some powerful, hideous, and abusive demons? That would have put fear in many of us.

Paul said that Jesus *"enabled"* him and put him into the ministry. Whatever your ministry may be, God gives an ability to match the obligation. This promise is true not only for a pastor but also for a soulwinner, Sunday School teacher, or bus worker. Go ahead and fulfill your calling in the strength of the Lord.

When you begin to feel overwhelmed at the responsibilities you have in God's service, remember what Jesus did for His other disciples— *"when he had called...he gave them power."* What more assurance do you need? What He has done for others He can do for you!

He that findeth his life shall lose it: and he that loseth his life for
my sake shall find it. Matthew 10:39

God's economy is unlike the world's. For example, a business man who loses money certainly does not think he has found it. Also, a child who loses a toy would never feel he has gained anything by the loss. So, people from all stations in life cannot understand how you can gain something by losing it.

However, God's ways outshine conventional wisdom. How can this truth of losing life lead to finding life? Let me illustrate by using a man who had been reluctant to go soulwinning. He finally decided to come out one Saturday for our church's soulwinning program. He and I visited his friend from work, and the next day that friend came to church and got saved. The one who lost his life by giving up part of his Saturday actually found it through the joy of his friend's salvation.

Although we say that we believe this truth, our daily experience is often just the opposite. We find ourselves trying to save our life rather than lose it. Why? We think we know better than God. Let go of your life today and see what God can do!

The Son of man came eating and drinking, and they say, Behold a man
gluttonous, and a winebibber, a friend of publicans and sinners.
Matthew 11:19

How quick the world is to accuse the righteous! Learn one thing— you can never please and satisfy the ungodly. They were upset because John the Baptist fasted and angered because Jesus ate with sinners. Both were sent from God, and the world found fault with both of them. However, what they saw as a fault, we see as a blessing!

Jesus went to the wicked, not to fellowship in their sin but rather to pull them out of it. We, too, have been guilty of terrible deeds at times and can take solace that the Lord is ready to visit us with merciful deliverance. Are you a sinner drowning in a tide of evil? If so, Jesus is your Friend, and He is quick to rescue all who cry out for mercy.

When I am out of sorts and overwhelmed with guilt, the devil wants me to forget about the kindness of my Friend. However, Jesus is a faithful Friend that *"sticketh closer than a brother."* Never fear that you are too wicked to receive help from Jesus. After all, He is *"a friend of...sinners."*

A bruised reed shall he not break, and smoking flax shall he not quench...
Matthew 12:20

A reed is not very strong to begin with, much less a bruised one. Its usefulness is limited, and its existence is precarious. Like the reed, we may become weak and wilted, but Christ is not ready to discard us!

Let us also consider the smoking flax. It may not be burning brightly; but as long as there is a little glow, there is yet hope for a flame. Our gracious Lord wants us to be on fire for Him; and if the flames of earnestness are but a faint glow, He will not extinguish them. He is kind and gentle when we are weak yet willing.

This is a great reminder of how Jesus deals with us, but it should also be an example of how we ought to treat others. As long as there is still hope for a fellow believer to be useful, we should never be so harsh as to break his spirit or extinguish his desire. He may yet gain strength and come ablaze for the Lord! Fanning the smoking embers with encouragement and prayer may bring back the fire in an erring one.

Rebukes are necessary at times, but they can be worked up in the flesh. On the contrary, gentleness is a fruit of the Spirit and a Christ-like quality. Let us be sure our attitude is what the Master would display!

He that is not with me is against me; and he that gathereth not with me
scattereth abroad. Matthew 12:30

Even in Jesus' day there were those who were uncommitted but thought they were not so bad. Man struggles with trying to be accepted by the world and by God at the same time, but no one has ever succeeded in this endeavor! Jesus made it clear that if we are not with Him we are against Him. There is no middle ground.

Are we with Him when we indulge in worldly amusements or when among bad friends? No. We are against Him at such times. If we are not actively gathering souls for His kingdom, we are scattering and preventing people from being saved. We cannot engage in worldly conversations and expect to win our friends to Christ. In such a case we are pushing them farther away from the Savior.

We like to justify ourselves by saying, "I may not be on fire for God as I should, but at least I'm not as bad as others." This kind of reasoning crumbles in the light of Christ's teaching. Get close to Him or you will be, in fact, against Him.

When any one heareth the word of the kingdom, and understandeth it not, then cometh the wicked one, and catcheth away that which was sown in his heart.   Matthew 13:19

When the Word of God goes forth, Satan is not happy because he knows that God's Word has power to save, sanctify, and settle our poor, destitute souls. Before the Word takes root in our hearts, the devil tries to snatch it away with doubts and disbelief. He wants us to question what we have heard and challenge it in our hearts. He wants us to rebel against it, or at the very least, ignore it.

Always receive the Word and endeavor to understand its application to your life. Rejecting it or resisting it surely invites the devil to work his wiles in your life and steal the blessing God wanted to give you. So, read your Bible with an open heart and listen to Bible preaching with a ready ear. Don't be quick to disagree or to justify yourself.

The seed is a source of life, and Satan wants to prevent every lost soul from being regenerated and every backslidden saint from being restored. He hates life! If you wish to receive eternal life or enjoy a revived spirit, you must accept the Word and seek to understand it.

And he did not many mighty works there because of their unbelief.
Matthew 13:58

How sad to see Almighty God limited by unbelieving men! This is a familiar verse and is often considered alone, out of its context. However, a deeper sense of the truth is gleaned when considering the full story. It is true that unbelief hinders the wonders that God is prepared to perform in our lives, but what is the source of our unbelief?

The people in Nazareth had either witnessed or heard of Christ's miracles. They said, *"Whence hath this man this wisdom, and these mighty works?"* The problem was not that they did not know of His power; the problem was that they did not accept His authority in their lives. To them He was just *"the carpenter's son."*

How often do we reject His authority in our lives? When we fail to submit and obey, He decides not to do many mighty works among us. If *"not many mighty works"* describes your life, it is because you have refused to let Jesus rule your life in some area; and that is the unbelief mentioned in this passage.

For Herod had laid hold on John, and bound him, and put him in prison
for Herodias' sake, his brother Philip's wife. For John said unto him,
It is not lawful for thee to have her. Matthew 14:3-4

Jesus said that John the Baptist was a great man, and one of the things that made him great was his frankness. He boldly proclaimed God's Word and preached righteousness at any cost. He did so to every individual regardless of his status or position in life, including the formidable king Herod.

Today, we call John the Baptist great, but in his day, many did not like him. Likewise, men of God in our generation are often despised for confronting us with things that are *"not lawful."* We need unflinching men to tell us what we may not always want to hear. Those who have such a man should not be offended when he does his job.

How many preachers would be in prison if angry people in the pews had the authority that Herod had? Pastors may not be bound with chains, but they are often locked out of the hearts of the people they are trying to help. Sadly, many preacher back down from their bold stand to regain favor with the rebels. We need men who will preach the truth at any cost!

JAN. 20   WHAT COMES OUT IS REVEALING   MATT. 15:1-20

But those things which proceed out of the mouth come forth from
the heart; and they defile the man. Matthew 15:18

What comes out of our mouths comes from our hearts. When our mouths reveal what is in our hearts, we go into denial saying, "Oh, I didn't really mean what I said." What kind of apology is that? A lie! Surely, foolish hearts utter foolish words, and angry hearts bring forth angry words. Something cannot come out unless it was first within.

After saying something terrible, have you ever cried, "Where did that come from?" It came from your corrupt nature! Discovering the hideousness of your heart may be humbling, but ignoring it is harmful. Jesus said that these utterings *"defile the man."* Ill speech has a way of tainting and tarnishing a man's character.

When a bucket draws contaminated water from a well, you understand that the problem is within the well—not the bucket. In the same way, the words of our mouths betray the pollution that is in our evil hearts. The next time ugly words come out, acknowledge the wickedness of your heart and make quick confession to God. Failure to deal with your heart will never correct the problem with your mouth.

But he answered her not a word. And his disciples came and besought him, saying, Send her away; for she crieth after us.   Matthew 15:23

The Syrophoenician woman had asked Jesus for help with her daughter, who was grievously vexed with a demon; and we can only imagine the deep distress she felt for her little girl. When no answer came from the Master, she turned to His disciples; but their response was cold and harsh as they said, *"Send her away; for she crieth after us."*

How often do we treat people in a similar fashion? We tend to run low on patience with some who demand our time and attention. The disciples were insensitive to her plight and bothered by her request. We must understand that people are hurting in this dark world, and we must not be hardened by their cries for help. Frequently, appeals for assistance are not as straightforward as the one made by the woman. Sometimes people hint around that they have a need in order to see if we are willing to recognize their distress, but we purposely ignore the hint.

Jesus was not callous toward the woman's problem. He eventually healed her daughter. Let us resolve to help those who are hurting instead of being annoyed with them. Be more patient with those who seek help from you, and rid yourself of the attitude which says, *"Send her away."*

But he turned, and said unto Peter, Get thee behind me, Satan: thou art an offence unto me: for thou savourest not the things that be of God, but those that be of men.   Matthew 16:23

These were indeed stinging words spoken by the Savior to Peter. Only six verses previously Jesus had called Peter, *"blessed."* From this we learn that our actions may please the Lord on one occasion, but that does not prevent us from backsliding soon after.

What was such an offense to the Lord? Peter had disagreed with Jesus. The Lord had foretold of His coming crucifixion, but Peter refused to accept it saying, *"This shall not be."* Can you imagine disagreeing with Jesus and trying to persuade Him that His will was not the proper direction to follow? I think we are guilty of this more than we realize. When we follow our reasoning over God's revealed will, it is always an offense to Him. It is not our position to argue but to agree.

Obviously Satan is the source of all rebellion and is ready to sow the seeds of discontent in our hearts. Therefore, no matter how difficult God's will may seem, be ready to accept it to avoid being an offense. Jesus followed the rebuke by saying, *"If any man will come after me, let him deny himself."* Deny the will of self, not the will of God.

Notwithstanding, lest we should offend them, go thou to the sea, and cast an hook, and take up the fish that first cometh up; and when thou hast opened his mouth, thou shalt find a piece of money: that take, and give unto them for me and thee. Matthew 17:27

God cares for His own, and this fact is visible throughout the pages of the Bible. He can send ravens to deliver food without nibbling on it themselves, feed thousands with a boy's lunch, and pay taxes with money from a fish's mouth. God is unlimited in His resources and unmatched in His delivery!

Should we ever doubt that He will take care of us and meet our needs? When our situation seems impossible, God's provision can come from the least likely places. Praise God from Whom all blessings flow!

In our text, the money was waiting to be found. Peter simply had to follow Christ's command. Likewise, God's provision for us is already prepared, and we will find it while on the pathway of obedience. How can we be idle and wait for God's portion to mysteriously appear when we fail to put our feet to work and move in the direction He has pointed us? Let us hasten to do our part knowing that God will do His.

Whosoever therefore shall humble himself as this little child, the same is greatest in the kingdom of heaven. Matthew 18:4

Mankind is obsessed with becoming great. Millions are trying to climb the ladder of success at any cost as they attempt to make a name for themselves. There are manuals and books about how to be the best in about any field imaginable. Believe it or not, this obsession with greatness is not a new phenomenon; the disciples had been infected by it.

When the disciples asked Jesus about the subject, He called a little child to illustrate His point. Children have no authority and little influence; they have a low station in society. Christ wants us to humble ourselves like a child, not seeking greatness or pompous position. Pride is the elevation of self, and humility is the opposite.

Jesus did not teach against holding important offices in life. Some of the disciples would later be called to fill such positions. Our Lord simply wanted His followers to be humble enough to be useful. He went on to say that the great one will *"humble himself."* So, greatness becomes a choice of the individual, but it is not attained by pursuit. It finds us when our quest for it dissolves. Then, God can lift us up in due time.

*Shouldest not thou also have had compassion on thy fellowservant,
even as I had pity on thee? Matthew 18:33*

Gratitude shows up not only in our attitude but in our actions. When
someone has done something wonderful for us, it ought to inspire us
to do the same for another. In our text, the servant who was forgiven
much was reproved for not treating his fellow the same way he had been
treated. Because he had received pity and forgiveness, he should have
understood the predicament of his own debtor. He knew the panic and
desperation of being unable to pay his bills, but how soon he forgot when
someone owed him!

Oh, how much the Lord has forgiven us! Shall we not be willing to
forgive others? If we have received mercy, should we not show the
same? We know what it is like to carry the load of guilt and misery
because of our foolish deeds, and we must empathize with those who
find themselves in the same dilemma. Having received the love and
forgiveness of Christ, we should give the same to others. *"Shouldest not
thou...?"* How can we forget the pity displayed by our loving Lord?
Pass on to others what Christ has done for you.

*Verily I say unto you, That a rich man shall hardly enter into the
kingdom of heaven... Who then can be saved?...With men this is
impossible; but with God all things are possible.
Matthew 19:23, 25, 26*

The disciples were astonished at how difficult it would be for rich
people to be saved. They even seemed to lose hope for the common
man when they asked, *"Who then can be saved?"*

However, those impossible situations should not discourage us from
praying and witnessing. Even the most difficult people can be saved
with the help of God. Some men are so hardened in sin that it seems
impossible for them to get saved, but God can soften their hearts and
make it possible if they are willing. He knows what can touch a heart
and influence the will. The impossible becomes possible when
individuals exercise their free will in response to God's conviction.

The same Lord that opened Lydia's heart has also promised to draw
all men to Himself. Jesus said, *"with God all things are possible."* So,
let us not give up hope for anybody. After all, even the chief of sinners
was saved! Be earnest in prayer and work to persuade men to trust
Christ. It is possible!

And when they had received it, they murmured against
the goodman of the house... Matthew 20:11

What an interesting paradox it is to murmur against the goodman. The men in the story had no job, but the householder agreed to hire them for a full day's wage. When the man hired others later in the day, he graciously paid them a full day's wage, too. The men who worked all day thought it was not fair and began to complain. However, they received what they had agreed upon before they started work that day, and they forgot that they were fortunate enough to have a job.

How frequently we think God is not fair to us! We see others who have it easier or seem to receive more blessings than we do, and our attitude sours to the place we begin to complain about the Goodman, God. We have forgotten that we have more than we deserve. Our Lord has been more than fair in all of His dealings with us. When someone else is blessed more than you, learn to rejoice instead of murmur. Because God has been good to others does not mean He has been unfair to you. Stop complaining, and be thankful for all you have received.

And Jesus stood still, and called them, and said, What will ye
that I shall do unto you? Matthew 20:32

A great multitude followed Jesus as He left the city of Jericho. There is no doubt that many crowded about Him seeking some sort of assistance; but of all the things that captured His attention that day, it was a cry for mercy. Jesus was interested in two blind men that the rest of the crowd had passed by with little or no concern. Do you feel overlooked by others? That is no problem because they can do little for you anyway.

Our Lord is never too busy to stop and listen to a humble appeal by the needy. Perhaps you really require assistance with something today. Follow the example of these blind men in our story who had no other hope than to cry out to God in desperation.

Religion has confused many about prayer with false notions such as "name it and claim it," vain repetitions, and demanding things from God. However, what grabs the attention of the Master is a cry for mercy; and without this attitude, He may pass us by. As we humbly cast ourselves and our needs upon the Lord, He will stand still and hear our requests. Then, we will hear those gracious words, *"What will ye that I shall do unto you?"* Can we not rejoice that He is willing and able to help?

....Verily I say unto you, If ye have faith, and doubt not...it shall be done.
Matthew 21:21

Doubt is the enemy of our faith and a hindrance to our prayers. It has prevented us from receiving many blessings from our benevolent God. He has not only told us that help is available but also how to gain that help. Oh, but then we hear the words, *"doubt not."* Doubt is a terrible thing. It kills a prayer before it even leaves our lips. Doubt is filled with suspicion and questions the character of the One who has spoken. Is there any shortcoming in our God? Has He ever allowed one promise to go unfulfilled? Has He failed you in the past in any way? What is there to doubt about God?

It may be that we doubt men because they have lied to us in the past or failed to keep their word. However, God is truth and has always kept every one of His promises. He is not a shady character with a bad reputation. Therefore, let us stop treating the all-gracious God as we do a proven sinner. Let us trust Him completely and cast away all doubt. Then, *"it shall be done"* as we have requested.

He answered and said, I will not: but afterward he repented, and went.
Matthew 21:29

These words were spoken by a son who had been instructed of his father to go to the vineyard and work. For a son to say, *"I will not,"* to his father is a serious offense and is nothing short of stubborn rebellion. We are shocked when we hear such language coming from children, but are we not guilty of the same attitude at times?

When our heavenly Father tells us to do a thing, what is our reaction? We may not be so bold as to utter the same words as the son in the parable, but we often have the same attitude of refusal. We make excuses why we can't do it, or we put it off until it is more convenient for us. No proper father allows such willful disregard of his commands. Shall our heavenly Father allow us to escape chastisement when we blatantly disobey? How can we expect the blessings of God in our lives when we are knowingly disobedient?

The only solution is to do what the obstinate son did—*"he repented, and went."* It may be that you have slipped into a slovenly, backslidden condition. Arise and go do the will of the Father! He will be merciful when He sees His prodigal coming back to Him in broken repentance.

Tell us therefore, What thinkest thou? Matthew 22:17

The Pharisees had sent men to set a trap for Jesus, hoping to entangle Him. Their question was not out of good will or from a desire to know the truth. They had no heart to hear the answer.

We may not set out to find fault with Christ's Words, but we may be guilty of disregarding what He thinks about certain matters. When we have no heart to receive God's instruction, we are not much better than the hypocrites in our text. They may have asked the question out of spite, but at times we fail to ask the question at all!

When contemplating decisions in life, we would do well to ask the Lord, *"What thinkest thou?"* We should ask Him that when sitting in church, reading our Bibles, and throughout the day. Shouldn't we want to know what He thinks about every area of our lives? Ask Him right now, and then be willing to accept His answers.

John said, *"God is greater than our heart, and knoweth all things."* (I John 3:20) Since He knows all things, why would we ever refuse to ask Him His thoughts? The truth of the matter is that we don't want to know because we don't want to be accountable to do what He says. How sad!

Jesus answered and said unto them, Ye do err, not knowing the scriptures, nor the power of God. Matthew 22:29

Not many of us like to be told we are wrong. Our text shows Jesus telling the Sadducees that they erred concerning their disbelief in the resurrection. Millions of people today are blinded by Satan and have been led into doctrinal error, too. How can this be?

Jesus gave us the answer: *"Ye do err, not knowing the scriptures."* When we trust the doctrine of men or our own human reasoning, it will surely lead to error. The diligent study of God's Word is the only way to be right in our thinking. If you do not faithfully study the Bible, you will err also.

The error is not only an intellectual failure but also a practical one— *"not knowing...the power of God."* Our ignorance of the Scriptures will definitely limit our faith in experiencing the miracles of God in our lives. Are you missing the power of God in your daily walk? If so, *"Ye do err."* Get your mind and life straightened out by getting to know the Scriptures!

But all their works they do for to be seen of men... Matthew 23:5

To be a man-pleaser ranks among the most shallow religious experiences. The "spiritual" leaders in Christ's day had degenerated to such a low state that they were more concerned about looking good than being good. Many Christians today are not much better, worrying more about what peers think than what God knows to be true. Religious hypocrites want *"to be seen of men,"* but true servants of God notice only the Lord in the audience! Children watch to see if their parents are looking, employees are concerned with what the boss sees, and church members are wary of how things appear to the preacher.

All of this preoccupation with what our fellows think would be sorted out if we remembered that God is watching! Live for Him, and you will have the approval of the right people as a consequence. Don't worry if your labor of love goes unnoticed. God won't forget your deeds when it is time to dole out the heavenly rewards. Have you caught yourself trying to display your good works to others? You will be tempted to compromise your convictions in order to please men, but yielding will lead to shame. The way to live a guiltless life is to strive to please only the Lord.

Ye blind guides, which strain at a gnat, and swallow a camel.
Matthew 23:24

The Pharisees were self-deceived, and Jesus revealed their attitude using the illustration of the gnat and the camel. The gnat is a very small insect that would get into their water and oil pots. Because gnats were considered unclean under Jewish Law, they would be strained out of the liquid before use. They took great pride in being right in the little areas of life but focused less on the more important areas.

The camel was also an unclean animal, and Jesus pointed out that they would easily partake of a large sin despite being right in the small areas of life. Don't be deceived into thinking you are spiritual because of the little things that you think you do right. Consider the example of a man who would not wear wire-rimmed glasses because he said they were worldly. Later, that same "holy" man was found to be an adulterer. He should have been more careful about what his eyes were looking at, rather than what his eyes were looking through! True holiness is not based on pride. Never neglect *"the weightier matters of the law."*

And many false prophets shall rise, and shall deceive many. Matthew 24:11

Jesus promised that many false prophets would rise in the end times and that many individuals would be deceived. The fact that they will be successful proves that they have some appeal. Naturally, the Lord does not want any of His people to be misled.

Already, many have risen and preach a false gospel. For example, men claim to be prophets with the ability to heal. When I was in the eighth grade, a classmate of mine went to a so-called healing crusade; he returned to school declaring that he was healed, but within a few months he was dead. He was one of millions who have been deceived by these false prophets Jesus warned about. Additionally, the prosperity gospel has become popular with promises of health and wealth. Unfortunately, the only ones getting rich are the crooked preachers! Now, we have the emerging church which dares to say they do not preach against sin, boasting that there is nothing negative in their message. We can be sure that there will be more similar false doctrines on the horizon.

All of these false teachings are popular today, proving that the Jesus' words are true, *"...many false prophets shall rise, and shall deceive many."* Determine to know God's Word so you won't be one of the many!

Therefore be ye also ready: for in such an hour as ye think not the Son of man cometh. Matthew 24:44

Our text contains a promise to hold dear and a prod to live right. Jesus is certainly returning, and we have been commanded to be ready. Truly, if you have never repented of your sin and received Jesus as your Savior, you are not ready. However, the state of readiness for those who are saved is determined by being a *"faithful and wise servant."* Doing the Father's will at the time of Christ's coming brings added blessings. Jesus said, *"Blessed is that servant, whom his lord when he cometh shall find so doing."*

Because Christ will come when we think not, we will hear no final warning to get ready. Therefore, a faithful believer will hasten to be ready and stay that way by daily fulfilling the will of God. Are you ready for Him to return today, or do you fear such a thought? Dear lost soul, are you ready to live an eternity in torment because you failed to receive Jesus as your Savior? Let His return be joyous, not disastrous.

We are so preoccupied with thoughts of this life that it is no wonder Christ's return will catch us off guard. Let us refocus on His possible return today! If we do, we shall surely live differently.

*His lord said unto him, Well done, thou good and faithful servant: thou
hast been faithful over a few things, I will make thee ruler over many
things: enter thou into the joy of thy lord. Matthew 25:21*

Many sermons have been preached prompting us to live in such a
way that we will one day hear the words, *"Well done."* Truly, we
ought to live a life that brings pleasure to our Lord, not self. So, what
must you do to hear the congratulatory words? The answer is simple: be
faithful with what God has entrusted to you.

Jesus praised the servants because they had been *"faithful over a few
things."* It should encourage us that we have all received *"a few things"*
from God to manage for Him, and all that is required of us is to be
faithful. We should not compare ourselves with those who have more
talent or opportunities. After all, the man with two talents received the
same praise as the man with five talents because he was faithful with
what he had. Use what God has given you by being dependable and
trustworthy. Never feel inferior because others seem to be used more
than you. Just be faithful with what God has given you, and you will
hear those precious words, *"Well done, thou good and faithful servant."*
How sweet that will be!

*And the King shall answer and say unto them, Verily I say unto you,
Inasmuch as ye have done it unto one of the least of these my brethren,
ye have done it unto me. Matthew 25:40*

How do you act toward the brethren? "Fine," you may say, but what
about the seemingly insignificant members of the church? How we
treat the *"least"* brethren is a reflection of how we treat Christ. This
should be a very sobering consideration!

To ignore, belittle, despise, or neglect them is to do the same to
Jesus. However, when we act kindly to those who cannot return the
favor and help those who cannot help us, we are discovering the true
meaning of righteousness. It is easy to regard those with money and
reputation, but that is no test of our goodwill.

The true test of our charity is how we treat the *"least"* of the
brethren. What we have done for them is what we have done for the
Lord Jesus, and every kind deed will be remembered in eternity. Have
we disregarded those brethren we deem lesser due to financial,
educational, or social status? Just remember that Christ was quite
comfortable with the common man, and we should be also.

When Jesus understood it, he said unto them, Why trouble ye the
woman? for she hath wrought a good work upon me.
Matthew 26:10

The disciples were upset that Mary had anointed Jesus with such valuable ointment. In their estimation it was a waste and could have been better spent. Jesus, however, saw the matter quite differently and said, *"Why trouble ye the woman?"*

Are we not like the blinded disciples at times? People do things out of a heart of love for God; and because we don't understand it, we criticize. Our pride is quick to condemn another, when in reality we may be the one at fault. If a person's service and worship to God is not unbiblical, leave them alone!

It is utterly detestable to trouble people who are attempting things for the Lord. This attitude usually arises from those doing little or nothing for God. Consider that the next time you begin to condemn someone. The disciples saw the matter as a waste, but Jesus called it *"a good work."* Oh, that we might see things the way the Master does!

Peter said unto him, Though I should die with thee, yet will I not
deny thee. Likewise also said all the disciples. Matthew 26:35

Jesus had just warned Peter that he was to deny him three times. Surely, this came as a complete surprise to Peter, and it hurt his pride to know that the Christ would think such a thing of him. However, the warning came because Peter confidently assured the Lord that he would never be offended. So, after Jesus prophesied of the denial, Peter denied the future denial! Self-confidence is doomed for failure because faith is placed in self and not in God.

Truly, we must pledge our allegiance to God and rally for His cause as Peter attempted, but we must never look to our own resolve for the strength to do so. Trusting self, no matter how noble the cause, is nothing short of pride. Our determination and confidence must not be rooted in our desire but in the mercy of God to infuse us with the necessary holy zeal to ensure the victory.

So, determination alone will bring the same result that Peter encountered. Be sure your drive is based on and backed with the power of God. Don't be like Peter and fail in the very thing of which you boast.

...Hereafter shall ye see the Son of man sitting on the right hand of power, and coming in the clouds of heaven. Matthew 26:64

Whatever your hardship here on earth, do not despair because one day all things will be made right! Today you may see storm clouds and darkness, but one day you will see glory and brightness as you behold Jesus on His throne! Notice also that Christ is on *"the right hand of power."* This is not only a future blessing but also a present reality we can enjoy. Surely, He is mighty enough to see you through your trial today.

Your mind may be preoccupied with present problems, but rehearse the encouraging words of the songwriter, "It will be worth it all when we see Jesus." Hence, renew your focus and look heavenward. He's coming! Nevertheless, while you are waiting for His return, envision Him *"on the right hand of power"* ready to assist your every need.

We end our thought for the day with the first word in our text— *Hereafter."* Too much of our focus is on our current situation, and we must remember that there is a *"hereafter."* The world lives for the pleasure of the present moment, but we look for better things to come.

Therefore when they were gathered together, Pilate said unto them, Whom will ye that I release unto you? Barabbas, or Jesus which is called Christ? Matthew 27:17

As we consider the question put forth by Pilate to the Jews, the choice seems simple. Barabbas was a worldly man full of sin and corruption while Jesus was the God-man from heaven full of grace and truth. Their choice reveals the perverse character of mankind who love *"darkness rather than light, because their deeds were evil."* (John 3:19)

We saw their selection, but what will your choice be today? *"Whom will ye...Barabbas or Jesus...?"* You say, "Oh, Jesus of course!" However, are you not prone to choose the world? Have you not chosen "Barabbas" over Jesus time after time by following the lusts of the flesh? Every time you listen to gossip, watch an unchaste video, view dirty Internet sites, or put on immodest attire, you have chosen Barabbas!

Why do we, in fact, refuse Jesus? It is because He is the Christ, and we do not want Him to rule over us. Instead, we want to fulfill our lusts and follow our own will. When our choice is selfish and worldly, it is a choice for Barabbas, the representative of worldliness and ungodliness. *"Whom will ye"* choose today, Christ or Barabbas?

And saying, Thou that destroyest the temple, and buildest it in three days, save thyself. If thou be the Son of God, come down from the cross.
Matthew 27:40

The harsh demands of the skeptics warranted no reply from our Lord. Jesus had nothing to prove to these unbelieving, hardened sinners. He knew that one day they would bow the knee and confess that He is Lord. Those cynics, if they were to see the power of God, only had to accept by faith who Jesus was; and then they would have had the assurance that He was the Son of God.

Do we find ourselves skeptical about who God is, what His motives are, and if His plans are right? Unfortunately, we make similar demands to God saying, "If you are really God, please do this for me." Let no such doubts arise in your heart. Faith in the character and nature of God will chase away those uncertainties and bring calm to your soul. Jesus has nothing to prove to the faithless individual. Sit back and watch His perfect will unfold for your life. When things do not go as you had hoped, rest in the promises of God.

And, behold, the veil of the temple was rent in twain from the top to the bottom; and the earth did quake, and the rocks rent... Matthew 27:51

The veil in the temple covered the entrance into the most holy place where only the high priest was allowed to enter to make atonement for the people. Entrance to this part of the temple was forbidden to the common man. However, symbolically this all changed when Christ died.

There is a wonderful picture of Christ in the veil. It shows that entrance into the presence of God is only through Jesus; and His blood makes atonement for our sin, allowing us to be close to God. Jesus Himself is the High Priest. When the veil was rent on the day of the crucifixion, it symbolized that the typology of the Old Testament sacrifices had been fulfilled. Thus, all who come to Christ are free to enter into the presence of God! This speaks, not only of salvation, but also of daily fellowship with God. Now, we have *"boldness to enter into the holiest."* (Hebrews 10:19) We are free to enter!

Because of Christ's sacrifice, we have direct access to God. Don't delay. *"Let us therefore come boldly unto the throne of grace, that we may obtain mercy, and find grace to help in time of need."* (Hebrews 4:16)

*He is not here: for he is risen, as he said. Come, see the place
where the Lord lay. Matthew 28:6*

God is not dead! Jesus arose and is presently in heaven interceding for His people below. Because He has conquered death, the Savior certainly has the power to triumph over your present difficulties. Are you feeling dead and defeated? Come to the One Who not only has life but gives life freely.

There is a second gem in this verse worthy of consideration, seen in the words, *"as he said."* Jesus did exactly what He said He would do. This is another affirmation that God always keeps His promises! Whatever promise you find for your need, plead it tirelessly in prayer, knowing that it will always be *"as he said."*

A last thought from our text points to an invitation—*"Come."* We are invited to partake of the promises offered by the risen, living, conquering Savior. Why delay any longer? Let us rush to His loving, pierced side with renewed faith, assured that He always does just as He promises! Never forget that Jesus is alive and able to intervene in any problem you currently face.

*And Jesus said unto them, Come ye after me, and I will make you
to become fishers of men. Mark 1:17*

Here we see the divine will of God expressed for each disciple: He wants us to go to Him so He can make us able to win souls. First, we must follow Jesus. How can we bid others to do what we are failing to do ourselves?

Coming to Jesus, on our part, requires us to abandon our own business and plans just as the disciples did in our story. We must be willing to change our schedules in order to witness to the ones God has prepared to listen. There are "fish" waiting to be caught! Can we not follow Him and leave some things behind for the sake of souls?

Second, there is a wonderful promise—*"I will make you."* We may feel inadequate or unequipped to catch men for the Master, but Christ promised to make us fit for the task. All we must do is go, trust, and allow God to work through us. We have no excuse! Let us follow Jesus today in every area of our lives and be yielded to witness for Him as opportunities arise. However, never forget that many opportunities to witness are created; they do not arise by chance. Go ahead and cast your line in the water. You might catch a soul today!

And in the morning, rising up a great while before day, he went out, and departed into a solitary place, and there prayed. Mark 1:35

Jesus was about to set out on a preaching tour in the neighboring towns, which was sure to be taxing on the body. How did He prepare for such a busy day? He rose up very early and prayed. Extra business demands more prayer.

Too often when we face a busy day, we are tempted to cut back a little on our time with God. However, do we not need more strength and wisdom rather than less? Let us learn from the Master and rise a little earlier so that the important things in our day do not overshadow the most important thing—fellowship with the Father!

Spurgeon once said, "All our strength lies in prayer!" If that be the case, the more strength we need, the more prayer we should muster. Jesus gave us the pattern that we must follow for a busy day—*"rising up a great while before day, he went out...and there prayed."* The results of failing to follow His example will show up later in your day, and you will wish then that you had taken time to pray.

And when they could not come nigh unto him for the press, they uncovered the roof where he was: and when they had broken it up, they let down the bed wherein the sick of the palsy lay. Mark 2:4

Life is full of obstacles! The four men in our text were on a noble mission—they wanted to get their friend to Jesus. Although *"they could not"* initially accomplish their objective, they refused to quit! Their example demonstrates that faith finds a way and keeps pressing on until the goal is reached.

How is it with you? Have you started something that you knew to be God's will and found, as the four men, that you *"could not"*? Dare to emulate the faith of the men who could not but did anyway! Faith without works is dead; therefore, God expects us to do our part. Faith looks for and finds a way when things seem impossible. This is not trusting self, but rather God Who alone can make all things possible.

The next time you attempt a great thing for God, rest assured that something will arise to hinder you. Perhaps you will encounter an unfavorable circumstance, uncooperative person, or unbelieving attitude. Don't let anything stop you. The disciples could not but did, and so can you!

And if a house be divided against itself, that house cannot stand.
Mark 3:25

Jesus warned us that a house divided against itself is in trouble. Sadly, many Christian homes are presently in such a state. Husbands and wives are at odds with one another, and in some cases they are prone to arguments or employing "the silent treatment." Moreover, children scheme behind the backs of their parents. What a mess!

How is it in your home today? How long can you pretend to be a good Christian when you are not working to bring unity to your home? Remaining divided will surely bring destruction to your marriage and wreck the future of your children. Do your best to mend any divisions today! A family that neglects its problems *"cannot stand."*

If there were ever a day that we needed our homes fortified, it is now. Satan wants to destroy our families and tries to infiltrate our homes through worldly attitudes and influences. Pride and carnality foster divisions. If you find yourself in a disagreement, be as quick to notice your own faults as you are to see the faults of others. When humility is found in a home, unity is found also. Humility unites a home so that it can stand!

But when the sun was up, it was scorched; and because it had no root,
it withered away. Mark 4:6

Our parable deals with surface growth. A seed germinates and begins to shoot upwards, but without properly being rooted in the ground it soon withers away. Such surface growth is not only detrimental to plant life but also to spiritual life. Sadly, many Christians vainly attend to the surface issues of life and neglect their hard, stony heart. Soon, signs of weakness and unfruitfulness are revealed.

Surface Christianity will be tested as the sun of affliction arises. Will you be *"scorched"* as the seed was in the parable? Only those who have dealt with the stones of sin can withstand the trials of life. You will surely wither when your focus is on the surface rather than on digging out deep-seated sins, and the sad result of being *"withered away"* is fruitlessness. If we fail to produce fruit for the Lord, what purpose do we serve in life?

Although the root system cannot be seen, it dictates the life of the plant. Spend more time caring for the roots than pruning the surface, or soon there will not be much to prune! You can only pretend for so long.

And he said unto them, Take heed what ye hear: with what measure ye
mete, it shall be measured to you: and unto you that hear
shall more be given. Mark 4:24

It is sad to see so many Christians become stagnant. Some have not grown for years, yet they go through the motions of attending church and may even faithfully fulfill a ministry. Why, then, do they fail to grow? Jesus set forth the condition for growth: *"unto you that hear shall more be given."* Thus, failure to listen leads to stunted growth.

At times we are blatant in our rebellion while on other occasions we justify shrugging off the conviction of the Holy Spirit. It may involve a problem at home, a lack of a burden for souls, a sinful habit, a covetous attitude, or insufficient faith to accomplish God's will. Whatever the case, when we refuse to listen, God turns off the tap of instruction!

The Lord is not likely to entrust us with more until we act upon what He has already spoken. Could this be the reason you have failed to grow sufficiently? Go do what He has already bidden you, and you will soon hear His sweet voice once again.

And they come to Jesus, and see him that was possessed with the devil,
and had the legion, sitting, and clothed, and in his right mind:
and they were afraid. Mark 5:15

If you think you have problems, consider the man from Gadara who was demon possessed! He wandered night and day, shouted at others, and cut himself. Moreover, people feared such a man who could break the chains with which he was bound. Truly, he was a menace to society. This man had all of these problems and more until he met Jesus.

When people saw him with Christ, he was no longer wandering about shouting but sitting quietly. Now the hideous scars of his self-inflicted wounds were covered with clothing provided by his new Master. Finally, he was in his right mind. The Lord offers a renewed mind to all who will spend time with Him.

If you truly come to Jesus the way you are, He can make a great change in you, too. Are you busy wandering through life without a purpose? Are you scarred with sin? Is your mind so cluttered that you cannot think clearly? What Jesus did for the demoniac He can do for you, but you first need to spend time with the Lord as he did.

When she had heard of Jesus, came in the press behind,
and touched his garment. Mark 5:27

The woman with the issue of blood was healed because of her faith, but someone else also had a part in this miracle. The account says that *"she had heard of Jesus."* She went to Him only after hearing. Therefore, we must conclude that she had responded to someone's witness! The great faith of the woman should not overshadow the great proclamation made by the unseen witness. Someone was used to point her to Jesus.

We may become weary trying to bring people to Christ, but don't give up because some do respond. Telling the good news still works, and we can have a part in the transformation of lives if we will be faithful to tell them about Jesus.

Notice also that the unseen witness remained anonymous in this story. There are too many glory seekers who love to boast about the numbers of people they have led to the Savior. Why not quietly go about your business, spreading the good news, and let God be glorified when He changes a life?

And they went out, and preached that men should repent. Mark 6:12

The message of the Bible is repentance, and God's men *"went out, and preached that men should repent."* What other theme should we preach? Mankind must see themselves as guilty sinners and turn to the Lord. The lost must repent to be saved, and the saved must repent to restore their fellowship with the Father.

Unfortunately, the preaching in most pulpits today is missing the all-important word *"repent."* The hirelings of today do not want to preach a negative message because they will lose their crowds and offerings. It may be time to find a new church when the preacher does not consistently challenge people to turn from their sin. Those of you who have a preacher doing his God-given job of keeping the sermons "hot," be thankful and learn to submit. Never complain that your pastor preaches too hard but rather rejoice that you have someone to call you back to God when you have gone astray.

One last thought: be sure that you include repentance when you witness to others. Nobody has ever gotten saved without repenting.

For they considered not the miracle of the loaves:
for their heart was hardened. Mark 6:52

The disciples had kept a busy schedule serving the Lord and had gone into a desert place to rest a while. Surely, they looked forward to the rest with great anticipation. However, upon reaching their destination, a great multitude of needy people met them; and once again, they were back to work. Howbeit, this work should have been delightful as they witnessed their Lord feed five thousand men with a boy's lunch.

What should have been a wonderful lesson to the disciples about the Lord's provision in time of need was missed altogether by the twelve. Later that day, they faced a trial of their own—a tempestuous storm. Now it was the disciples, not the multitude, that needed help; but they were filled with fear. Why? They had hardened their hearts while feeding the five thousand. They begrudged the needs of others and now had a need of their own. Failing to consider the great miracle that God had just performed prevented them from seeking one for themselves.

A hard heart will surely rob you of many blessings and leave you unprepared for future trials. Beware of becoming weary in your service for Christ as it will lead to a hard heart.

There is nothing from without a man, that entering into him can defile
him: but the things which come out of him, those are they
that defile the man. Mark 7:15

This verse has been used by foolish hypocrites to justify many sinful deeds. The argument goes like this, "Jesus said that nothing you put into your body makes you a sinner. Therefore, beer, wine, and smoking are all okay." Depraved men love to twist God's Word to approve their sin.

In context, Jesus had rebuked the Pharisees for elevating their tradition above inner holiness. They stressed the importance of hand-washing before eating. Certainly, it is good hygiene to wash your hands, but dirt does not corrupt your heart as the Pharisees taught. So, Christ's teaching in this verse was that eating with dirty hands does not make you a sinner. The verse goes on to stress that what comes out of the heart actually defiles the man. Obviously, drunkenness will cause many bad things to come out of the heart. Isn't it amazing that the verse some people use to justify their actions actually condemns them? Don't miss the main point: guard what comes out of your heart today!

And were beyond measure astonished, saying,
He hath done all things well... Mark 7:37

These are good words to remember during times of triumph and tragedy. God makes no mistakes, and the disappointments in life are no less part of His plan than the victories.

He does well when He answers our prayers, delivers us from temptation, and does exceeding abundantly above all that we could ask or think. However, He also does well when fiery trials afflict us, heartaches come, and persecutions arise. He tests our faith during the difficult times, and that is part of doing all things well. When Job lost all that he had, did not God do all things well? Was there not a purpose for the trial? Did He not reward Job in the end and bless him more than at his beginning? Surely, Job would say that God did well. Will He do less for us in our troubling times? Certainly not!

Our text reminds us that, *"He hath done all things well."* Let us accept the good and the bad that may come our way today. Jesus has never failed us and never will. How will He do things well for you today? Watch and see!

Having eyes, see ye not? and having ears, hear ye not?
and do ye not remember? Mark 8:18

The disciples had just witnessed the feeding of the four thousand, and this was the second time they had witnessed such a miraculous provision by the hands of Christ. Now they are in a ship worrying because they had forgotten to bring bread for their journey. Jesus' response was, *"do ye not remember?"*

Hadn't the Lord fed them from little in time past? How could they forget the former deliverances? How terrible our memories are when it comes to the goodness God has shown us! We recollect our miseries but not His mercies. Oh, how soon we forget!

When trials come, we must remember how the Lord solved our past troubles. Don't you recall how He lifted you, comforted you, delivered you, and encouraged you in times past? True Christianity is a thoughtful religion; and faithful believers will consistently reflect upon who God is, what He has done, and what He is capable of doing.

Jesus was astonished that they had forgotten their former provisions. Let us not disappoint our Lord in such a fashion today!

For whosoever will save his life shall lose it; but whosoever shall lose his life for my sake and the gospel's, the same shall save it. Mark 8:35

We are prone to protect ourselves and our own interests but fail to acknowledge that self-preservation actually leads to self-destruction. For the sake of happiness, we guard ourselves from the things that we think may hurt our own welfare. For example, one may refuse to give his tithe because he would rather spend it on himself. However, he is not the happy one. The one who gives up his pursuit of materialism has the real joy. The same is true of a man who willingly gets more involved in ministries and activities at the church rather than wasting his time on temporary pleasure. We find our life by giving it up and handing it over to the Lord, and He can do more with it than we can!

Our text speaks of one who loses his joy by trying to save it. In reality, the person who gives up what he thinks will bring happiness is truly blessed. Let us lose our life for Christ today and accept the challenges He has for us. Holding back and saving our time, money, and energy will surely end in eternal loss. Beware of the sin of self-preservation.

After that he put his hands again upon his eyes, and made him look up: and he was restored, and saw every man clearly. Mark 8:25

There are times when our spiritual vision is blurry. We don't see clearly and run into obstacles on life's path. It is a burdened existence and should come as rarely as the extra day in leap year.

Many foolish decisions are made when we are out of fellowship with God and don't see things as He does. Problems in marriages go unnoticed, children's inconsistencies are overlooked, and besetting sins are undetected. It is a terrible thing when our vision is obstructed. Problems that are not seen do not go away. Instead, they can grow into life-threatening situations. As cancer spreads when unidentified, so sin permeates its toxin throughout our entire lives. It is extremely dangerous to live with obscured vision.

What is the solution? First, we must get close to Jesus because He is the only One Who can straighten out our spiritual eyesight. Second, notice that Christ *"made him look up."* If we are ever to see properly, we must get our eyes off of the affairs of this life and learn to look up. Only, after the man looked up was his vision restored and he saw clearly.

...but if thou canst do any thing, have compassion on us, and help us.
Jesus said unto him, If thou canst believe, all things are possible to
him that believeth. Mark 9:22-23

Here was a desperate man who wanted Jesus to help him with a tremendous problem. In his petition he asked the Lord to help if He could do so. The man said, *"if thou canst do,"* but the Savior replied, *"If thou canst believe."*

Frequently we are guilty of the same initial lack of faith displayed by the man in our story. We present to Jesus our request, but then we add an "if" to the prayer where one does not belong. "If" is suitable when we are asking whether or not a thing is God's will. However, "if" never should be tied with whether or not God has the ability to do a thing because God can do anything!

We clearly see that the problem is not "if" the Lord can do it, but rather "if" we can believe it. All things are possible if we truly believe! Let us come with renewed confidence that our God can indeed assist us. He can help "if" you can believe! Will you trust Him for your need today?

Salt is good: but if the salt have lost his saltness, wherewith will ye
season it? Have salt in yourselves, and have peace one with another.
Mark 9:50

Salt has many properties: it cleanses, preserves, and promotes healing. However, salt is used in another wonderful sense in this passage—it seasons. Salt can add much flavor and enhance the taste of a meal. In fact, some food is quite bland until salt brings out its appeal.

Here, Jesus warns us not to lose our saltiness. When we cease to make a difference for the better in this world, we have failed to fulfill God's plan for our lives. Look where you can season some soul today. It may be a lost sinner or a discouraged saint that needs a sprinkling.

We are commanded to have salt in ourselves, and part of that means to *"have peace one with another."* Bitter food can be altered by adding salt, and we should be so full of seasoning that any bitter conflicts with the brethren will be quickly made palatable. Have you lost your savor?

"Salt is good," but when we have lost our saltiness we cease to be good. Surely, staying close to the Lord will keep the necessary salt in our soul that is needed to be a blessing to others. How salty are you?

And he was sad at that saying, and went away grieved... Mark 10:22

The rich young ruler had come kneeling before Jesus and asked Him, *"Master, what shall I do...?"* The Lord exposed the man's covetousness and told him to sell his belongings and follow Him. Instead of rejoicing at Christ's answer, he went away sad.

How often do we act in the same manner? We say, "O God, show me Your will so that I may do it." Then, when His way does not seem agreeable or appealing, we are grieved. This is nothing less than self-inflicted grief because the Scriptures plainly teach that *"his commandments are not grievous."* (I John 5:3) Why do we often think that following God's will is going to make us unhappy? It is just the opposite! God promises peace: *"O that thou hadst hearkened to my commandments! then had thy peace been as a river..."* (Isaiah 48:18)

Oh, if we would just trust that the Lord is only good, and that He will lead us to paths of peace! Grief does not come from following God's Word but rather from disobeying it. Had the young ruler followed Christ, he would have had the joy he was seeking—not sadness. Do you want to be happy? Ask God, "What shall I do?" and be willing to do it!

And Jesus answered and said unto him, What wilt thou that I should do unto thee? The blind man said unto him, Lord, that I might receive my sight. Mark 10:51

What if Jesus asked you the same question, *"What wilt thou that I should do unto thee?"* What would you want Him to do? By faith, Bartimæus received what he needed because he cried, *"have mercy upon me."*

We must remember that the Lord truly wants to do things in our lives and make great changes as He did for Bartimæus. If we are to experience the blessings that he received, we must demonstrate the same kind of humble faith. Our prayers must not be demands, but rather cries for mercy. This is the way to get God's attention!

So, what would you like Jesus to do in your life? Go ahead and ask Him! He has the same love for you as He had for Bartimæus. His power has not diminished one iota. Let us ask for new courage to witness, victory over sin, deliverance from temptation, true revival, transformed marriages, godly children, and a heart of gratitude. *"What wilt thou..."* is like a blank check, and this is a thrilling opportunity when the account belongs to One with inexhaustible riches!

And Jesus answering saith unto them, Have faith in God. Mark 11:22

This is a seemingly simple command, *"Have faith in God."* However, much of what we call faith is empty or meager at best. How many times do we pray for God to meet our needs, but do not expect Him to do so? How often do we serve Him without the faith that our witnessing efforts will be fruitful? How frequently do we get discouraged when we intercede for others and wonder if it does much good? True faith moves mountains and obtains promises! We cannot be satisfied with a feeble faith that limps through life accomplishing little.

Furthermore, our faith must not be misplaced. The command is to *"Have faith in God."* We are not to have faith in ourselves, our works, or our righteousness; and if we do, we will fail miserably. We must remember that the Lord is generous and ready to play an active role in our lives. He desires our fellowship and dependence upon Him. He wants to glorify Himself by doing for us what we cannot do for ourselves. Therefore, let us be sure that what we do today demonstrates that we believe God is going to be involved directly in our lives.

MARK 12:1-27   **JESUS KNOWS THE REAL YOU**   **MAR. 6**

...But he, knowing their hypocrisy, said unto them, Why tempt ye me?
Mark 12:15

Not much has changed since Jesus' day. The religious people pretended to be something they were not, and it greatly disturbed our Lord. The text clearly reminds us that He perceives our hypocrisy, too. Even when others are fooled, He knows when we are merely acting and pretending to be sincere.

It is true that many Christians do not even try to be holy or pretend that they have a real relationship with the Father. That is quite sad in itself, but equally distressing is the fact that many who attend vibrant, fundamental churches are more concerned about looking spiritual rather than being so. Parents try to look good at church but live differently at home, and eventually their hypocrisy is revealed when their children don't even try to pretend. Kids tend to follow our true character, not the phony one. What we are will be exposed sooner or later.

It actually takes more effort to pretend to be spiritual than it does to be spiritual. Christ knows all such hypocrisy, and it tempts Him! Cease from pretending and just be real, or you may face God's judgment.

...Thou shalt love thy neighbour as thyself. Mark 12:31

This is a very difficult command! Loving our neighbor is not always easy, but loving him as ourselves makes it all the more challenging! We all tend to love ourselves very much. Most of our time, thoughts, and energies are expended on making ourselves happy and comfortable.

Turning our attention to the needs of others takes sacrifice and determination. Yet, we are called to bear one another's burdens and fulfill the law of Christ, which is love. It is easy to rejoice with those who are rejoicing but tough to enter into the sorrows of those who are grieving. It is too easy to excuse ourselves from getting involved, but this violates Christ's great command.

Determine to be thoughtful of others this day and look for a needy individual that requires your assistance. You could be the one that God has chosen and equipped to be a blessing to them, and neglecting that duty would mean the need would go unfulfilled. Would you deprive yourself of relief in trouble? Then, don't fail to succor that one who is in such a case when you find him. A deep sense of joy will fill your soul when you have so done!

MAR. 8   BE LOOKING   MARK 13

And what I say unto you I say unto all, Watch. Mark 13:37

Jesus has promised that His return could be at any moment, and tied to that promise is a simple command—*"Watch."* Why should we watch? The answer is quite simple: looking for His return implies a state of readiness, and being on the lookout for Him prevents backsliding. If we lived each day as though it may be the time of His return, we would be more careful to maintain a holy life. Who would wish to be found indulging in carnal pleasure or lounging in laziness at His return?

So many live without the fear of God in their lives and have no expectation that He could come at any moment and find them in a shameful condition. What is worse is that many do not even seem to care how Christ finds them.

We have been called to holiness and activity for the Master's sake, and we must be about our Father's business. He is definitely coming! Are you ready? Are there things you must change? Watch for Him today and notice how your life will be different as you focus on the right things. Jesus' command to us today is, *"Watch."* Will you?

And his disciples went forth, and came into the city,
and found as he had said unto them...
Mark 14:16

The Lord had told the disciples to go into Jerusalem and that they would find a man carrying a pitcher of water. They were to follow him and ask the owner of the house where the guest chamber was for them to observe the Passover. In human reasoning, it seemed highly unlikely that this scenario would come to pass. Surely there would be many bearing a pitcher of water in a city of thousands of people.

No matter how improbable God's will may seem, trust Him and it will always work. In every case you will find it to be just as He said! How exciting it is to face a difficult challenge and see it resolved by following God's wisdom rather than conventional thinking.

The disciples did not find it *"as he had said"* until they *"went forth."* The key to the whole matter is faith, and as we act upon what He said we shall find that His Word never fails. Do you have a difficult decision facing you today? Does it seem impossible that things will work the way God is leading you? Learn to walk by faith, not sight!

And he said, Abba, Father, all things are possible unto thee; take away
this cup from me: nevertheless not what I will, but what thou wilt.
Mark 14:36

To learn anything in life it is always wise to study the best person on the subject. Therefore, the greatest lessons on prayer can be gleaned from the Master Himself. Notice first that Jesus communed with a special *closeness* as He cried, *"Abba, Father."* These are precious words depicting a dear relationship and showing the love between Father and Son. We, too, must endeavor to live so close to God that prayer is natural instead of a formal procedure.

Also, we notice the *confidence* that Christ had in prayer as He said, *"all things are possible unto thee."* We must be absolutely convinced that God can do anything and meet any need we bring to Him. Do you always have that assurance that God can intervene?

Lastly, we see *submission* in the words, *"not what I will, but what thou wilt."* Although God can do anything we ask, He may choose not to do everything we ask. Seek answers to prayer, but desire His will more than your own, even if it means your request may be denied.

...Art thou the Christ, the Son of the Blessed?   And Jesus said, I am...
Mark 14:61-62

The name *Christ* is synonymous with the name *Messiah*, the promised Deliverer. The high priest who was speaking to the Lord should have been looking for the Messiah, but his question to Jesus was far from sincere. He had already refused to believe that Jesus was the Christ. Some people today like to say that Jesus never claimed to be the Messiah, but listen to His own words—*"I am."*

Never doubt that Jesus is Jehovah God. He came as the Savior of the world to deliver us from our sins. The Jews are still waiting for the Messiah, the Muslims believe Jesus was only a prophet, and the Watchtower organization has distributed millions of pamphlets throughout the world attacking the Deity of Christ. If you are saved, be glad you know the truth and be diligent to tell people who Jesus really is.

Are you as busy promoting Christ as much as others are denying Him? Instead of letting others shake your faith with their lies, attempt to shake their misplaced faith with the truth. Don't keep this wonderful assurance to yourself.

And so Pilate, willing to content the people, released Barabbas unto them, and delivered Jesus, when he had scourged him, to be crucified.
Mark 15:15

Pilate knew he was wrong to condemn Jesus, but he did it anyway. This much we know, but why did he do it? Our text gives us the key to his cowardly behavior. He failed to do the right thing because he was *"willing to content the people."* Although he had the authority to set Christ free, he became spineless when he faced opposition. It is amazing how often right causes crumble because people try to protect themselves from criticism!

Many of our worst decisions result from the same weakness that Pilate displayed. We must not live to be accepted by others, especially when it requires us to do wrong in the process. In fact, who is it that we are trying to please when we compromise? Is it not the ungodly crowd?

Perhaps you are facing pressure from family, friends, co-workers, classmates, or neighbors to concede to their wishes instead of remaining loyal to Christ. Don't be a Pilate! Determine to please God rather than anyone else in the entire world. Contenting the people leads to abusing Christ. Let no redeemed child of God thus spit in the Savior's face.

And at the ninth hour Jesus cried with a loud voice, saying, Eloi, Eloi, lama sabachthani? which is, being interpreted, My God, my God, why hast thou forsaken me? Mark 15:34

P art of God's wonderful, sacrificial plan for our salvation was that Jesus would become sin for us. As that transpired on the cross, the Father turned from Jesus and forsook Him as He poured out all of His wrath and fury against our sin. If it were not for the love and mercy of God, we would have to experience His anger and be punished in eternal fires.

Christ was innocent yet God forsook Him; we are guilty, but God has promised never to forsake us. What a paradox worked by grace! Jesus knows how horrible it is to be forsaken by God and has promised that such loneliness and terror will never be experienced by us who are saved. Because of Christ, we have been treated better than He Himself was treated on the cross. Can we render sufficient thankfulness to our Savior? Thank you Jesus for bearing what I could never bear and preventing me from ever having to cry, *"My God, my God, why hast thou forsaken me?"*

And they went forth, and preached every where, the Lord working with them, and confirming the word with signs following. Amen. Mark 16:20

T his is the last verse in the Book of Mark, and it is quite a fitting conclusion. After seeing who Jesus was and what He had done, it spurred the disciples into action: *"they went forth, and preached every where."* Should we not put into practice what we hear?

Christians ought to set time aside on a regular basis to go forth and proclaim the gospel to the lost. Those who get involved have a wonderful promise, *"the Lord working with them."* Perhaps you are discouraged from seemingly fruitless soulwinning efforts; don't lose hope now. The Lord has promised to work with us in this great endeavor. It may be that you are fearful of witnessing to certain individuals, but remember Who has promised to confirm the Word!

Never allow the devil to hinder you from going out with the best message the world has ever been given. The songwriter wrote, "If Jesus goes with me, I'll go anywhere." Whether you go across the seas or across the street to witness for the Lord, He has promised to go with you. How can we fear when the King of the Universe stands by our side?

And they were both righteous before God, walking in all the commandments and ordinances of the Lord blameless. Luke 1:6

Our text speaks of Zacharias and Elizabeth, the parents of John the Baptist. The development of any child depends upon the character of the parents. Jesus proclaimed that John the Baptist was the greatest man ever born. However, it was not his birth that made him great but rather his upbringing! Simply put, he was great because he had outstanding parents.

Notice Luke's words, *"And they were <u>both</u> righteous before God."* It takes two godly parents to raise godly children. Husband and wife must work together and not undermine one another with the children. It is difficult for a child to rise above the spiritual level of the parents if the parents are carnal and careless. If you are a single parent, remember that God is merciful and will help you when you follow Him.

No parents are perfect, but good kids will be the result when both parents are *"walking in <u>all</u> the commandments and ordinances of the Lord."* Are you trying to follow the Lord, or are you hindering your children from reaching their spiritual potential by living a disobedient life?

MAR. 16   NOTHING IS IMPOSSIBLE   LUKE 1:26-56

For with God nothing shall be impossible. Luke 1:37

These words were spoken by Gabriel to Mary. Elizabeth, who was barren, was now with child; Mary, who was a virgin, was to give birth to the Messiah. These were two, humanly speaking, impossible situations, but they both happened!

Throughout both the Old and New Testaments, we are reminded that God is the God of the impossible. The text gives *us* hope, too, because it says, *"nothing <u>shall</u> be impossible."* The promise is given in the future tense, *"shall be."* Our mighty God is not limited to the past but is quite capable of doing what is deemed unfeasible today!

Don't be discouraged when the skies are at their darkest and you feel no ray of light can shine through to cheer you. Sometimes things have to get worse so the deliverance can be all the more spectacular. God is glorified when things become hopeless. Go immediately to the Lord with your impossible situation and make *your* request known to Him. If it is within His will, the impossible will become possible.

To give light to them that sit in darkness and in the shadow of death,
to guide our feet into the way of peace. Luke 1:79

Jesus came, not only to be a light, but to give us light. How many days have we sat in the darkness of sin and self-deceit? Truly, sin brings death, and we have sat in those shadows, precariously awaiting sentencing. Praise God for Jesus, though!

The Lord wants to give us light to guide us on the right path, and that pathway leads to wonderful peace. Do you not long for peace? Too often we think that following God's way will bring disappointment or a terrible burden; this is selfishness and unbelief. Receiving light from Jesus will lead us into a happier state and put us on the pathway of peace. Furthermore, beams of righteousness will expose our sinful ways; and as this happens, we should seek the necessary cleansing that will enable us to stay on God's path of peace.

The light guides, but peace is only promised to those who follow it. Therefore, a choice must be made to stop sitting in darkness. Arise and run to Jesus, the Light! You cannot have your sin and peace at the same time. Make your choice today.

Glory to God in the highest, and on earth peace, good will toward men.
Luke 2:14

At the birth of Christ, the heavenly host rang out these words, *"good will toward men."* It is amazing that God would leave heaven, come to earth, and dwell among sinful men; this is definitely good will demonstrated toward us. Let us never forget the goodness of our God, especially when we start to feel sorry for ourselves during stressful times of difficulty or discomfort.

Not only has God shown good will toward us, but we must also follow His example and do likewise to our fellow man. This, of course, must be practiced more often than at Christmas time when there is an emphasis on the subject. We have received mercy undeservedly and must demonstrate the same kindness toward others. We have freely been forgiven; should we not exercise good will in forgiving others' trespasses against us?

In conclusion, good will must be enjoyed and appreciated as we reflect upon God's goodness. Additionally, we must rally to express the same to our fellows.

*And he said unto them, How is it that ye sought me? wist ye not
that I must be about my Father's business? Luke 2:49*

Jesus was in the temple as a twelve-year-old boy, confounding the
doctors of the law. At an early age, His purpose in life was apparent
to us: He wanted to do His Father's business. Twelve-year-old children
of our generation are more interested in computers, TV, video games,
text messaging, or sports. What a contrast between the childhood of
Jesus and that of today's youth!

What is your purpose in life? Whose business are you attending to
most frequently? So often we forget that we must be about the Father's
business. It should be the driving force in our lives and dictate all of our
decisions. There is no time to procrastinate when we know God's will
for our lives; we must consider it a *"must."* Have you allowed your
plans, ambitions, and aspirations to crowd out the business of God?

Perhaps we should take a few moments today and reevaluate our
priorities. Once that is done, let us consider the priorities of our children
to be sure they have not neglected their heavenly Father's business.

Bring forth therefore fruits worthy of repentance... Luke 3:8

John the Baptist's message was quite clear; if a person had truly
repented, there would be some evidence. John would not even baptize
this crowd until they understood a change was expected. Even in his
day, people talked as though they were spiritual; but without the proof of
a changed life, there was no real repentance.

So often people say they are sorry when they have been caught in
sin, but that does not mean they have repented. The command is, *"Bring
forth fruits worthy of repentance."* We must not simply say we have
repented but, instead, demonstrate it. As a seed brings forth fruit, so
repentance produces something good. Repentance changes complaining
to thankfulness, laziness to diligence, pride to humility and rebellion to
obedience. A noticeable change always results!

Have you repented of what God has convicted you? Prove it! Bring
forth some real, conclusive evidence. When there is no change, there has
been no repentance. Do not deceive yourself by accepting a half-hearted
confession when God does not accept it. Could it be that we do not have
the joy of forgiveness because we have not truly repented?

*And Jesus answered him, saying, It is written, That man shall not live by
bread alone, but by every word of God. Luke 4:4*

Satan tried to tempt Jesus to turn stones into bread to satisfy His
hunger. This temptation placed an undue emphasis on the needs of
the body. Of course, Jesus knew that spiritual sustenance was of greater
importance and would not succumb to the devil's trickery.

Now that we have considered Jesus' reaction, let us ponder our own
priorities. Do we not neglect the Word of God at times because of the
temptation to cater to the flesh? Our true strength in life comes from
"every word of God." When running behind schedule, too many
Christians are more willing to neglect their Bible than they are their
breakfast. However, we must realize that our soul cries out for
something to feast on as much as our belly does. Some have made a
good rule for themselves: "No Bible, no food." Would you be willing to
choose time in the Word over time at the table?

Let us remember that spiritual nourishment is of utmost importance.
As Satan attempted to get Jesus to neglect it, he will do the same to you.
Will you have the same victory as Jesus? By the way, this book is not
meant to be a substitute for the real meat of personal Bible study.

*And he stood over her, and rebuked the fever; and it left her: and
immediately she arose and ministered unto them. Luke 4:39*

Peter's mother-in-law had been sick, but Jesus came to the rescue and
healed her. This shows the great power Jesus has over our infirmities
and illnesses. When it is according to His will, complete healing can
result. Therefore, we must never fear to ask the Master for help.

However, another important lesson unfolds in the story. What did
the woman do once she was healed? She expressed her gratitude, not
only with words, but with action. Luke's record says, *"immediately she
arose and ministered unto them."* There were no empty promises of
future service, but rather an immediate display of her gratefulness.

Our thankfulness to God is best seen in renewed, fervent service to
Him. It may be that He has done some great thing for us. Can we not
render a great act in return toward Him? When He has given much to us,
can we not be excited about giving back to Him? The Old Testament
saints offered sacrifices of thanksgiving. What sacrifices have you made
to show your gratitude?

...And Jesus said unto Simon, Fear not;
from henceforth thou shalt catch men.
Luke 5:10

Peter had fished all night and caught nothing, but Jesus went out to sea with him again and told him to expect a big catch. At first, Peter was skeptical, but he soon found more fish than his net could hold! Christ taught him an important lesson that we must also learn: on our own we can do nothing, but with Jesus we can be extremely productive.

As usual, God had more in mind than merely giving Peter a net full of fish. The Lord's intentions were not to encourage Peter to continue as a fisherman; the multitude of fish represented something much greater. Jesus promised him that he would now fish for the souls of men.

It is one thing to try and another to succeed; but the Lord makes it clear that while fishing with Him, we cannot fail. When we are walking with the Lord, we will surely catch some souls for Him. This should encourage us to witness with renewed hope and optimism as we remember the words of Christ, *"thou shalt catch men."* How many we catch is His business, as it was in Peter's case. Leave the numbers up to God, and just get busy casting out the net.

MAR. 24   HAPPINESS ON THE HORIZON   LUKE 6:1-26

...Blessed are ye that weep now: for ye shall laugh. Luke 6:21

It is difficult to imagine that we are actually blessed while we endure a time of weeping. However, Jesus said it, and that guarantees it! Instead of considering our miseries, we ought to focus on our current blessings. It may be hard to see God's goodness through the mist of tears, but it is there nonetheless. Isn't it better to wipe away those drops that blur our spiritual vision? Those weepy eyes have prevented you from beholding the joy that is set before you.

There is a bonus promise in this verse, too. Not only do we have current blessings, but there is a pledge of more to come! Although we may need to weep for a short season, we shall laugh once again. Never allow yourself to become so discouraged that you think all is doom and gloom. The sun is rising, and happiness is shining on the horizon. Don't lose hope now. Be comforted with the Master's assurance, *"ye shall laugh."* Today may be the day that the dark clouds clear; so, be on the lookout! We are promised that *"weeping may endure for a night, but joy cometh in the morning."* (Psalm 30:5)

And as ye would that men should do to you, do ye also to them likewise.
Luke 6:31

Our text today gives us the principle of treating others the way we would like to be treated. It has been called the Golden Rule, and it is so famous that even the unsaved crowd refers to it. Imagine how peaceful the world would be if everybody practiced it! Crime would stop, wars would end, and gracious words would always be spoken.

Unfortunately, not everyone follows the Golden Rule, but every Christian should. Just because others fail to observe it does not justify our neglect of it. We live in a wicked world whose motto is more like, "Do unto others before they do it unto you." That is the exact opposite of Christ's instructions! Never be caught up in the "dog eat dog" world.

If we want people to forgive us, we should be forgiving. If we would like to be treated fairly and honestly, we must do likewise to others. You want people to be kind to you, but are you always kind to your fellow man? Let us endeavor to follow this principle, and when others fail, we shall be a candle that ever shines to show others the right way.

And blessed is he, whosoever shall not be offended in me. Luke 7:23

Do you want to be blessed? Those who are not offended about their Lord have been assured of definite blessings. You may say, "That is an easy requirement to fulfill." Is it? All of Christ's disciples were offended and left Him when He was arrested in the garden. Have you ever felt ashamed as they were? Did not guilt and sorrow follow?

To be offended means to be disgraced, scandalized, or reproached. Are we willing to receive such treatment on behalf of our Lord? It is a high cost to pay to receive the blessing, but what more could honor our precious Lord who was disgraced for us? Yet the promise is to those who *"shall not be offended."* Never feel shame or disgrace no matter what the world hurls at you by way of insult or jeering.

The world never liked Christ or His followers, and the same is true today. Hollywood has defamed Jesus by attacking His character and purity, and those who try to live a holy life are labeled as crazed fanatics. Christ has done great things for us and deserves our unwavering faithfulness and loyalty. Be true when tested and joy will follow.

And he said to the woman, Thy faith hath saved thee; go in peace.
Luke 7:50

Jesus was dining at Simon the Pharisee's house when a woman of disrepute entered the place. She was burdened with the guilt of her sin, and her heart was full of repentance. After washing Jesus' feet with her tears, wiping them with her hair, and anointing them with precious ointment, the Lord spoke to her. His words were, *"Thy faith hath saved thee; go in peace."* It was not the works that she did which saved her, but rather her faith in Jesus. Those humble deeds were only the evidence of the change in her heart.

There are two lessons for us to consider from this account. First, faith in Christ should produce a noticeable change in our lives. The hardened, unchaste woman was transformed. Has your faith made that much of a difference in your life? Many professing Christians have little to show for their "faith."

Secondly, those who come in faith to Jesus in deep remorse for their sins can be assured of His reply, *"go in peace."* If you are lacking peace within, perhaps you have not brought your sins to the Master. He is ever ready to cleanse and fill that void in your heart with blissful peace.

And he said unto them, Where is your faith? Luke 8:25

Here is a question we would all do well to contemplate. The disciples were in trouble and began to panic. They seemed to run to Jesus more as a miracle worker than as the One who cared for their well-being. Jesus stilled the storm but was displeased that the disciples were filled with fear. Fear shows mistrust and questions the character of Christ.

Are you facing a tempestuous storm in life? How have you pled with the Master, out of fear or in faith? Jesus wants to know, *"Where is your faith?"* We must remain calm and come to God in full assurance that He is in control of our fate. His care has never ceased during our affliction. With faith, there is no need for panic or alarm. Unfortunately, we are very often like the disciples—filled with worry.

The next time the raging waters threaten you, ask yourself, *"Where is your faith?"* Look for it and display it with confidence and courage! That faith will carry you through with an expectant eye that will see calm waters ahead. Faith sees deliverance, not destruction.

Return to thine own house, and shew how great things God hath done unto thee. And he went his way, and published throughout the whole city how great things Jesus had done unto him. Luke 8:39

The maniac of Gadara was healed of his demon possessed condition and transformed completely by the power of Christ. This new man wanted to return with Jesus and spend more time with Him, but Christ said, *"Return to thine own house, and shew how great things God hath done unto thee."* It may seem odd that Jesus did not allow the man to follow Him, but the Lord had a good reason.

This account demonstrates the importance that Christ puts on the family and His desire for our loved ones to hear the good news of salvation. It may seem that our close relatives are the most difficult to witness to, but they should be the ones with whom we start.

Do you have a lost father, mother, husband, wife, or child? Should you not go and show them what great things God has done for you? Is not this the first priority that Jesus placed on the former maniac? We must start at home, and then we may freely publish the gospel elsewhere.

And he said to them all, If any man will come after me, let him deny himself, and take up his cross daily, and follow me. Luke 9:23

When applying for loans, universities, or military positions, certain requirements must be met. When contemplating becoming a disciple of Jesus, we must see if we meet the criteria He set forth. Not everybody is willing to follow the strict guidelines; and, therefore, they cannot be one of His disciples. What is required?

First, Jesus said, *"let him deny himself."* Every disciple will constantly be faced with opportunities to please himself, but he must learn to say, "No." Second, Jesus said a disciple must *"take up his cross daily."* The cross refers to death, and we must be willing to put to death carnal appetites. Each day we must carry a burden for the Lord and not grow weary in our pilgrimage. Lastly, Jesus instructed the interested candidates of discipleship, *"follow me."* By definition, a disciple is a follower; therefore, when we fail to do the things Jesus did and live the way He lived, we cease to be disciples. Will we follow Him when others don't? Will we do so when it leads to mockery and shame? Do we really meet the standard of being a true disciple?

51

And I besought thy disciples to cast him out; and they could not.
Luke 9:40

A man, out of desperation, had brought his demon-possessed son to the disciples for help. The disciples tried to cast out the demon; but, sadly, *"they could not."* Previously, in verse one of this same chapter, Jesus *"gave them power and authority over all devils."* They had been given the power to do the job but failed!

Have we not also been promised power in our lives to do *"all"* that God requires? There are promises for soulwinning, victory over sin, raising our children, having a good marriage, peace, joy, *etc.* We have been given power through His promises but often fail to use it as did the disciples in this account. Consequently, we accomplish much less for God than what He intended for us to do. The cause of all our failures is summed up in one word by Jesus in the next verse—*"faithless."*

Let us believe in the power that He has promised to give us, and do what is expected of us. Not only do we fail the Lord when we lack faith, we also fail others who are counting on us for help. Let it not be said of us, *"they could not."* Are you a powerful or powerless disciple?

APR. 1   **HELPING THE HARVEST**   LUKE 10:1-22

Therefore said he unto them, The harvest truly is great, but the labourers are few: pray ye therefore the Lord of the harvest, that he would send forth labourers into his harvest. Luke 10:2

O ur Lord spoke of a *great potential*: *"The harvest truly is great."* Whether we realize it or not, there are many souls ready to be saved throughout the world. However, there is a *great problem*: *"the labourers are few."* It is well and good that we do our part to win souls, but the dilemma still exists as to who will win the others waiting to be saved.

What we need is *great prayer*—such prayer that will meet the great need. Herein I believe we fail miserably. Because we are not convinced of a great harvest, we pray so little for more laborers. When is the last time you asked the Lord to send hard-working laborers, new recruits as it were, to go win souls at home and abroad? It was a burden upon the heart of Jesus. Should not your heart yearn for what Christ yearns— more laborers? We need *great producers*, but that will only happen as we look to the Lord of the harvest to send them. Trying to rally lethargic saints may yield a few workers, but don't overlook a greater source for potential laborers—new converts. Let's work and pray to get some!

But he, willing to justify himself, said unto Jesus,
And who is my neighbour? Luke 10:29

To be justified means to be made and pronounced righteous. As odd as it sounds, one of man's biggest sins is to justify himself. Why is this so terrible? First, we have no power to make ourselves righteous because we are sinners; only Jesus can justify. Second, it is deceitful to pronounce ourselves as being righteous when, in fact, we are not. Third, it is wrong because there is no admission of guilt or confession of sin, which is nothing short of the hideous sin of pride.

The lost sinner tries to save himself by his works but can never manage to do so. The erring Christian often tries to justify himself by making excuses for his sins. He goes to great pains to cover his sins, trying to make himself look good when, in truth, he is not!

The man in our text was *"willing to justify himself."* He thought he had good reasoning skills to dodge his true condition. Are you guilty of the same? Is it not better to come to Christ in your broken condition, confess your sin, and let Him pronounce you clean and right? Learn to be unwilling to justify yourself so Christ can do for you what you cannot do for yourself.

And I say unto you, Ask, and it shall be given you; seek, and ye
shall find; knock, and it shall be opened unto you. Luke 11:9

Here is a very familiar promise given to those who are willing to understand its depth and try it. The way to get what we need is to go to our Father in *dependence*, along with an eye of expectation. Jesus made it simple: ask and receive, seek and find, and knock to have it opened. How often do we take Him at His word?

The words *ask, seek,* and *knock* imply work and *determination*. We may have to ask more than once! Perhaps we must become a bit more *desperate* and set aside extra time with the Lord to seek our desired answer. When we resolve to seek for a thing, it is because it has previously eluded us; and a casual attitude will not prevail to find it.

Why would we have to knock? When a door is closed, the way to get it opened is to knock. Does it not seem that, at times, God has not opened a way for us? We must knock until it is opened. To be effective in prayer, we must employ all three avenues of prayer: ask, seek, and knock. Be dependent, desperate, and determined!

The light of the body is the eye: therefore when thine eye is single, thy whole body also is full of light; but when thine eye is evil, thy body also is full of darkness. Luke 11:34

Jesus gave us the key to open the door to a happy life. Failure to use this key will lead to a dark, miserable existence. So, our text has both a promise and a prod to consider. Our eye, or focus in life, affects our entire well-being. When the eye is single, we see clearly. It is the opposite of having double vision, which is typified by having an eye towards worldliness and another towards heaven. Having a clear, upward focus on the Lord will make us full of light! Don't we want a bright, beaming radiance within our souls?

When we fail to have a singular eye, Jesus frankly says it is really an evil eye. Low, earthly vision is filled with fleshly desires and brings our whole body into darkness and bondage. Are you living in the sunlight or the shadows today? It is wise to get a vision check before entering your busy schedule. Go to the Great Physician and get your focus adjusted!

Set both eyes on the Lord today and gaze not at the temptations this evil world has to offer. Remember, low looks lead to low living.

Beware ye of the leaven of the Pharisees, which is hypocrisy. Luke 12:1

There are only a few occasions in the Bible when Jesus used the alarming word *beware*. Such a word is saved for dangerous situations and is meant to cause us to seriously consider a matter. As surely as DDT eliminates mosquitoes, hypocrisy wipes out vibrant Christianity. Far too many Christians pretend to be spiritual but are more concerned with looking good than being good. This kind of façade is tolerated and accepted by others who have the same worldly tendencies. Like leaven, it has a permeating effect. It often starts with parents who live differently at home than they do at church; soon the hypocrisy is instilled in the hearts of their children. If not dealt with, hypocrisy spreads, not only through homes but also through churches.

Many churches which were once strong contenders for the faith have become mere entertainment centers. By succumbing to the pressure of being accepted by the world, they have forfeited holiness. Though they claim to be spiritual, they have been affected by the leaven of hypocrisy.

We are losing our homes, our churches, and our future through pretending to be godly. It is no wonder Jesus said, *"Beware."* We need some Christians who will just be real! Will you be one of them?

But I have a baptism to be baptized with; and how am I straitened till
it be accomplished! Luke 12:50

There is no question that the baptism Jesus referred to here was His coming death. He would be immersed in pain, sorrow, and suffering. Despite knowing the pending hardships, He was focused on accomplishing the Father's will.

Jesus said He was "straitened." What does that mean? It literally means to be compressed, and it carries the idea of being preoccupied with the necessity of a task. How often do the cares of life distract us and prevent us from fulfilling the will of God? We must allow ourselves to feel the pressure of completing each task the Master sets before us. Like Jesus, we must not allow anticipated hardships to deter us from our appointed duty.

Are you ready to get immersed in doing the will of God? We cannot rest until the *"baptism"* that has been assigned to us has been accomplished. Do you have the drive and determination to finish your course? Ask God to help you shake off lethargy and get refocused.

Then said he unto the dresser of his vineyard, Behold, these three years I
come seeking fruit on this fig tree, and find none: cut it down;
why cumbereth it the ground? Luke 13:7

A man planted a fig tree in his vineyard so he could enjoy some figs. Certainly, it took space that could have been used for expanding his vineyard, but he desired the taste of figs. How disappointed he was when after three years he found none.

Is not our Lord also seeking fruit in our lives? Has He not come year after year looking, waiting, and longing for us to fulfill His purpose? God is gracious to give us time for growth; but when we have reached His appointed time of maturity, He becomes much more demanding.

God is seeking fruit in your life. Perhaps there are yet some areas of your Christian walk in which He has found none. The fig tree was dear to the owner of the field and had a special purpose to fulfill. As the fig tree differed from the vines of the vineyard, you also differ from all other believers. The fig tree was to bear a particular fruit, and God has created you to produce something unique for Him. Ask the Lord to help you produce the things that are pleasing to Him.

*And the lord said unto the servant, Go out into the highways and hedges,
and compel them to come in, that my house may be filled. Luke 14:23*

Do you get the idea from this verse that God wants His house to be filled? Many who have been invited to come to Christ have made excuses, but God still wants heaven to be as full as possible. To accomplish this important task, He commands His servants, *"Go out into the highways and hedges."* We must not be content to witness only where and when it is convenient but in all places and at all times: from the nice neighborhoods to the ghettos, from the cities to the small towns, and from modern countries to remote villages. The servant in the parable was obedient, and we are expected to be the same.

Furthermore, we must have fervent zeal when we go. Our job is to *"compel them to come in."* There ought to be radiance in our witness. When our hearts are right with God and we are filled with His Spirit, there is a natural burden for the unsaved; and we will earnestly and sincerely invite men to Christ. Do you have such a burden? God wants His house full, but He relies on His servants to do the bidding.

*I say unto you, that likewise joy shall be in heaven over one sinner that
repenteth, more than over ninety and nine just persons,
which need no repentance. Luke 15:7*

Yesterday's reading discussed the importance of winning souls, and today's discussion does the same. One may say, "Enough is enough. Move on to another subject." Sorry, but we cannot. This entire chapter deals with lost things being found: lost sheep, lost silver, and a lost son. The best thing about each situation is that the lost was found!

Our text says that there is joy in heaven when one sinner repents. In fact, there is more joy from that than from ninety-nine people who are saved and sitting in the pews at church. Churches are filled with saved people who think their presence in church brings great joy to the Lord. Obviously, God gets some pleasure from our faithfulness, but He rejoices more when a single lost soul is saved. This should tell us where our focus should be!

A church should be a working force engaged in finding the lost. If you really want to make God happy, win souls for Him. Perhaps you could look for a lost one today!

And he called him, and said unto him, How is it that I hear this of thee?
give an account of thy stewardship; for thou mayest
be no longer steward. Luke 16:2

F irst of all, let us be clear that stewardship refers to more than money. Whatever God has entrusted to you, He expects you to manage it well. We have all received something from God; it could be children, wealth, time, talent, position, or possessions.

What is certain is that God wants us to be responsible to fulfill our assigned duties; and we must give an account to God concerning our stewardship, not only on judgment day but also in this life. The verse warns, *"thou mayest be no longer steward."* It is, therefore, possible that we may lose what God has committed to our trust. Are you prepared to lose those things He has entrusted you to manage for Him?

This should cause us to stop being so complacent in our responsibilities and presumptuous that our unfaithfulness will go unchecked. What has the Lord endowed you with to serve Him? Are you faithful with those things? Have you lost opportunities already? Be serious about your duties so you don't lose your stewardship!

And it came to pass, that, as they went, they were cleansed. Luke 17:14

A s Christ entered into a village, ten lepers saw Him as their only hope and pled, *"Jesus, Master, have mercy on us."* They were told to go to the priests and show that they had been cleansed, but one problem remained: they were not yet cleansed! Jesus was about to perform a miracle which could only be accomplished if the lepers did their part.

What did the lepers have to do? They were expected to, by faith, go to the priests even though the leprosy was still in their bodies. They had to expect that at some point before reaching the priests they would, in fact, be healed. This required faith!

What is the lesson for us? Faith obeys first, and then it is rewarded. Notice the narrative, *"as they went, they were cleansed."* God is willing to answer our prayers and perform miracles, but He is looking for us to do our part. We need to put some feet to our prayers and do what He commands us. Then, as we go, God will intervene. If the lepers had refused to start off towards the priests until they were healed, the healing would not have come. When we refuse to obey God's commands, we cannot expect a miracle. Do your part so God can do His!

And shall not God avenge his own elect, which cry day and night unto
him, though he bear long with them? I tell you that
he will avenge them speedily. Luke 18:7, 8

When a saint pleads day and night with God, we can be sure He hears his petitions. However, there is a supposed contradiction in the wording found in these two verses, but no such malady can ever exist in Scripture. Consider the words of Christ, *"though he bear long with them...he will avenge them speedily."*

It may seem that you have been knocking on the door of heaven repeatedly with no answer. To you, God is taking a long time to respond; but our perception of time is much different than the everlasting Lord's. We are promised that He will answer *"speedily."* This means that as soon as He deems it best, He will grant our request. God is ready and willing to answer us; and when the time is right, He will move at lightning speed to accomplish His will. We must resolve to keep knocking and patiently trust that God's timing is best. A delay just makes the answer sweeter! *"Hope deferred maketh the heart sick: but when the desire cometh, it is a tree of life."* (Proverbs 13:12)

APR. 13   BLESSINGS NOW AND LATER   LUKE 18:18-43

And he said unto them, Verily I say unto you, There is no man that hath
left house, or parents, or brethren, or wife, or children, for the kingdom
of God's sake, Who shall not receive manifold more in this present time,
and in the world to come life everlasting. Luke 18:29-30

One of the greatest hindrances to walking with God is the fear of giving something up for Him. We know we are called to live a life of sacrifice, and when it isn't too much, we cheerfully follow. However, when we are asked to leave something very dear to us, it becomes more difficult because we do not want to lose the current blessing.

By failing to make that sacrifice, we not only lose out on eternal rewards but also miss present blessings. A poor man may be down to his last ear of corn and struggles with a decision. He can eat it and be satisfied for that day, or he can plant the kernels and have an abundance later. To gain more, he has to sacrifice what he has, as precious as it seems to him at the present moment.

When we put Christ first, the promise results in *"more in this present time and in the world to come."* We can be blessed now and later! Will you give up that special object of your affection in faith so God can give you more?

And he ran before, and climbed up into a sycomore tree to see him:
for he was to pass that way. Luke 19:4

Zacchaeus was a sinful man but wanted to get a view of the One who had the power to forgive sins. Like many of us, he was hindered from reaching the Savior. He was short in stature, and we are often short in seriousness. His desire for Christ drove him to find a tree for a better view of the Lord.

Likewise, a true longing to get closer to Jesus will require some effort on our part. We may have to climb a little higher in our attempt to get a better view of the Holy One. We will have to leave the lowland of sin and worldliness to set our affections on things above. A higher level of dedication to fervent prayer and meditative Bible study will also be required. Climbing may be tedious but is rewarding.

For Zacchaeus, *"Jesus came to the place...and saw him."* Will He not see us when we make a greater effort to gain a better glimpse of Him? Surely He is a *"rewarder of them that diligently seek him."* So, make the effort to climb a little higher!

...It is written, My house is the house of prayer: but ye have made it a den
of thieves. And he taught daily in the temple... Luke 19:46-47

Clearly, Jesus referred to the temple as being God's house. There is no temple today; we worship at the local church, which is commonly referred to as God's house. Christ was visibly upset at the activities going on in the temple in His day. How do you think He would react if He attended the average church in modern times? Churches are filled with entertainment: jazzed up music, dancing, activities, and worldly movies. Would there not be some cleansing of the sanctuary?

Our text gives two purposes for God's house: prayer and instruction. Church is a place to meet God and elevate our hearts toward Him in the *"house of prayer."* We also see that Jesus *"taught daily in the temple."* When God's Word goes forth, we are to examine our lives to be sure we are in accord with it. As Jesus taught in the temple, both believers and unbelievers were present. We must conclude that God's house is a place for the saved to be edified and the sinner to be evangelized. Two verses later, we see that *"he taught the people in the temple, and preached the gospel."* Sadly, many churches make little or no effort to bring the lost to God's house to hear the gospel.

And they could not take hold of his words before the people: and they marvelled at his answer, and held their peace. Luke 20:26

The religious leaders of Christ's day sent spies to try to trick Him with difficult questions. Christ answered them with such wisdom that they stood in amazement and were left speechless. They understood that they were no match for the Words of the Master.

People will pester you and question your faith, too. Many think they are clever as they frame their arguments against Biblical truth, but we should have no fear. The same Word that silenced the skeptics in Christ's day is available to us. Simply turn to the Word of God because it has all of the right answers!

After Christ's words were spoken, the opposition *"held their peace."* There is no need to argue with people; simply start quoting the mighty Word of God. Having God's Word hidden in your heart is invaluable in such situations. However, if you do not have the needed verses memorized or the Bible with you, be sure to go home and study the matter. This will give peace in your heart and prepare you for the next encounter with those who seek to shake your faith.

For he is not a God of the dead, but of the living: for all live unto him. Luke 20:38

The thought of death is chilling and sobering. However, life brings warmth and vibrancy. In Christ, no man is ever dead! How could He reign over a kingdom of dead people? What ruler has dead subjects? Jesus assures us that *"he is not a God of the dead, but of the living."* He is alive and so are the souls of departed believers!

In life, our soul has been renewed and regenerated, and in death that same soul never ceases to exist or fade into oblivion. Whether in this world or the next, we have life! The Christian is alive forevermore.

The text further reveals why we have continual life—*"all live unto him."* It is certain that departed souls who enjoy His presence are busy serving Him, and it should be equally the same for the living who are still on earth. We should *"live unto him"* every day, not unto self. So, the purpose of our life is to give it back to the One who gave it to us. Has He given you life? If so, have you given it back to Him? Do you need reviving? Perhaps you have forgotten for Whom you are to be living. Purpose to renew your dedication *"to live unto him"* today.

And he looked up, and saw the rich men casting their gifts into the
treasury. And he saw also a certain poor widow
casting in thither two mites. Luke 21:1-2

The contrast in this story is so striking that one might be tempted to think it was a parable designed to get our attention. However, this is not a fictional account for the narrative explains that Jesus *"looked up, and saw."* He beheld several things: He saw who gave, what they gave, how they gave, and what was remaining after they gave.

It is interesting that the word *tithe* is never mentioned in the story. The rich men had lots of money and gave of their abundance, but it could have been less than the required tithe. Even today, people think they have done well for throwing a few large bills into the offering plate while they know it is far less than a tithe. The poor destitute widow in the story obviously gave more than the tithe; she gave *"all the living that she had."* It may have been small in men's eyes, but it wasn't in Christ's!

This touching account of love and sacrifice should motivate us to be sure that we give from the heart, not what is convenient. What the widow gave was not much in man's eyes but great in God's! Never feel compelled to give in order to please man—One far greater is watching!

LUKE 22:1-23   THE DANGER OF YOUR OWN WAY   APR. 19

And he went his way, and communed with the chief priests and captains,
how he might betray him unto them. Luke 22:4

Can we learn a lesson from Judas Iscariot? Just hearing that name makes a godly man cringe with disgust, but we must beware that we never stray down the same path that he took. Is it possible we could act like such a traitor? You may be surprised!

Before the infamous kiss of betrayal, we see two fatal mistakes. First, *"he went his way."* God never intended for man to go his own way, and from the onset of creation He has given instruction to man in the way he should go. When we do our own thing and go the direction in life that is pleasing to self, we walk in the footsteps of Judas, rather than those of Jesus.

The second step Judas took towards betraying the Lord was that he *"communed"* with the enemy. What business do Christians have desiring fellowship with the wicked? A longing to be with worldly ones reveals a betrayal of Christ, and seeking to benefit from their company is surely Judas-like. Oh, forsake your own way and never be allured by the world's rewards!

And when he rose up from prayer, and was come to his disciples, he
found them sleeping for sorrow, And said unto them, Why sleep ye?
rise and pray, lest ye enter into temptation. Luke 22:45-46

Our Lord prayed in agony in the garden, and He had instructed the disciples to do likewise. After submitting to the will of the Father, Jesus was strengthened by an attending angel. The disciples could have received the same strength had they prayed, but instead their weakness was apparent when they all forsook Christ.

The fruit of prayerlessness was twofold: sorrow and sin. Why were they sleeping? They were *"sleeping for sorrow."* When we fail to pray, we ensure that sadness will follow. So many depressed people try to sleep their troubles away; but rather than slumbering in faithlessness, we need to rise and be earnest in prayer. Prayer is not only the best solution for discouragement; it also prevents it from taking root in the first place!

The second result of failing to pray is sin. Jesus made it clear, *"pray, lest ye enter into temptation."* Refusing to take prayer seriously, the disciples became backslidden. Can we expect to avoid the same fate if we fail to pray as we should?

APR. 21   **STAY CLOSE TO THE MASTER**   LUKE 22:47-71

...And Peter followed afar off. Luke 22:54

Peter found himself in quite a dilemma. He wanted to follow Jesus, but not so closely that it would bring personal discomfort. Instead, he resolved to follow *"afar off."* Is this not the same attitude of many Christians today? When we are in the company of fellow believers, we are bold to claim Christ and stand for righteousness. However, when the world surrounds us and snarls at our godliness, many of us tend to take the *"afar off"* approach.

Of course, we know what this led to in Peter's life. He got too close to the unbelieving crowd, denied the Lord, changed his behavior in an attempt to fit in, and brought disgrace to himself. Had Peter prayed as mentioned earlier, he would have received the necessary strength to stay close to the Master. Nobody has ever successfully followed *"afar off,"* and it is certain that you won't be the first to succeed.

When following someone in a vehicle to an unknown destination, you always stay as close as possible, not far away. The danger of losing your way is multiplied when you are *"afar off."* So, stay close to Jesus!

And they cried out all at once, saying, Away with this man... Luke 23:18

S ince the day Jesus entered the world, He has been hated. At His birth, Herod wanted the True King killed and slew the children at Bethlehem. At His death, the religious leaders cried, *"Away with this man."* Is it not the same still? In public schools, where prayer was once commonplace, they cried, *"Away with this man,"* and banned prayer. In court houses where the Ten Commandments had been on display as a model of law, the world said, *"Away with this man."* At Christmas time they demanded, *"Away with this man,"* and replaced "Merry Christmas" with "Happy Holidays" or "Compliments of the Season."

Can we expect the world's attitude to change? Never! The time is coming when true Christians will have to pay a severe price for their faith. Other generations faced harsh persecution, and we can expect the same. This is not a time to be ashamed of Christ! We must proclaim His name with at least as much fervor as they shout, *"Away with this man."* Be of good cheer because nobody can do away with our Jesus! Only beware that you have not squeezed the Lord out of any corner of your life. Satan relentlessly tries to get us to replace Christ with other things!

LUKE 23:27-56   A GOOD MAN CONSENTS NOT   APR. 23

And, behold, there was a man named Joseph, a counsellor; and he was a good man, and a just: (The same had not consented to the counsel and deed of them;) Luke 23:50-51

J esus had just been horribly mistreated and crucified at the demand of the Jewish elders. However, there was a certain counselor who refused to give his consent to their evil deeds. The Bible says that Joseph *"was a good man."* Surely his peers criticized and derided him for not agreeing to their plans. The lesson for us today is quite clear: good men never follow the crowd. Many will do right when it is easy and convenient, but few will bear the shame of being godly when all others are against them. Joseph not only faced the ridicule of the Jewish elders, he also faced the evil ruler, Pilate, who gave Christ's death sentence.

Although Joseph could not stop the crucifixion, he did what he could to honor the Lord. While others fled, he bore the shame of being associated with Jesus by burying Him. There were not many heroes on that grim day, but Joseph was certainly one. Will you rise up and stand for Christ regardless of the cost? Will you be a hero or a coward?

And he said unto them, What manner of communications are these that ye have one to another, as ye walk, and are sad? Luke 24:17

We find two discouraged disciples leaving Jerusalem and discussing the event that had just taken place. They witnessed Christ's death, heard about the women finding the empty tomb, knew that the angel said He was alive, and bare witness that Peter and John had *"found it even as the women had said."* They had all the evidence they needed that Christ was raised from the dead, but they were still sad!

Christ had fulfilled His plan, but the disciples left Jerusalem. If Christ were alive, that was certainly not the time to leave Jerusalem! So, when Jesus found them, He asked them why they were sad. They mumbled a bit, and then Jesus gave them the real reason for their sadness, *"O fools, and slow of heart to believe all that the prophets have spoken."* Why do we get sad? Do we not fail to believe God's Word at times? We foolishly set out onto the sad road to Emmaus because of unbelief, while the living Christ is ready to help us.

One more cause for their sadness stands out. It is certain that the *"manner of communications"* they had *"one to another"* added to their grief. Be careful not to talk yourself into discouragement!

And they said one to another, Did not our heart burn within us, while he talked with us by the way, and while he opened to us the scriptures? Luke 24:32

Something special and wonderful happens when you walk with Jesus. Although the two men in our story were foolish, faint, and faithless, spending time with Jesus changed all of that. Their testimony was, *"Did not our heart burn within us...?"* That burning heart came when Christ *"talked"* and *"opened...the scriptures."*

The fire of God's Word will revive us as we meditate on it. When fire burns, it has a warming effect. Just as a cold automobile engine is sluggish until it gets warmed up, we do little for God until we get a fire in our hearts. Fire also has a comforting effect. The disciples had been discouraged, but the message of the Master brought encouragement. Is your soul a bit chilly? Why not snuggle up to the Word of God and get renewed?

We should also consider that fire illuminates. The sad disciples could not understand why Jesus had died but found the answer while He spoke to them. We often misunderstand many events of life, but God's Word will be a light to our path. Oh, how we need a fire raging within!

There was a man sent from God, whose name was John. John 1:6

Let every servant of God learn a lesson from this short text. John the Baptist was only a man, but he was greatly used of God. Men have weakness, but God still chooses to use us. Although John was only a man, he *"was sent from God."* At times we are tempted to think that God cannot use us because of our frailties and frequent failures, but we must remember that God uses us in spite of ourselves—not because of our own strength. If you are sent by God to do a thing, never fear; God is with you to accomplish His will.

Additionally, if a man is to be used, he must be manly. We know John had a masculine appearance; he did not array himself in smooth, gorgeous apparel. Too many men of modern times have become feminine, but God does not choose such men to represent Him! God wants men who look, act, walk, talk, and smell like men, not women. God possesses no feminine characteristics, and His men must not either.

The best thing parents can do in raising their sons is to make men out of them. By instilling toughness of character we prepare them to endure hardness as good soldiers of Jesus Christ. The world needs men sent from God, but God relies on fathers to train boys who can be those men.

Jesus answered and said unto him...thou shalt see
greater things than these. John 1:50

What a reassuring God we have! These words were spoken to Nathanael who stood in amazement after Jesus proved to be all knowing. The man had witnessed a great event but was promised to see many more!

What have we already seen God do in our lives? Has He not demonstrated His power repeatedly to us? Have we not had answers to prayer and witnessed miracles from God? Don't think that God has run out of mercy and kindness. You will see greater things than these! A farmer is not satisfied by reaping one apple from his tree; he expects many more. In the same manner, we can return to God for a full harvest, knowing that He will produce the best fruit in His season.

Do you need such a promise today? Have you forgotten what God has done in the past? Are you discouraged by a long delay regarding a request you have brought to God? He has not failed you. He has many more wonderful things planned for your life and is anxious to reveal Himself again. Take Him at His word, claim the promise, and wait until He blesses you once again!

...Whatsoever he saith unto you, do it. John 2:5

These were the words spoken by Mary to the servants at the wedding. She knew Jesus could perform a miracle and gave some good advice for preparing for one. Before we can expect to see God do something wonderful in our lives, we must be obedient. *"Whatsoever he saith unto you, do it."* *"Whatsoever"* is the key; therefore, be willing to do anything and everything that God directs you to do.

Jesus issued the command, *"Fill the waterpots with water."* Did they obey? Oh yes, *"they filled them up to the brim."* They did not fill them halfway but to the brim. Here we see complete obedience by the servants, and the miracle followed soon after. God is looking for people who will not only obey but do so with little hesitation and much expectation!

So, do you want a miracle? You cannot anticipate God doing anything for you until you have followed His will. Neglecting God's commands is a sure way to prevent the miraculous. As we ponder what we want from God, let us also consider what He wants from us!

He must increase, but I must decrease. John 3:30

We live in the age of the mega-church syndrome. All we hear about is this "great" man and that one. Men are building empires for themselves and becoming known for church growth techniques or new ministry philosophies. We hear much of men but not much of Jesus!

John the Baptist had the best ministry philosophy: *"He must increase, but I must decrease."* We see this emphasis in his message which was, *"Behold the Lamb of God."* He pointed people to Christ and was not interested in attracting others to himself. Consequently, he lifted up his voice against sin and hypocrisy, even daring to call some in the audience a *"generation of vipers."* If he were alive today, I think he would remind us that church growth occurs when people are confronted with their sins and God's men cry, "Repent!" Mega-church builders and compromising pastors are afraid of God's method of old-fashioned, red-hot preaching. It worked in John's day and still works in ours!

Beware of new ideas and movements that rally around men. We don't need to hear more about Rick Warren, Joel Osteen, or Bill Hybels—we need to hear about Jesus! Don't become enamored with self-promotion. Magnify Christ—not self or any other.

...the true worshippers shall worship the Father in spirit and in truth: for the Father seeketh such to worship him. John 4:23

The Samaritan woman had made a distinction between the worship of the Jews and that of her own people. Both had some form of religious worship, but Jesus was clear that the Father was seeking more than form. Religious activity and ceremony may abound in the churches of our day, but true worship is lacking.

In modern times, worship has been equated with feeling good. People get mesmerized as they sway to heavy rhythms and breathy ballads. As they "lose themselves" in the music, they feel that their hearts are somehow being lifted up to God. However, this is not worship *"in spirit"* but rather engaging the flesh. Any activities that are contrary to the revealed truth of the Bible cannot be considered as worship.

Truth must be present if worship is to be legitimate. Therefore, we must conclude that the true worshipers are those who are much in the Word and agree with it in their spirits. As you meditate therein and commune with God in your heart, that is true worship! Beware of what the world calls worship.

Jesus saith unto them, My meat is to do the will of him that sent me, and to finish his work. John 4:34

The meat that Jesus referred to was not physical food; He used the term to relay a spiritual application. Food is not only essential for strength: it also brings satisfaction to the body. Without food, our whole being is disturbed and unfulfilled.

Christ made it clear that what sustained Him was not partaking of this world's goods. Real satisfaction was gained as He carried out the will of the Father and labored to finish that work. Hence, no Christian can ever have the strength, sustenance, or satisfaction that he craves until he is focused on the will of God.

What is it that God wants you to do today? You will never be complete without accomplishing it. Some sense of satisfaction is gained by starting a task, but true fulfillment comes when we *"finish his work."* Real happiness will elude you until you get hungry for the right type of meat. Nothing is more gratifying than finding God's will, doing it, and obtaining the blessings tied to it.

Afterward Jesus findeth him in the temple, and said unto him, Behold, thou art made whole: sin no more, lest a worse thing come unto thee.
John 5:14

How happy the man at the pool of Bethesda must have been when he was healed after thirty-eight years! There is no indication why he had been sick for so long, but we do know the healing was a demonstration of God's mercy.

Later, the man apparently went to the temple to worship God. Jesus made a point to seek him out and deliver an important message—*"sin no more, lest a worse thing come unto thee."* After God does great things in our lives, He expects us to serve Him out of gratitude. We should determine to forsake every sin and purpose to be more consecrated.

Failing to allow God's blessings to change us can lead to bigger troubles than we previously faced. I am sure the man that was healed was thinking, "What could be worse than thirty-eight years of sickness? I don't want anything worse!" The same Lord Who shows tender mercy also afflicts and scourges. Therefore, we must resolve to *"sin no more"* when we have been pardoned. Nobody wants to face *"a worse thing."*

MAY 3   BURNING AND SHINING LIGHTS   JOHN 5:24-47

He was a burning and a shining light: and ye were willing for a season to rejoice in his light. John 5:35

John the Baptist was a true witness for Jesus Christ in both word and deed. His life and message challenged those around him. Some, evidently, only took pleasure in his ministry *"for a season."* Although initially enlightened, they later counted the cost of repentance too high.

Regardless of how our light is received by others, we must determine to be *"burning and shining."* A *burning light* refers to a fire which consumes, and our lives must be totally obsessed with glorifying God. We must be set ablaze by His Word and emit the warm love of God. In regards to being a *shining light*, we must lighten the dark corners of this world where sin abounds by a radiating testimony of true holiness.

Finally, we must note how John burned so brightly for God. The oil lamp was the commonly used light of the day. Oil is an emblem of the Holy Spirit, and only He can supply us with the ability to burn and shine. As a lamp without oil fails to fulfill its purpose, so a Christian without a filling of the Holy Spirit cannot bear a true witness of Jesus. Is your lamp full?

There is a lad here, which hath five barley loaves, and two small fishes: but what are they among so many? John 6:9

A dilemma of mammoth proportions faced the disciples: there were five thousand men who needed to be fed. Jesus, in an attempt to test Philip's faith, said *"Whence shall we buy bread that these may eat?"* Philip's response was not, "Oh, we can't find a place that has that much." Neither did he suggest that Jesus perform a miracle. Instead, he looked on the financial side of the crisis. It would take over six month's wages to feed this many men!

Andrew wasn't looking at the money issue; he considered what was available. By doing so, he showed some initiative to see if they could meet the need with the resources at their disposal. However, when he discovered there were only five loaves and two fishes, he exclaimed, *"what are they among so many?"* What he failed to realize is that little is much when placed in the hands of the Master. What you have available by way of talent, treasure, and time is sufficient when put into God's hands. Don't fail the tests God puts before you by looking at the circumstances. The eye of faith sees something special on the horizon.

JOHN 6:22-48   SEEKING JESUS FOR WRONG REASONS   MAY 5

...Verily, verily, I say unto you, Ye seek me, not because ye saw the miracles, but because ye did eat of the loaves, and were filled. John 6:26

A fter feeding the five thousand, Jesus crossed the sea of Galilee to Capernaum. The next day, a group from the feeding began looking for Jesus but could not find Him. Therefore, *"they also took shipping, and came to Capernaum, seeking Jesus."* On the surface, their actions seem commendable because they were, after all, *"seeking Jesus."* What could be wrong with that?

When they found Christ, they were confronted with the words of our text. Instead of blessing them, Jesus reproved them! Why? The people were not interested in who Jesus was nor amazed at the glorious power He possessed. They simply had enjoyed receiving a big, filling meal the day before and hoped to get the same again. They only sought Him for physical provision.

When we are only concerned about what we can get from Jesus, are we not guilty of seeking Him for the wrong reasons, too? Should we not seek Him for who He is and praise Him for His loving kindness?

Many therefore of his disciples, when they had heard this, said,
This is an hard saying; who can hear it? John 6:60

Some of the disciples were offended when they heard Christ's teachings; they believed that what He said was too difficult to accept. Consequently, we read of their fate, *"From that time many of his disciples went back, and walked no more with him."* There is a direct correlation between how we receive the Word and how we react to it. When we think it is too hard, we cease to walk with Him and go our own way.

Is it not interesting that followers of Christ decided to follow no more? Many people will listen to the Lord as long as it is not too harsh or intolerable; but when it goes against their will or understanding, they rebel. It is not so much a matter of a hard saying, but rather of a hard heart!

Jesus knew that some of those disciples did not trust Him, and He turned His attention to the twelve saying, *"Will ye also go away?"* When things get too tough for you, will you go away? Will you follow no more? Either we accept the hard sayings or develop hard hearts.

MAY 7   PROPER JUDGMENT   JOHN 7:1-27

Judge not according to the appearance, but judge righteous judgment.
John 7:24

Judgment is not condemned in the Bible as some would have us to believe. Notice that there are two commands issued in this verse, *"Judge not"* and *"judge."* There is, then, a type of judging we should abstain from and another we should engage in.

The Pharisees were scolded by Jesus because they had condemned Him for healing a man on the Sabbath. In their minds He broke God's law by working. However, they made exceptions for themselves to be able to work when they deemed it necessary. Christ's actions did not fit into their idea of what was acceptable; so, they criticized Him.

Jesus' response to those hypocrites teaches us not to judge according to personal biases. How a thing appears to us is not the final consideration to be made. We must judge righteously, and that is done only by examining the situation in the light of God's Word. If the Bible condemns a thing, then you may safely do likewise. However, don't be a self-righteous hypocrite going about finding faults in others when they do not meet your own personal expectations.

...If any man thirst, let him come unto me, and drink. John 7:37

Thirst is a natural sensation in the body aroused when we are low on fluids. A refreshing drink will revitalize our body and boost our energy level. All men thirst physically, but not all acknowledge being spiritually depleted. Neglecting the body's need for liquid will lead to the dangerous condition of dehydration. Likewise, Christians who attempt to go on in their own strength will become spiritually dehydrated, which leaves them languishing in a backslidden condition.

The invitation is given to all men to *"come"* to Jesus. The unsaved can come and drink the waters of salvation freely, and the saved can come and partake of a fresh filling of the Spirit. In both cases, Jesus says, *"come unto me, and drink."* Do you run to Jesus when feeling spiritually dry? So often we sense the lack of living waters flooding our souls but fail to go to the Fountain to quench our thirst.

We rarely neglect a drink when our body demands it, but we treat our soul quite differently. Is this not strange? Go at once to the Savior and partake; strength and satisfaction await you! The only way to be refreshed is to be refilled with the Spirit of God.

...I am the light of the world: he that followeth me shall not walk in darkness, but shall have the light of life. John 8:12

Jesus proclaimed Himself to be the light of the world, but why does the world need light? Obviously, it is because it is in utter spiritual darkness. The religious people of the day had brought a woman guilty of adultery to Christ for judgment. They were not interested in helping her; therefore, they were in as much darkness as she was!

The answer to every man's need, whether he is religious or not, is Jesus. For the Christian, we have to beware of being influenced by the gloomy world around us that ever seeks to cast its shadows on our path. Our only safety is to stay close to the Light!

One evening, in Zambia, my daughter went outside on an errand, and on her way she encountered a large black snake, doubtless a spitting cobra. Had she not followed the beams of her flashlight, she could have gotten dangerously close and been attacked. Likewise, the Christian must follow Jesus to avoid the danger posed by the old serpent, the devil, who blends in so well under the cover of this world's darkness.

Walking in darkness is not only dangerous but scary. Therefore, let us mind Christ—*"he that followeth me shall not walk in darkness."*

...Whosoever committeth sin is the servant of sin. John 8:34

A servant is one who is under the control of another. In our text, Jesus warns us how sins can enslave us if we are not careful. The road to slavery is quite simple: commit a sin just one time!

Although sin promises liberty, it delivers just the opposite. We must realize that a decision to sin is a request to be brought into bondage. When a person tells a lie, he then becomes a servant of that lie and will have to tell several more to protect the first one. The sin dictates his future thoughts and actions.

A Christian cannot take a short visit to the land of sin. Once there, he is not free to leave when he desires; he is held as a prisoner and forbidden to leave the gate he entered. Whether it is the land of worldly music, gossip, pornography, drinking, stealing, or fornication, the moment you go for a visit you have surrendered your freedom and can be held captive at any moment.

If you are in such bondage today, run to Jesus! *"If the Son therefore shall make you free, ye shall be free indeed."* Once free, never forget the horrors your soul experienced while in sin's shackles.

Ye are of your father the devil...When he speaketh a lie, he speaketh of his own: for he is a liar, and the father of it. John 8:44

I suppose that few would openly express a desire to be like Satan. However, many reflect his character more frequently than they realize, and it occurs each time they tell a lie. Jesus said of the devil, *"he is a liar, and the father of it."*

Can we argue against Christ? One who lies is acting just like Satan! In fact, the devil is the originator of lying, being called, *"the father of it."* To tell a lie is to support his cause and reinforce his crafty invention.

A Christian must not only hate lies spoken by others; he must also recognize and detest them in his own life. We excuse our lies as being innocent or unintentional, but in reality they are Satanic! Our deceitful hearts certainly do not help the matter either as we are prone to lie even to ourselves. What then? Is there no hope?

Surely we can escape the snare of telling falsehoods. How? We must saturate our minds with the truth of the Bible and be led by the Spirit of truth. God's people must be representatives of the Father of Truth, not the father of lies. Let us proclaim as did the psalmist, *"I hate and abhor lying: but thy law do I love."* (Psalm 119:163)

*I must work the works of him that sent me, while it is day:
the night cometh, when no man can work. John 9:4*

How much time do you have remaining on this earth? Most of us have no idea; and consequently, we live as though we have many years ahead of us. This attitude often leads to procrastination or laziness when it comes to the Lord's work, and many opportunities for service are squandered away.

Jesus knew when He would die and diligently went about His duties. He was focused and determined to accomplish all His work in His allotted window of time. We, too, have been granted a specific timeframe to fulfill our mission and must get busy while *"it is day."*

Jesus used a common example of a working day to illustrate this idea. People in those days could only work while the sunlight was available; and once the sun had set, their work ceased. Certainly, many would get an early start and work harder to finish their task as the sun began to set. For us, every day brings us closer to the final sundown of our lives. Knowing that *"the night cometh, when no man can work,"* we must work harder than ever. There is no time to procrastinate!

*And some of the Pharisees which were with him heard these words,
and said unto him, Are we blind also? John 9:40*

Although the Pharisees asked many provoking questions, occasionally they posed some very good ones like the one in our text for today. Unfortunately, even when they put forth a good question, they had no heart to receive the answer.

All men are born with spiritual blindness and must come to Christ for sight. Jesus came *"that they which see not might see; and that they which see might be made blind."* Blindness speaks of a frail, humble condition, and Christ delights to illuminate those in such a state. The Pharisees claimed to know all and see the Scriptures clearly, yet they were blinded by their pride. A saved person must guard against pride and maintain a humble disposition before God and man. Sin will blind us so that we cannot see clearly, and many Christians needlessly stumble through life. We would do well to ask Jesus today, *"Are we blind also?"*

It could be that you are blinded to sinful habits, haughty attitudes, bitter feelings, worldly vices, or bad friends in your life. The only way to find out is to humbly, honestly ask God to show you.

*And when he putteth forth his own sheep, he goeth before them, and the
sheep follow him: for they know his voice. John 10:4*

Herein lies a beautiful illustration of how the Good Shepherd and the
sheep work together. The Shepherd *"putteth forth his own sheep"*
into fields of service, and we must gladly move at His bidding. Being
"his own sheep" reminds us that we have been purchased and are
assured of His protection. We will never be left in a place of jeopardy by
the Good Shepherd. Therefore, we should rejoice in His ownership, not
bemoan it.

Another blessing is that our Shepherd *"goeth before"* the sheep.
Going where Jesus sends me is my duty, but knowing that He has gone
before me to prepare the way is my delight. When I obey Him and go to
His fields of service, I will meet Him there. Amen!

Lastly, *"the sheep follow him."* It is contrary to our new nature to
refuse to follow the Shepherd, and sheep easily follow because *"they
know his voice."* Failure to listen leads to a failure in obedience. Take
time to listen to the Shepherd each day and you will hear His voice
calling you where His presence awaits. Is there not fullness of joy there?

*And I give unto them eternal life; and they shall never perish,
neither shall any man pluck them out of my hand. John 10:28*

Unfortunately, there are occasions in some believers' lives in which
they begin to question or doubt their salvation. The only people
who should ever doubt are those who are not born again, and they should
repent and receive Christ to end their doubts. However, the devil knows
that if he can introduce such troubling questions into a believer's life, he
will cripple their effectiveness for the Savior.

Consider the words of Jesus and take hope if you are in such a state
today, *"I give unto them eternal life."* Notice that eternal life is a gift. A
person does not gain salvation by earning it, nor does he keep it by being
good. Sinful failures will not cause you to lose your salvation; however,
they will disturb your fellowship with God. Allowing sin into your life
may make you feel unsaved; but in reality, you have lost your closeness
to God, not your home in heaven.

Salvation cannot be lost because Jesus called it *"eternal."*
Something eternal cannot end! Further, He said, *"they shall never
perish."* Clearly, a saved person can never go to hell. So, rejoice if you
have received Christ and confess your sin if out of fellowship.

Therefore his sisters sent unto him, saying, Lord, behold,
he whom thou lovest is sick. John 11:3

Many times when we are faced with sore afflictions we are tempted to wonder why God permits such troubles into our lives. Christians even find themselves saying, "I thought God loved me; why is He doing this to me? This isn't fair." Our text shows us a marvelous truth that we would do well to keep in mind. Jesus loved Lazarus, but that did not prevent bad things from happening to him. In fact, he got so sick that he died. We must remember that bad things happen to good people; and when such events occur in a Christian's life, it can never be considered as a lack of love on God's behalf. No matter what happens in your life, God's love remains constant and faithful.

Another consideration from this story reveals that the "bad thing" in Lazarus' life was not so bad after all! He lived again! Jesus said, *"This sickness is...for the glory of God."* Even the deepest trials of life have a master plan behind them to bring glory to the Father. We may not see the result in our time of grief, but faith counts on God as being perfect in all His ways. Never question God's love; trust Him that He has a purpose for your current troubles.

Jesus wept. John 11:35

Crying is a true expression of grief and sorrow. There were occasions in Jesus' life in which He wept. You may recall when He beheld Jerusalem and wept over their pending judgment due to unbelief.

In today's passage, we find the Savior about to raise Lazarus from the dead. He was not weeping, as some supposed, because Lazarus had died, but rather because of the unbelief of the people. He *"groaned in the spirit and was troubled"* because the people demonstrated no faith in Him to handle the problem. Some even murmured, *"could not this man, which opened the eyes of the blind, have caused that this man should not have died?"* They questioned His goodness and power.

Herein lies food for thought. When we fail to trust God by doubting His character, it hurts Him terribly. Unbelief not only prevents peace in our hearts, it also produces pain in Jesus' heart. Would it not be better to bring joy to His heart by expressing unwavering faith?

How often have you caused Him to weep because of your unbelief? Have you failed to trust Him in the midst of your problems? Let's be more concerned about His feelings than our own this day.

*Verily, verily, I say unto you, Except a corn of wheat fall into the ground
and die, it abideth alone: but if it die, it bringeth forth much fruit.*
John 12:24

God's creation preaches yet another sermon to us. The kernel of
wheat can bring limited satisfaction if consumed by itself.
However, if it falls and dies, a bountiful harvest is sure to result. The
lesson is simple: death brings life.

Consider the process involved with the kernel of wheat. First, it
must *"fall into the ground."* This speaks of humility! Our carnal nature
is always trying to elevate self and never wants to be cast down; but until
we fall prostrate at the throne of grace, we shall be fruitless Christians.
As we *"fall into the ground"* we are burying selfish desires, plans, and
pursuits. When buried, self is out of sight so that the glory of God may
spring forth. Secondly, observe that the kernel must *"die."* Death
speaks of pain, and truly it is a painful process to deny our carnal
appetites and crucify the flesh. However, like a seed, without death fruit
will never be produced. The saint who will fall in humility and die to the
world will indeed bring forth *"much fruit."* Death turns into a blessing!

*Now is my soul troubled; and what shall I say? Father, save me from this
hour: but for this cause came I unto this hour. John 12:27*

Doing the right thing will at times bring trouble to the soul. God's
will is not always easy to follow because of the opposition we will
receive by doing it. Jesus not only faced rejection, He also had to deal
with being made sin for us. Consequently, the thought of losing
fellowship with the Father troubled Him. So, what did Jesus do with a
troubled soul?

He brought His concern straight to the Father of mercies and cast His
care upon Him. The first One we should ever consult is our loving
Father whose ear is always awaiting our appeal. Further, we read Jesus'
request, *"save me from this hour."* If it is at all possible for God to
deliver us from the affliction, He will. However, some troubles are
meant to be endured, not avoided. Therefore, we must submit to His
plan and resign to follow, whatever the cost. In the end, Jesus admitted,
"but for this cause came I unto this hour." Although we wish the trouble
to flee, our faith must prevail by crying out as did Christ, *"Father,
glorify thy name."* We are to live for His glory—not for our deliverance!

Jesus answered and said unto him, What I do thou knowest not now;
but thou shalt know hereafter. John 13:7

J esus had begun to wash the disciples feet, but Peter protested when it
was his turn.   He obviously did not understand why Jesus was
engaged in such a lowly activity. Our Lord responded, *"What I do thou*
knowest not now; but thou shalt know hereafter."

Are there not times when we fail to understand what God is doing in
our lives? It should be comforting to know that He is wisely arranging
every detail, even when things make no sense to us. We must learn to
exercise patience and wait for the *"hereafter."* The disciples saw Jesus
at work, and their curiosity should have been piqued as they wondered
what the Lord was going to do next. Never fear when you cannot grasp
the workings of God; be excited that He is at work! Faith accepts that
His dealings with us will be fair and right.

You will soon discover the reason for what seems to make little
sense now. It is not for us to wonder but to wait. It will be clear one
day! Strike up a tune in your heart and sing, "We will understand it
better by and by."

By this shall all men know that ye are my disciples,
if ye have love one to another. John 13:35

J esus wants all men to know that we are His followers, but that requires
more than just talk. It demands an adequate display of Christian love
towards the brethren.   Because Jesus loves others, we ought to do
likewise. After all, a disciple is one that follows the Master in action and
attitude.

So, how can we demonstrate love toward other Christians if we are
never around them? In most churches, there are some who sit on the
sidelines and observe. They never jump in and really get involved.
Perhaps they are timid, feel unneeded, or fear getting hurt by others; but
none of these excuses are Biblical. A hen that neglects her eggs can't
warm them, and a Christian who avoids the brethren can't love them. If
we limit our participation in the lives of others, we hinder opportunities
to help and show concern. Life is not about us—it is about loving others!

Sometimes we are amazed at how much a son acts likes his father.
He does so because he has spent much time with him and has learned his
ways. Likewise, if we spend much time with Jesus, we will learn to love
as He does. Is there enough evidence to prove you are His disciple?

...I go to prepare a place for you...that where I am, there ye may be also.
John 14:2-3

How sweet are the words, *"a place for you."* Every child of God has a home in heaven. Let this cheer your soul today as you trudge through this wicked, defiled world. One day, our earthly pilgrimage will be over and we will reach the Celestial City! No more sin, sorrow, or disappointments. Despite failures and faithlessness, we still have *"a place."* Salvation is not determined by our works, but our rewards are. Notice Jesus' words, *"I go to prepare a place for you."* I believe that each saint will have something prepared uniquely for him, and that will be based upon his service to God in this life. Are we not to lay up treasures in heaven?

Next, we must look at His wonderful promise, *"where I am, there ye may be also."* Those intimate times of fellowship here when God manifests Himself in a special way are precious, but sin so quickly severs that blessedness. However, in heaven, nothing exists that can interrupt our communion with God. Won't that be eternal bliss? The best is yet to come! So, fight the good fight always looking to your heavenly abode.

If ye abide in me, and my words abide in you, ye shall ask what ye will,
and it shall be done unto you. John 15:7

Wonderful promises which guarantee answers to prayer abound; and when they are considered as a whole, we discover that there are conditions placed on obtaining what we desire. The "name it and claim it" principle asserts that you are entitled to anything you ask regardless of definite stipulations mentioned by Christ.

Our text provides two conditions that must be met. First, Jesus said, *"If ye abide in me."* To abide means to continue or remain, and Christ wants us to remain in fellowship with Him. A fruit tree that abides in the soil bears much fruit; but if it is plucked out, it withers. Those who abide in communion with Christ will have fruitful prayers, and those who don't abide will have a barren prayer life.

The second condition reads, *"If...my words abide in you."* We must fill our hearts with God's Word and allow it to rule our actions throughout each day. If you are disobedient to His Word, He is not inclined to listen to your words. However, when you meet the conditions of faithfulness and obedience, then *"ye shall ask what ye will, and it shall be done unto you."*

I have yet many things to say unto you, but ye cannot bear them now.
John 16:12

The Christian life is a series of steps, and there is much to learn. In school, children do not start with algebra, trigonometry, or calculus while studying math; they begin with simple addition. Why? It is because they cannot bear more difficult lessons until they master the basics. Likewise, we can rest assured that God has many more things to teach us, but we must learn the lessons set before us each day if we ever hope to advance to a more mature Christian experience.

Some may despair that difficult lessons lie ahead, but be not frightened because the Lord will only send them when you are ready. We should look forward to new challenges, knowing that they will strengthen us to be more effective in our Lord's service.

Lastly, the next verse shows us how we will learn, *"the Spirit of truth...he will guide you into all truth."* Praise God for the Comforter who is our constant Teacher and Guide! We are not left alone to face the difficult lessons that await us. There is much to learn; so, determine to tend to this day's set of instructions in order to be fit for future ones.

...your sorrow shall be turned into joy...and your joy no man taketh from you...ask, and ye shall receive, that your joy may be full.
John 16:20, 22, 24

Situations that we fail to understand are bound to arise and occasionally bring sorrow. Perhaps you are sad at this hour as you ponder events and circumstances that do not seem fair or appropriate. Cheer yourself with the words of our Savior, *"your sorrow shall be turned into joy."* You have not been forgotten by God, and He has a plan for the troublesome developments. Trust Him that joy is soon to come.

Once you have secured that inner peace the Lord promises, claim His next promise—*"your joy no man taketh from you."* It is God's will that your joy remains! Regardless of what man may say or do unto you, your joy does not need to flee.

Lastly, we see that God not only wants us to gain and retain joy, He also wants it to abound. He said, *"ask, and ye shall receive, that your joy may be full."* As a vehicle runs out of fuel, it begins to sputter and chug to a stop. A Christian will do the same without fullness of joy. So, ask for a "full tank" of joy today!

As thou hast sent me into the world, even so have I also sent them into the world. John 17:18

The Father sent Jesus into a dark, evil world with a mission to seek and to save. Christ has returned to His glorious abode in heaven but has sent us into this bleak world as the Father had sent Him. His love for the Father was displayed in obedience. Likewise, our love for our Savior is manifested as we boldly go into this Christ-rejecting world and hold His name up high.

Was Jesus ashamed of the Father when the world scoffed at Him? Should we ever blush when insults are thrown at us for piety and devotion to our Savior? Because He was sent before sending us, He fully understands the perils and heartaches that we will encounter. Let us run to Him as He went to the Father for fellowship in uncertain times.

We are sent to be a light as Jesus was; so, let us burn brightly. We are sent to preach repentance as He did; so, let us proclaim boldly. We are sent to love; so, let us do so with the same filling of the Spirit that Jesus had. As He made a difference on earth, He has sent us *"into the world"* to do likewise. Will you go represent Him today?

Then said Jesus unto Peter, Put up thy sword into the sheath: the cup which my Father hath given me, shall I not drink it? John 18:11

A cup represents a portion allotted for the sake of drinking. In Jesus' case, the cup represented His suffering, mistreatment, and awful death on the cross. In short, the cup is the will of God for our lives regardless of the circumstances.

Notice that we do not choose the cup that we want. Jesus said, *"the cup which my Father hath given me."* The Father gives us a portion that He knows is best for His glory. The cup may not be pleasant, and in Christ's case was full of pain and agony. At times, following God's will may come at a great cost; hence, many Christians refuse the cup, preferring a more palatable course in life. Further, we must not consider another man's cup but accept the one that God has chosen for us.

Although the cup was bitter, Christ said, *"shall I not drink it?"* As He partook of the cup, our salvation was secured. After His resurrection, the disciples saw a glorified Jesus, not a suffering one. Partaking of the cup will, in the end, bring bountiful rewards. Go ahead and drink the cup! God's richest blessings await those who are willing to trust Him.

Peter then denied again... John 18:27

Have you ever wondered why Peter denied Jesus repeatedly? It was not because Jesus had prophesied it; He was simply stating what He knew would happen. So, why did Peter do it again and again? The frightening reality of sin is that once you engage in it, you are enslaved by it. Have you not found this true in your own life?

"Peter then denied again." What is it that you have done *"again"*? A word of gossip, a lustful look, a covering lie, and an evil thought are all sins which are easily committed a second time or more. When a person skips his devotions, it is easier to do the same the next day, and soon a week passes. What about the one who refuses to follow the leading of the Spirit to pass out a tract; he may go weeks without handing another to a needy lost soul. Those who used to come to prayer meeting missed only once in the beginning, but now they rarely come.

Before we get too hard on Peter, we should see if we are not also guilty of sinning *"again."* The best way to prevent the *"again"* syndrome is to never start the evil practice. If you have entered a sin, confess it at once and seek deliverance. You do not have to continue!

Jesus answered, Thou couldest have no power at all against me, except it were given thee from above... John 19:11

Pilate had boasted that he held in his hand the power to kill Jesus or to spare Him. He uttered such words because he was frustrated that Christ did not answer his question, but Jesus reminded him that his authority had been granted by God.

Power can be used for great good or great evil. Those of us who have any positions of authority would do well to remember where it came from. As Jesus said, *"it were given thee from above."* Power from above is to be used for causes for above, not for self. Pilate had abused his authority by flaunting his power in an effort to manipulate Jesus. How often do Christians similarly? Pastors, missionaries, deacons, bus captains, and Sunday school teachers must all remember to use their positions to serve those under them. In the home, husbands must not abuse their headship over the wife, and parents must utilize their authority to mold godly children. Never allow yourself to be elevated in heart above what you really are, or you may soon *"have no power at all."*

Now there stood by the cross of Jesus his mother... John 19:25

Jesus was fulfilling the will of His Father as He agonized on the cross. It must have been an incredibly painful ordeal for His mother to behold her Son while He suffered greatly. However, we do not see her wailing out of control or bitter towards God for her bereavement. Instead, we see that she *"stood by the cross of Jesus."*

Oh, for more mothers like Mary who do not interfere when their children follow the will of God for their lives! We need mothers who will stand with their children when they bear their crosses. So often mothers are guilty of clinging to their children, and they try to discourage them from following God's leading if the cost is too high. Even when trials, disappointments, and suffering threaten those precious children, each mother must not question God's goodness in the matter.

We are to raise our children to follow the will of God. If it leads to dangers on the mission field or perils at home, we must not fret. Raise them for God, give them to God, and entrust them to God's care. Mary was a woman of faith and stood with Christ in His time of need. Will you also stand with your children and support them while they endure their cross for Christ? It may be difficult to do, but we must have faith.

...Then were the disciples glad, when they saw the Lord. John 20:20

Christ had been crucified, and the disciples were gathered together behind closed doors out of fear that the Jews might assault them next. In their time of trouble, Jesus appeared to them and said, *"Peace be unto you."* Isn't it great that the Lord thinks upon us in our distress? His message to us is the same, *"Peace."*

It was only after they had seen the Lord that their countenances changed. We will not experience a visible manifestation of God, but we can see Him by the eye of faith. After all, we are to walk by faith—not by sight.

When trials come, we must look for His message of peace in the Scriptures. Moreover, let us be watching for Him at work in our midst. Answers to prayer and turning of events must be recognized as His presence among us.

When were the disciples glad? It was *"when they saw the Lord."* If you look closely, you will see Him at work today in your life. When you catch a glimpse of Him, you will also be glad! So, be on the lookout.

Simon Peter saith unto them, I go a fishing. They say unto him, We also go with thee...and that night they caught nothing.　John 21:3

Although Peter had been sent to go preach the gospel, he decided to go back to his former vocation of fishing. He told some of the others, *"I go a fishing."* Unfortunately, he persuaded six fellow disciples to join him in his backsliding. However, after these expert fishermen fished all night *"they caught nothing."*

The next morning, Jesus called to them from the shore, *"Children, have ye any meat?"* The Lord knew that they had caught nothing and confronted them with their failure to find happiness. It was as if He had said, "What did you find in your old life? Are you satisfied now?"

We must learn that when we go back to our old ways, we will be very disappointed. The disciples did not find what they were seeking in their former life, and neither will we. Now that we are new creatures in Christ with a new purpose, what can we expect to find in our previous life? We think happiness and pleasure are waiting for us, but we will find *"nothing."* Never let discouragement or temptations lead you backwards. It is only by obeying God's commands that we will find the joy and satisfaction that we seek!

ACTS 1　　**DON'T WORRY ABOUT KNOWING**　　JUN. 2

And he said unto them, It is not for you to know the times or the seasons, which the Father hath put in his own power.　Acts 1:7

The disciples had just been promised the baptism of the Holy Ghost, but their minds were on something else. They wondered if it was time for Jesus to set up His earthly kingdom; however, Jesus simply replied, *"It is not for you to know."* Oftentimes, we become so curious about what God is going to do in the future that we get distracted from the business at hand. Do you ever wonder what the Lord is doing in your life? Rather than focusing on what He has not revealed to us, we must attend to the things He has clearly shown us.

Notice that Jesus brought the focus back to the matter of being filled with the Holy Ghost. In the next verse He said, *"But ye shall receive power, after that the Holy Ghost is come upon you: and ye shall be witnesses unto me."* The disciples wondered when the kingdom would be set up, but Jesus wanted them to forget about when it would be set up and get busy trying to win others for it. So, don't worry about things you don't know and get busy following what you do know! When you find yourself preoccupied with the unknown, remember that some things are *"not for you to know."*

And suddenly there came a sound from heaven as of a rushing mighty wind, and it filled all the house where they were sitting. Acts 2:2

Jesus had instructed the disciples to wait in Jerusalem for the promise of the Father. They obediently met together and prayed for God's enduement with power. At last, God's time had *"fully come."* When the Lord is ready to fulfill His promises, He does so with grandeur!

Observe that the promise came *suddenly.* We may think that God has tarried long, but the fulfillment is always on time and never late. Also, the promise was *heavenly.* We are never left to doubt if God really answered our prayer or not. As the disciples received their promise *"from heaven"* so will our petitions be evidently heaven sent.

Notice also that the promise arrived *mightily* in the form of a *"rushing mighty wind."* God loves to display His power to those who not only seek Him but do so with patient expectation. Is not the Lord ready to demonstrate His might to us also? Lastly, see that the promise arrived *completely* as the wind *"filled all the house."* This account should bolster our faith in the promises that God has given to us. When He is ready, the promise will be fulfilled suddenly, heavenly, mightily, and completely. What more could we ask for?

JUN. 4   GOOD CHURCH MEMBERS   ACTS 2:22-47

And they continued stedfastly in the apostles' doctrine and fellowship, and in breaking of bread, and in prayers. Acts 2:42

The church in Jerusalem gloriously witnessed three thousand people getting saved, baptized, and added to membership. That must have been an exciting day to observe so many decisions for the Savior! However, what followed is equally as exciting.

Our text indicates that these new converts were not ones who made shallow, fleeting commitments. It says, *"they continued stedfastly."* Oh, for more converts like these! Too often people take a long time to become faithful, dedicated church members. Why is it such a struggle? I believe many are holding onto their sins and not truly hungry for God's Word.

What made these early church members so good? They continued in doctrine, fellowship, observance of the ordinances, and prayers. Are you such a member? To be a good member you must actively participate in the local church. This early church understood three important truths: doctrine is needed for growth, fellowship is necessary for encouragement, and prayer is imperative for the power of God.

*And he leaping up stood, and walked, and entered with them into the
temple, walking, and leaping, and praising God. Acts 3:8*

The lame man who was laid at the gate of the temple had been in that
condition since birth. Perhaps he had previously seen Jesus at the
temple but lacked the necessary faith to be healed. Regardless of
possible lost opportunities in the past, he experienced a wonderful
miracle the day Peter and John passed his way.

Can you imagine the scene? Peter told the man, *"rise up and walk."*
Being overwhelmed with joy, the man did more than get up—he leaped!
How much excitement do you show when God pours out His blessings
on you? We ought to be overjoyed every time He reveals Himself to us.

This man's happiness was not motivated solely because of his healed
condition; he rejoiced in the One who made it possible. He did not
immediately run home to tell family and friends the good news. Instead,
he *"entered with them into the temple...praising God."* His first desire
was to glorify the Lord, and he was not shy about it either as he went
leaping through the temple. When God intervenes on our behalf, we
ought to get a little excited and let it come out in heartfelt praise.

ACTS 4:1-20   THE POWER OF A CHANGED LIFE   JUN. 6

*And beholding the man which was healed standing with them,
they could say nothing against it. Acts 4:14*

Not much has changed since the days of the apostles. As it is now, so
it was then that many rejected Jesus and detested the proclamation
of the gospel. Because Peter and John had healed the lame man, they
gained a large audience with a wonderful opportunity to preach Christ.
The results were stunning—about five thousand responded to their
message and believed!

The Jewish rulers despised the success of the apostles and felt they
were losing their own influence over the people. Although they detained
God's spokesmen, they could not refute the undeniable proof of a healed
man standing before them. In fact, *"they could say nothing against it."*
People may reject the One Who has so wonderfully regenerated us, but
they cannot deny the changes He has made.

When Christ transforms a life, there is little that people can say
against it. Do you have a life like the man in our story—one that silences
the critics? Remember that a changed life verifies and validates the
message we proclaim. Our walk is just as important as our talk.

And when they had prayed, the place was shaken where they were
assembled together; and they were all filled with the Holy Ghost,
and they spake the word of God with boldness. Acts 4:31

A tremendous change had transpired in the lives of the apostles. Think back to the closing pages of John's gospel when they were gathered together behind closed doors for fear of the Jews. Now, we see them boldly proclaiming Christ. Even after their lives were threatened by the ones they once feared, a holy zeal prevailed. What happened to bring about such a transformation? Pentecost had changed them.

This time, when faced with fear, they did not hide but prayed. What was the result? First, *"...the place was shaken."* God begins to move when we begin to pray! Second, *"...they were all filled with the Holy Ghost."* The Lord longs to fill us with His Spirit so that His power may be displayed through us. Third, *"...they spake the word of God with boldness."* Two verses earlier they had prayed for boldness, and they received an answer immediately. There is no need to be timid. As they overcame fear, so can you. Ask for a fresh anointing and new filling of the Spirit. Then, you will experience the same change as the apostles did. Prayer and the Spirit-filled life make the difference!

Jun. 8   EXPECT OPPOSITION   ACTS 5:1-20

Then the high priest rose up, and all they that were with him...and were
filled with indignation, And laid their hands on the apostles,
and put them in the common prison. Acts 5:17-18

We have heard the words of television evangelists, "Something good is going to happen to you today!" It is a nice thought but not always true! The apostles had experienced many blessings: they worked signs and wonders, saw multitudes saved, and healed many. Some great things had happened as they faithfully served God, but then something bad happened to them. The more you serve the Lord and see His power manifested, the more you will irritate the devil and his crowd. The opposition was *"filled with indignation."* They hated those godly apostles with all their might and threw them in prison for no good reason.

Satan has people in high places who work at his bidding. Expect opposition, but don't fear it. Never think the Lord has let you down after you suffer a temporary setback. As the apostles were soon set free, so your trial will come to an end also. So, whether it is something good or bad that happens to you today, accept it as the will of God and trust Him. Do you live in fear of trials? It's better to anticipate God's deliverance.

And they departed from the presence of the council, rejoicing that they were counted worthy to suffer shame for his name. Acts 5:41

The apostles had been arrested and cast into jail for preaching Christ, but God intervened by sending an angel that night to release them. Having been commanded to return to the temple and preach, they were seized once again by the enraged Jewish council. The apostle's victory was only temporary. Now they were not only threatened but beaten.

They were abused for serving the Lord, but they were not discouraged. Instead of feeling sorry for themselves for being so poorly treated, *"they departed from the presence of the council, rejoicing."* What true, trusting servants of the Lord they were! Had that been many of us, we would have walked away disappointed, dejected, and discouraged. Self-pity seems to be a common plague these days, but we become no stronger by feeling sorry for ourselves. Are you prone to complain or to rejoice during tribulation?

Although their release from prison proved to be a short-lived deliverance, the apostles maintained an upbeat attitude. We can do likewise when our joy comes from the Lord, not from our circumstances.

And they were not able to resist the wisdom and the spirit by which he spake. Acts 6:10

Praise the Lord for godly laymen who yield themselves as honorable vessels for the Lord's use! Our text refers to Stephen who was challenged by highly educated men of an elite synagogue. They engaged him in a dispute, thinking that their intellect and extensive training would easily defeat such a common man.

Stephen, however, was better equipped than the men who attacked him because he was *"a man full of faith and of the Holy Ghost."* Consequently, the men with the natural advantage *"were not able to resist the wisdom and the spirit by which he spake."* Stephen's consecration to God gave him an obvious supernatural advantage, and you can have the same thing.

No Christian has to be intimidated by those with intellectual prowess. As ordinary as we may be, we need only to be filled with the Spirit of God. Strong faith brings irresistible wisdom that will prove victorious. Those who claim superior knowledge but deny Biblical truth are, at best, educated idiots. Be confident—we have what they don't.

And God spake on this wise, That his seed should sojourn in a strange land; and that they should bring them into bondage, and entreat them evil four hundred years. Acts 7:6

God had made a promise to Abraham that his seed would, in fact, inherit the land of Canaan. However, that promise would be delayed for a long time. The children of Israel would have to dwell in Egypt four hundred years and eventually endure terrible affliction.

Abraham must have rejoiced as he received the promise of a land filled with his offspring. Likewise, Moses celebrated as God delivered His people from bondage when they crossed the Red Sea. Both of these men had joy, but what about the generations in between? Millions of Jews lived in Egypt during those four hundred years, and some of them were treated cruelly. Was God unfair to them? No!

They were just as much a part of His plan as Abraham and Moses were. They were the generations who had to wait for the promise by faith, and faith is always rewarded! Surely God sustained those who trusted in Him. Never be discouraged as you wait and long for God to fulfill His promises. Even if we are like the generation in between, we can still rejoice by placing our faith in the promises of God.

JUN. 12   RIGHT BUT WRONG   ACTS 7:20-40

For he supposed his brethren would have understood how that God by his hand would deliver them: but they understood not. Acts 7:25

Moses saw the affliction of his people while he lived luxuriously in Pharaoh's house. When he was forty years old, *"it came into his heart to visit his brethren."* It is fair to believe that God had put this in his heart and had revealed to him that he would one day deliver them from bondage. However, something went terribly wrong!

Although Moses was the chosen deliverer, he went about it wrongly. He thought that killing an oppressive Egyptian would demonstrate his authority to the Israelites. He obviously took matters into his own hands and ended up doing the right thing in the wrong way. It was not Moses' power but God's that would bring the desired deliverance.

Is there not a lesson here for us? When you do the right thing in the wrong way, it is bound for failure. Could this be the reason you have lacked success, even though you thought you were right? Moses had to reflect on his error for forty years. Don't wait too long to re-evaluate your actions, or you may find yourself in a desert-like situation living with regrets. Careful consideration now can prevent misgivings later. So, be careful about doing the right thing in the wrong way.

But he, being full of the Holy Ghost, looked up stedfastly into heaven,
and saw the glory of God, and Jesus standing on the right hand of God...
Acts 7:55

S tephen faithfully stood for Jesus Christ against a stiff-necked crowd by exposing their sin. As a result, *"they were cut to the heart, and they gnashed on him with their teeth."* He knew the end was near but *"looked up stedfastly into heaven."* When all is against you, the best place to look is up! What did Stephen see as he looked to God for help? He saw *"Jesus standing on the right hand of God."* Let us be encouraged that the Lord will stand for those who have stood for Him. Never fear your earthly audience for One much greater is observing.

Notice that Jesus stood *for* him. Standing shows respect and honor, and we are assured that God honors his faithful saints. Your uncompromising stand against ungodliness will not go unnoticed or unrewarded. Also, see that Jesus stood *with* him. As the angry mob grabbed him, threw him out of the city, and stoned him, he was strengthened by God's presence. Not only did he commune with God in prayer, he was able also to say, *"Lord, lay not this sin to their charge."* God always stands with you and gives grace for your trials.

Therefore they that were scattered abroad went every where
preaching the word. Acts 8:4

A fierce persecution arose against the church in Jerusalem. Not only was Stephen martyred, but Saul tried his best to bring devastation to the church as he put both men and women into prison. What was the result? Our text tells us that, although people were scattered abroad, they *"went every where preaching the word."*

Satan had tried to stop God's work, but his plan of persecution backfired on him! Instead of wiping out Christianity, it spread to other regions. During the Dark Ages, the Roman Catholic Church murdered multitudes of true believers, but their actions only sparked a reformation movement that has never been extinguished.

Conclusively, there is reviving power in times of persecution. As the world waxes worse and governments become less tolerable of the true King, we can expect more persecution on the horizon. However, we must not dread it but fulfill our duty. The Lord just may use our hardship to advance His kingdom as He did in times past with the early saints. How could that be disappointing?

And the angel of the Lord spake unto Philip, saying, Arise, and go toward the...desert. And he arose and went... Acts 8:26-27

Philip had enjoyed a tremendous revival in Samaria. Many turned to Christ, which led to *"great joy in that city."* No doubt, there was still much work to be done there, but God had other plans for Philip. An angel appeared to him and directed him towards the desert with no further details as to what he would find. He simply commanded, *"Arise, and go."* So, Philip *"arose and went,"* never questioning the command.

Certainly God knows what He is doing even when His ways make little sense to us. Although there was a need in Samaria, God had a divine appointment for him with an open-hearted Ethiopian in the desert. Never doubt God's wisdom; simply obey with no questions asked.

Furthermore, this principle must be instilled into our children as well as ourselves. A child should never question why an instruction must be followed. They must move with swift obedience without dragging their feet. As Philip discovered why he was to obey, so will they in due time. God is looking for people to use mightily, but they must first learn to go when bidden. Surely our world is in dire need of more obedient Philips!

JUN. 16   SELF-INFLICTED PAIN   ACTS 9:1-21

...it is hard for thee to kick against the pricks. Acts 9:5

Our gracious Lord appeared to the villain, Saul, who was on his way to capture and kill Christians. Confronting Saul with his sin, Christ said, *"I am Jesus whom thou persecutest."* That must have been a shock to Saul's ears! God is in the business of pointing out our sin, and we need to accept it.

Evidently, the Lord had been working in Saul's heart for a while, as He often does with us concerning our sin. Jesus mentioned, *"it is hard for thee to kick against the pricks."* To understand Christ's terminology, we should consider the use of the ox goad in their day. It was a pointed stick used to poke and prod a team of stubborn oxen. At times, the oxen would get annoyed with the prodding and kick back; but in so doing, they would only cause more pain for themselves. This was a picture of Saul kicking against the conviction of the Holy Spirit.

How often do you resist the pricks of the Spirit in your heart? Fighting against God when He attempts to poke you in the right direction is *"hard for thee."* The more you kick, the more pain and problems you will face. Stop resisting and say, *"Lord, what wilt thou have me to do?"*

Then had the churches rest throughout all Judœa and Galilee and Samaria, and were edified; and walking in the fear of the Lord, and in the comfort of the Holy Ghost, were multiplied. Acts 9:31

Up to this point, the Book of Acts has provided us with many examples of persecution, imprisonments, and mistreatments of God's people. The Christian life certainly is properly likened to warfare as there are many hardships and conflicts to face. At times, it seems as though it is one difficult battle after another with no end in sight.

Let our text cheer us today if we have become weary by extended duty on the battlefield. Despite all that the churches had been through, God gave them a reprieve. *"Then had the churches rest."* We ought to thank the Lord for such times of refreshing we get to experience along the way. Take this verse as a promise that good times are yet to come!

We see that the rest provided by God was not the only blessing. They *"were edified...and in the comfort of the Holy Ghost."* God is certain to encourage, comfort, and strengthen His soldiers. He even sends fresh recruits as we read that they *"were multiplied."* Don't give up the fight now! So many blessings await faithful soldiers of the cross.

ACTS 10:1-22   **ACCEPT GOD'S WILL**   JUN. **18**

But Peter said, Not so, Lord; for I have never eaten any thing that is common or unclean. Acts 10:14

At times we may not understand why God is leading us in a certain way, but His will is always right. Peter had seen a vision of a great sheet with many unclean animals, and God told him, *"Rise, Peter; kill and eat."* However, instead of obeying Peter cried, *"Not so, Lord."* He thought God had made a mistake and argued that he had never eaten an unclean animal. Ironically, he called Him *"Lord"* while refusing to obey!

We, too, boast that God is the Lord of our lives while rejecting His clear commands. When His will is acceptable to our understanding we gladly follow; but when it goes against conventional wisdom, we refuse. How can we still call Him Lord and Master while refusing His will?

The Lord wanted Peter to go to the wicked city of Cæsarea to witness to a particular Gentile, but Peter first had to get past his prejudices and go to those he deemed unclean. We must learn that the will of God is not determined by whether or not a thing is acceptable to us. If He is Lord, we must accept any assignment given.

...Stand up; I myself also am a man. Acts 10:26

When Peter arrived in Cæsarea, he found Cornelius full of gratitude and anticipation. Unknowingly, Cornelius gave more honor to Peter than was due when he *"fell down at his feet, and worshipped."* It is common for people, overwhelmed by God's goodness, to transfer some of their praise to the individual that God uses to be a blessing. Peter, however, would not take any of the glory and quickly exclaimed, *"Stand up; I myself also am a man."* Man deserves no such recognition!

Too many, who claim to be servants of God, are glory seekers. I have witnessed the smug expression on a priest's face as a follower bowed and kissed his hand. Further, many television evangelists strut in front of the cameras with every move choreographed to receive the greatest amount of applause. Sadly, many preachers are striving for recognition and have begun to promote themselves more than Christ.

True servants of God must be humble and grateful that God is willing to use them. Resist any temptation to accept praise for what God does through you, and always point those thankful for your service to the One who truly prepared the blessing for them. You are only a conduit!

For he was a good man, and full of the Holy Ghost and of faith:
and much people was added unto the Lord. Acts 11:24

The revival that broke out under Saul's persecution had spread wonderfully. The Lord blessed the zeal of those early converts; and when tidings reached Jerusalem of the need for help, the church sent Barnabas to Antioch. Why did they choose Barnabas for the mission?

The answer is in our text, *"he was a good man, and full of the Holy Ghost and of faith."* There is no mention of talent or popularity—just simple devotion to God! His character provides an example to all who want to be successful Christians. First, be a good person. Allow God to change your bad habits into good practices. Next, be full of the Holy Ghost. This involves denying fleshly appetites and yielding to the Spirit. Ask God for a filling, and be quick to confess any sin that quenches His influence. Finally, be full of faith. Faith simply believes what God says despite the circumstances. All may look impossible, but faith clings to the promises of the Word.

What are the results when these traits are in our lives? In Barnabas' case, *"much people was added unto the Lord."* If we want the same results, we must follow the example provided for us.

*Peter therefore was kept in prison: but prayer was made without
ceasing of the church unto God for him. Acts 12:5*

A horrible event troubled the church when Herod killed James, one of
the "sons of thunder," and proceeded to capture Peter for the same
purpose. There seemed to be no hope for Peter while he sat in prison
awaiting the executioner's sword, *"but prayer was made without ceasing
of the church unto God for him."* There was hope after all! One of the
joys of being part of a good local church is having a Christian family that
intercedes on the behalf of one another.

What a difference those prayers made for Peter! An angel was sent
to release him from his bonds and prevent his premature death. God had
further plans for Peter and used the prayers of the saints to intervene!

Are there any in your church who are going through deep valleys?
Are there missionaries facing dangers, afflictions, or perils unknown to
most?   Perhaps   Satan   has   oppressed   people   you   know   with
discouragement or temptation. There must be prayer *"without ceasing of
the church."* As we pray, God can strengthen, comfort, or deliver those
facing the hour of darkness. Prayer made a difference for Peter, and it
will for others, too!

*...I have found David the son of Jesse, a man after mine own heart,
which shall fulfil all my will. Acts 13:22*

D id you know that God is looking for people?   He scans the
multitudes to anoint some for His great cause. Occasionally, His
chosen rise to become men of renown such as Moses, David, Paul,
Spurgeon, Torrey, and Rice. However, God is not necessarily looking
for men to lift up but rather to use. In order to be *"found"* as David was,
we must meet the simple criteria.

First, God said, *"...a man after mine own heart."* God's heart loves
righteousness and hates sin. It is filled with kindness and mercy. His
heart is affected by the needs of the afflicted, and He has a great
inclination to give and forgive. Do you long to have a heart like God's?

Secondly, God said, *"...which shall fulfil all my will."* Our lives
must be completely surrendered to God, setting aside desires of the flesh
and allurements of the world. When we can cry, *"Not my will, but thine,
be done,"* then God is sure to discover us! Will He find you? If the Lord
does choose you for a task, remember that a great deed done is better
than a great name earned.

And the disciples were filled with joy, and with the Holy Ghost.
Acts 13:52

Does your joy depend upon the events of daily life going in your favor? If so, you do not fully comprehend Holy Ghost given joy. Our text reveals happy disciples whose circumstances were far from desirable. Let's consider their situation.

Paul had preached a strong message in the synagogue, and a great crowd gathered the next week to hear more. However, the Jewish leaders became envious of Paul and Barnabas and raised a persecution against them that eventually *"expelled them out of their coasts."* They had been maligned and mistreated, but they *"were filled with joy, and with the Holy Ghost."* Could you be happy in such a situation?

God-given joy does not depend upon favorable circumstances. True joy is associated with an obedient life that is blessed by the Spirit. The disciples, though rejected by some, had obeyed the Lord and thereby had great reason for heartfelt joy. Are you prone to be sad when rejected, disappointed, or misunderstood? Away with such self-pity, and rejoice!

And when they had preached the gospel to that city, and had taught many, they returned again to Lystra, and to Iconium, and Antioch...
Acts 14:21

Have you ever had a bad experience and became reluctant to expose yourself to the same situation again? Our text shows the strength of Paul and his commitment to a purpose greater than self-preservation. After preaching in Derbe, he *"returned again to Lystra, and to Iconium, and Antioch."* You may say, "What is so difficult about that?" Well, at Lystra they had stoned him and left him for dead, at Iconium they plotted *"to use them despitefully, and to stone them,"* and at Antioch they had already persecuted them and chased them away. Humanly speaking, those three cities would be the last on the list for another visit, but Paul would not be thwarted. Surely he must have wondered what treatment awaited him, but he had a job to do. New disciples needed to be strengthened and encouraged. Paul faced his fears!

How often do we let difficulties stop us from continuing in the will of God? Maybe a bad experience has discouraged you. Face the trouble, and press on victoriously. God often desires for us to leave our comfort zone to help those who need His Word.

Known unto God are all his works from the beginning of the world.
Acts 15:18

God knows what He is doing at all times. In fact, He has known everything He is going to do since the very beginning of time. Therefore, we are assured that nothing takes Him by surprise!

Every disappointment that we face in life has not only been known but also planned of God. We get discouraged when sickness disrupts our schedules. Financial setbacks throw us into despair as we wonder how we will ever recover. Have you been mistreated, persecuted, misunderstood, or maligned? Never forget that the Lord is fully aware of your plight? All these things are *"known unto God,"* and He has a plan to assist you in every malady.

Oh, for the faith to trust the all-wise God implicitly! He has never failed us in the past and never will. He has known *"all his works"* and in due time will perform them. Deliverance is on the way! The next time trouble or tragedy takes you by surprise, remember that God has known about it since *"the beginning of the world."* It will all work out as we cast our cares upon Him.

And the contention was so sharp between them, that they departed
asunder one from the other... Acts 15:39

Paul and Barnabas had been friends for a long time. It was Barnabas who took Paul under his wing in the early days of their ministry. Together they traveled, preached, endured persecution, and disputed with troublemakers. They were good friends and compatible co-workers, but something went wrong.

By this time Paul had risen as the leader and was seen as the *"chief speaker."* After spending much time in Antioch, Paul led in the decision for a second missionary journey. There were no problems until Barnabas *"determined to take with them John."* Paul did not think it was a good idea because John had previously deserted them. Instead of deferring to Paul's decision and leadership, Barnabas was determined to bring his nephew, John Mark. Consequently, contention needlessly ended a solid friendship. Proverbs 13:10 says, *"Only by pride cometh contention."* Sharp contention is sure to ruin many of our relationships when, out of pride, we push our own ways. Have you had tense words with someone you know? Take a tip: swallow your pride, and save a friendship!

...forbidden of the Holy Ghost...the Spirit suffered them not. Acts 16:6, 7

There are times when a right thing is wrong because it is not God's timing. Paul had tried to go to Asia to preach, but the Lord clearly forbade him to do so. Was it not a noble endeavor? Certainly, but Asia was to wait for another season. Had Paul gone to Asia, ignoring the Holy Spirit, he would have created a terrible mess.

God wanted Paul to pass through Troas because there was a certain physician-preacher, Luke, who needed to join the team. Also, the Lord was taking him step by step into Europe by way of Philippi. Had Paul gone to Asia, Lydia's family, the demoniac girl, and the jailor's household would not have been saved. Furthermore, the church at Philippi would not have been started, and the epistle to the Philippians would probably not have been penned. Can you imagine not having all of the precious promises that are found in the Book of Philippians? So much depends upon our obedience to the guidance of the Holy Spirit!

Sometimes we will be *"forbidden of the Holy Ghost."* Whether told to abstain from evil or from a good work, we must obey. It is vital that we are filled with the Holy Spirit and sensitive to His leading.

And they went out of the prison...and when they had seen the brethren, they comforted them, and departed. Acts 16:40

Do you frequently feel the need to be comforted by the brethren? Are you prone to look for pity from others by sharing all your woeful experiences with them? These are not traits of a true servant of God. Instead of constantly seeking comfort, we should be looking for those who need to be comforted. Our text shows the hearts of Paul and Silas. They had been imprisoned wrongfully and beaten terribly. Their wounds were fresh, and their stripes had just been cleansed. Truly, they needed to be solaced. However, when released from prison, they went to the brethren and comforted them. These faithful Christians were giving to others what they needed themselves!

Paul later wrote that the God of all comfort will comfort us so we can comfort others. (See II Corinthians 1:4) Run to God for your comfort, and once received, you will become a blessing to others. How did these men receive the comfort to comfort others? When in distress, they *"prayed, and sang praises unto God."* Do likewise!

...These that have turned the world upside down are come hither also...
Acts 17:6

Paul had preached to the Jews that Jesus was the Christ; and, as usual, some believed while others rejected. In Thessalonica, *"the Jews which believed not...set all the city on an uproar."* They were angry that Paul's company had come with their life-changing message. Their argument was that they had *"turned the world upside down."*

What happened to Jesus in Jerusalem was over a thousand miles away from Thessalonica, and Paul's group had been in Europe for only a short time before reaching Thessalonica. Without the means of modern communication, it is incredible that people had heard of the effectiveness of their activity in other regions. Simply put, early Christianity was so powerful that it made a huge impact on the world!

Oh, how we need a renewed dedication to have such power on our lives! To turn something upside down is to create a stir and disturb business as usual. We need the kind of lives that will cause heads to turn in awe over the dramatic changes in our lives. We need lives completely overturned for God. As individuals we may not turn the world upside down, but we can beg God to help us impact our corner of it!

And when they heard of the resurrection of the dead, some mocked: and others said, We will hear thee again of this matter. Acts 17:32

While Paul waited for Silas and Timothy in Athens, he was deeply stirred in his heart at the grip idolatry had on the entire city. He began preaching Christ in various places, and soon the philosophers were interested in hearing him. Thus, he was brought to Mars' Hill where the intellectual people met to discuss new ideas. His zeal opened doors of opportunity to witness for the Lord.

Paul boldly preached about the God they did not know and of the resurrection. Consequently, he called upon them to repent of their empty, ignorant religion. Many of these philosophers, however, were only interested in having their ears tickled, not their hearts pricked.

We, too, will encounter many in life who do not want to hear the convicting message of repentance. However, we must be faithful to give what the people need, not what they want. What will be the result? Paul's audience had three responses: some mocked, some delayed, and some believed. Be encouraged that even among the intellectual crowd, some will believe!

...Be not afraid, but speak, and hold not thy peace: For I am with thee, and no man shall set on thee to hurt thee: for I have much people in this city. Acts 18:9-10

As Paul traveled from city to city, he preached in the synagogues to convince people that Jesus was the long-awaited Messiah. Here in Corinth, many of the Jews *"opposed themselves, and blasphemed."* He had met such opposition before and it had resulted in great persecution, oftentimes causing him to flee for his life. At Iconium, they wanted to stone him, and at Lystra they succeeded in doing so! He was beaten and imprisoned in Philippi, driven from Thessalonica, and pursued to Berea. He knew full well that his life was now in danger at Corinth, and he could have easily been sidelined by the current threat. Therefore, along with the command to endure, the Lord gave a promise to sustain him.

Have you grown weary in the battle? Perhaps your current situation reminds you of a previous occasion which ended in trouble. Will you respond with faith or fear? God's message to you today is, *"Be not afraid."* Press on in your mission for God and cling to His promise, *"I am with thee."* What could be greater than knowing God is with you?

...I will return again unto you, if God will. And he sailed from Ephesus. Acts 18:21

It is always wise to include God in your plans. Paul was on the last stretch of his second missionary journey. He had spent over a year and a half helping the church at Corinth and would soon be home in Antioch. However, he first stopped in the busy, worldly city of Ephesus. The need for gospel preaching there was great. In fact, many people *"desired him to tarry"* much longer with them. Certainly, it must have been difficult for Paul to leave while many wanted to hear more, but he promised only to return if *"God will."*

Many opportunities arise in our lives that we think would be gratifying and fulfilling should we follow them. A cause may be noble and proper; however, we should pursue nothing if it is not in accord with God's will. Although Ephesus was an open door for Paul, God had other plans for him in the meantime. Disciples in Galatia and Phrygia needed to be strengthened. At last, Paul did return to Ephesus, but only when he was sure it was God's will. From this we can learn a valuable lesson: God's will includes doing the right thing at the right time!

Many of them also which used curious arts brought their books together, and burned them before all men: and they counted the price of them, and found it fifty thousand pieces of silver. Acts 19:19

These early Christians got a good dose of life-changing salvation! After they got saved, they wanted to put their past life behind them so they could move forward for God. So, they brought their evil possessions and *"burned them before all men."* Oh, if we only had more like-minded believers today who would not be ashamed to make a bold stand for Christ! Isn't it sad that many Christians are more ashamed of Jesus than they are of their sin?

We must learn to deal thoroughly with sin and destroy it before it destroys us. The cost was high for these early saints—*"fifty thousand pieces of silver."* In any age, that would be considered a lot of money! Just as they counted the cost, we must also be willing to pay the price to be free from our sin. Unfortunately, many Christians leave sinful possessions around their home. After being saved, why would someone hang onto worldly music, filthy videos, or immodest clothing? In most cases, sinful belongings remain just in case there is an urge to go back to them. Arise and wait no longer—rid yourself of any sinful temptations.

...almost throughout all Asia, this Paul hath persuaded and turned away much people, saying that they be no gods, which are made with hands... Acts 19:26

Demetrius, the silversmith in Ephesus, was unhappy with Paul who had effectively turned many people from idolatry. The words of our text were spoken by Demetrius out of contempt, but they reveal a glowing testimony of Paul's purpose in life. Paul *"persuaded and turned away much people"* from sin.

Our hearts should break to witness the empty and broken lives of those living without Jesus. As Paul faced criticism, so will we. Today, those who confront others with their waywardness are called judgmental and hateful. Making matters worse, an increasing number of pastors are trying hard not to present a negative message that would offend anyone. The pressure is mounting upon us to lower our standards and soften our message, but God has not told us to appeal to the world but rather reprove it. Although our message may be strong, our method should be humble and full of compassion.

Let us determine that, by God's grace, we will persuade many to turn from their sin and come to Christ. Is this your purpose in life?

*And we went before to ship, and sailed unto Assos, there intending to
take in Paul: for so had he appointed, minding himself to go afoot.*
Acts 20:13

Our text for today may seem a little lackluster, but I believe there is a great truth tucked away in it. We must understand that Paul was in a hurry to get to Jerusalem for the feast of Pentecost; but despite his haste, we see a peculiar decision to *"go afoot."* He and his company were in Troas, and Paul sent the others by boat to Assos while he walked there. Why would a person who was in a hurry take time to walk 20 miles when he could go faster by boat?

The truth for us today is that when in a hurry to do a work for the Lord, we must prepare by slowing down. Paul had much time for prayer and meditation while walking alone. His next big mission was days later at Miletus where he addressed the Ephesian elders. Knowing it would be the last time he would see them, his heart and message had to be just right! He had to be sure he was ready for such an important task.

Always take time with God to be sure you are what you need to be for the pressing duties ahead of you. Slow down before moving full steam ahead because people are depending upon you.

*And now, brethren, I commend you to God, and to the word of his grace,
which is able to build you up, and to give you an inheritance among
all them which are sanctified. Acts 20:32*

The Ephesian elders were indebted to Paul's ministry and had grown fond of his counsel, but soon they would *"see his face no more."* Out of Paul's heart poured great affection, comfort, instruction, and warning. However, his greatest encouragement was, *"I commend you to God, and to the word of his grace."*

Paul pointed them to God and His Word for continued guidance. Although the man of God would not be around forever, God and His Word would always be available. While it is good to enjoy the advice and instruction of the preacher, he cannot be with us at all times. We must, therefore, remember to rely upon God and cling to His Word!

Some Christians are content to feast only on the message prepared by their pastor, but that is not enough. We must learn to go to God for ourselves and obtain strength from the Bible daily. God's Word is *"able to build you up."* Don't you want to be stronger, more fruitful, and more deeply rooted in the faith? Go to God and His Holy Book! This is the best advice you will ever receive.

...they all brought us on our way, with wives and children, till we were out of the city: and we kneeled down on the shore, and prayed. Acts 21:5

Paul and his companions had made a brief stop at Tyre, and when they found disciples, they stayed seven days. I am sure the fellowship and encouragement meant much to both groups. As the time drew near for Paul's departure, they escorted him to the shore. They were especially concerned for his safety as they knew of the danger that he faced upon his arrival in Jerusalem.

What a blessing to envision the believers gathering on the seashore with their entire families to pray! It was a spontaneous, impromptu event. Certainly, this was a busy public area along the seacoast with many coming and going, but nothing could stop their heartfelt prayer to God for His protection and blessing. What real prayer!

We need a return to this type of old-fashioned prayer meeting. We talk much about our troubles and future turmoil. However, we tend to talk more than we pray! It's time to gather together and sincerely seek the Lord's help. Luke records their humble devotion, *"we kneeled down on the shore, and prayed."* Isn't it time for a prayer meeting?

(For they had seen before with him in the city Trophimus an Ephesian, whom they supposed that Paul had brought into the temple.) Acts21:29

The Jews in Jerusalem were filled with rage towards Paul, and part of the reason is found in our text for today. The Jews had made false accusations and were guilty of supposing things to be true that were, in fact, not true at all. The dangerous words recorded are *"they supposed."*

Although the guilty men in our text were unsaved, Christians must also beware of possessing such fleshly actions. Making quick judgments of others with no real basis is a trap we can easily fall into if we are not cautious. We must watch our tempers and realize that uncontrolled anger will lead to other sins. If we are not careful, we will soon be supposing things to be true about fellow Christians that are completely unfounded. This can lead to gossip, hurtful accusations, and severed friendships.

Supposing bad things of others comes from an evil heart. Are you guilty of blowing things out of proportion? Do you assume things of others because of your own insecurity, fear, or self-righteousness? Away with such attitudes! Learn to think the best of others—not the worst.

And they gave him audience unto this word, and then lifted up their voices, and said, Away with such a fellow from the earth: for it is not fit that he should live. Acts 22:22

S imilar words were spoken of our Lord Jesus when the angry mob cried, *"Away with him."* (John 19:15) Truly, the disciple is not above his Lord! What caused the crowd to speak such words of Paul? He simply had told of his conversion to Christ and how the Lord worked a great change in his life. What was such a blessing to him was a threat to them. You must remember that some people will not appreciate the changes God has made in your life. Our righteousness makes their wickedness appear so much worse, and we make them look bad. Do you remember what happened after Jesus cast the demons out of the maniac of Gadara? Instead of rejoicing, many wanted Jesus to leave their region.

Have you ever been ridiculed for your new life in Christ? Don't be alarmed when the world lifts its voice against you saying, *"Away with such a fellow from the earth: for it is not fit that he should live."* In reality, your faith in the Lord has actually made you fit to live! Never regret the transformation that Christ has made in your life, and don't allow your critics to silence your testimony for Jesus.

And the night following the Lord stood by him, and said, Be of good cheer, Paul: for as thou hast testified of me in Jerusalem, so must thou bear witness also at Rome. Acts 23:11

P aul had been falsely accused, beaten, taken captive by the Romans, and questioned by the Jewish counsel. It certainly was what we would call a bad day! After he was nearly pulled apart by the angry mob, he was rescued by the soldiers and brought into the castle. That night, God revealed Himself to Paul in a special way.

In the midst of uncertainty and deep sorrow we read, *"the Lord stood by him."* How comforting it is to know that God is very near to us even when trouble obscures our consciousness of His presence. Not only is He there, but He will make it so obvious that we cannot possibly despair.

Further, He comes to us with a strengthening message—*"Be of good cheer."* God does not want us in a gloomy state of misery—He wants us full of joy. Things will get better, and we will once again be at liberty to serve our Lord with new opportunities. Therefore, we must hold onto these precious promises when we face occasional adversities. The One who stands by you will surely uplift your spirit. Are you sad today? There is no need to sulk—just look at Who is standing beside you!

But after two years Porcius Festus came into Felix' room: and Felix,
willing to shew the Jews a pleasure, left Paul bound. Acts 24:27

Paul had travelled freely for several years, evangelizing vast regions. He enjoyed a fruitful ministry, but now we find him bound in Cæsarea for two years. It must have seemed to him that his time could have been better spent. However, God never makes mistakes. These were not wasted years at all.

Let us not be discouraged when we are in the crucible being refined for long periods of time. Certainly, some of the trials God sends will last longer than we desire and may seem very difficult to endure. Are you in such a state right now? Don't lose hope or get bitter, but rather learn to serve God in your present situation. Even though in bonds, Paul had enough liberty to receive guests and serve the Lord in some capacity. Additionally, he had several opportunities to preach Christ to the governor, Felix. Paul did what he could where he could, and this is a valuable lesson for us all to learn.

How did Paul endure? As we read yesterday, God promised that he would also preach in Rome. Paul had God's promise to cling to during those two years. Should you not also find a promise upon which to lean?

For if I be an offender, or have committed any thing worthy of death, I
refuse not to die: but if there be none of these things whereof these
accuse me, no man may deliver me unto them. I appeal unto Cæsar.
Acts 25:11

Being falsely accused, Paul was left in bonds. When he was questioned by the new governor, Felix, he was daring in his defense. He refused not to die if he were guilty of wrongdoing. However, he was innocent, and that gave him great boldness. Living right brings great confidence, even in troubling circumstances. Had Paul been at fault, he could not have been so emboldened to appeal unto Cæsar.

How is it with you? Are you facing tribulation? If you are living in sin, you can have no confidence that God is going to deliver you. Instead, anxiety and fear will grip your heart. Are you energized because of righteous living, or are you intimidated due to a distant relationship with God? It is difficult to be bold against our adversary, the devil, when we know we are backslidden! Let's remember that David only defeated Goliath because he was walking with God. David's own son testified, *"In the fear of the LORD is strong confidence."* (Proverbs 14:26)

Having therefore obtained help of God, I continue unto this day,
witnessing both to small and great... Acts 26:22

Do you need some help today? Allow this verse to lift your spirit.
First, let's consider the setting. Paul testified of his faith in Christ
to King Agrippa and related how the Jews savagely attempted to kill him
for that faith. Then, he uttered the words of our text as a marvelous
testimony of God's watch-care over His saints, *"Having therefore*
obtained help of God, I continue unto this day."

Although most of us are not in as desperate a condition as was Paul,
we can rest assured that we, too, can obtain help from God. If the Lord
could shield the apostle from murderers, He can surely rescue us from
those who trouble us. Whatever your dilemma or burden is today, God is
ready and able to help.

Paul boldly proclaimed, *"I continue unto this day."* Once help is
obtained from God, no plot against you can prevail. The devil himself
cannot destroy the one whom God has protected with His Almighty
hand. Truly, we shall be tested to some degree as was Paul, but we can
expect assistance as he did. Then, we can rejoice by proclaiming that we
have *"obtained help of God."* Won't that little trial be worth it then?

And when neither sun nor stars in many days appeared, and no small
tempest lay on us, all hope that we should be saved was then taken away.
Acts 27:20

Paul and Luke were en route to Italy by ship when caught in a terrible
storm. The crew had already taken drastic measures to keep the ship
afloat, but there was no hope. Destruction was inevitable. We will all
face perils so difficult that deliverance seems impossible. We can endure
tremendous hardships as long as we have hope; but when hope is taken
from us, life becomes most miserable.

Thankfully, God sent a message to Paul—*"Fear not."* In the midst
of the raging storms of life, the Lord always has a reassuring *promise* for
those who serve Him. Notice also the *peace* this promise gave to Paul:
he was able to say to the others on board, *"be of good cheer."* We not
only have comfort within but are able to console others facing the same
struggles. Lastly, we observe the *persuasion* that God's promise worked
in the heart of Paul. He said, *"I believe God, that it shall be even as it*
was told me." When hope is gone, remember that *"the God of hope"* is
still alive! Secure a promise and cling to it until deliverance comes. Are
the waves of impossibility crashing upon you today? Trust in God.

And the soldiers' counsel was to kill the prisoners, lest any of them
should swim out, and escape. But the centurion, willing to save Paul,
kept them from their purpose... Acts 27:42-43

We find Paul in another precarious predicament indeed. The ship, which carried nearly three hundred people, ran aground and was beginning to break in pieces by the fierce waves that battered it from behind. The soldiers, fearing what reprisals may befall them should the prisoners escape, decided to kill every one of the captives. Once again, Paul's life was in jeopardy, but praise God for His intervention!

When all counsel is against you and evil is purposed toward you, rest assured that God can deliver you. Notice that the Lord had a centurion on board who *"kept them from their purpose."* It is comforting to know that God has His "centurions" posted to assist us.

We have no cause for alarm or fear when Satan's minions threaten us. God is well able to suppress the enemy and prevent their wicked objectives. How many times had God previously delivered Paul from certain destruction? Many times! What about David? If God rescued these faithful servants repeatedly, can He not spare you? Just be faithful and you will see the Lord intervene on your behalf.

And he shook off the beast into the fire, and felt no harm. Acts 28:5

After escaping the shipwreck, Paul was stranded with the others on an island inhabited by barbarians. Miraculously, those uncivilized islanders were kind to them. It was cold and rainy, but Paul was helping out by collecting firewood so everyone could dry off and get warm. Then, seeming tragedy struck again. A poisonous snake sunk its fangs into Paul's hand, and death was certain. As a missionary in Africa, I watched our dog swell and suffer before dying from a venomous snake bite. Just the thought of getting bitten is enough to cause one to panic. However, we observe that Paul calmly shook off the viper and *"felt no harm."* He did not scream or look for sympathy. His faith was so great that he refused to fear what would frighten most of us.

Surely, Paul remembered yet again God's promise that he must preach one day in Rome. God had not spared him from the soldiers only to kill him by the serpent. It would have been treasonous to imagine that God would fail to keep His Word. When a crisis threatens to prevent us from fulfilling the will of God, we must never lose hope. A "serpent" may strike, but we must learn to shake it off!

Be it known therefore unto you, that the salvation of God is sent unto the Gentiles, and that they will hear it. Acts 28:28

Although kept as a prisoner in Rome, Paul was allowed to proclaim the gospel to all who visited him. Within three days of arriving in Rome, he called for the chief men of the Jews and made a strong witness for Christ. What was the result? *"...some believed the things which were spoken, and some believed not."* Paul then addressed the unbelievers with the words of our text, *"the salvation of God is sent unto the Gentiles, and that they will hear it."* What can we glean from this?

God wants us to bring the message of salvation to the Gentiles, and there is a guarantee that some will receive the message. Let us rally around this promise and renew our interest and investment in foreign missions. Billions of souls still wait to be evangelized at this very moment. Meanwhile, we have not only a charge to bring them salvation but absolute assurance that *"they will hear it."* Did not Livingstone, Carey, Judson, and Taylor find it so? Will we find the promise less reliable? Never! Let us labor where there are promised results. The darker the region, the more brightly the gospel shines. Although we cannot all go to foreign lands, we have plenty of needy sinners around us.

JUL. 18   GET READY   ROMANS 1:1-17

So, as much as in me is, I am ready to preach the gospel to you that are at Rome also. Romans 1:15

Did the Lord mightily use the Apostle Paul? The answer is obvious, but the reason He used him is often missed. Sometimes we think that Paul had something special which made him different than we are and, therefore, more useful than we could be. However that is not true.

The secret to Paul's effectiveness is no secret at all. He gave us the key that unlocks the door of opportunity to serve the Lord in a greater capacity. Observe his testimony, *"So, as much as in me is, I am ready..."* He had made himself available to the Lord and prepared his heart so God could use him. He was in a state of readiness.

The Lord delights to use those who are ready. On the mission field, I kept a couple of guns ready at all times to protect my family. On several occasions, I killed poisonous snakes that were a threat. That was only possible because I kept the firearms in a state of readiness. Likewise, the Lord is quick to use those who are prepared for the battle. Be sure that your sin is confessed, things are right in your home, vices are set aside, and your devotional time is warm and consistent. When you are ready, God can use you. So, get ready.

Professing themselves to be wise, they became fools... Romans 1:22

The way up is down, and the way down is up. Those who humble themselves will be exalted, and those who lift themselves up will be brought low. Our text conveys this truth vividly.

Those who reject God's authority in their lives begin to act foolishly. How can people believe it is okay to murder babies by calling it abortion? How can states pass laws allowing men to use a lady's restroom because he feels more like a woman? How can people refuse to accept that the increase of promiscuity and violence in the public schools is directly related to the removal of the Bible and prayer? The answer to these questions is clear. Those who reject God's ways become fools.

Every time man exalts himself over the truth of the Bible, he is doomed. Sadly, this error is even common in churches. Members who reject the counsel of the Word of God and their pastor are no better. They think their way will work, but in the end they are utterly confounded. Marriages struggle, children never reach their potential, finances are in disarray, and peace is lost because people have been too "wise" to follow God's plan. Do you want to be a fool? Simply embrace your own way. Fools always resist the Word and Spirit of God.

Or despisest thou the riches of his goodness and forbearance and longsuffering; not knowing that the goodness of God leadeth thee to repentance? Romans 2:4

God is good to us even when we do not deserve it. In most cases, He provides an interval of time to repent before executing judgment on our sin. Too often, however, we abuse this time and continue in our wayward direction. Thus, our text poses this question. Have you despised His goodness?

The Lord is merciful and longsuffering towards us. He does not enjoy inflicting pain and punishment upon His children. Therefore, time to repent is given before His rod of chastisement strikes. Further, God's Holy Spirit will work to convict your heart and prick your conscience. However, when you resist His reproof, quench His Spirit, and shake off His commands, do you not also despise His goodness?

When the Lord finally chastens us, it is because we fully deserve it—not only for the initial sin but for the second sin of despising His goodness. If God has shown longsuffering toward your waywardness, do not repay Him with stubbornness. Allow His goodness to lead you to repentance. Rejoice that He has given you space to repent.

For what if some did not believe? shall their unbelief make the
faith of God without effect? Romans 3:3

O ur text poses a good question—*"what if some did not believe?"* If someone refuses to believe what God says, does it make it untrue? No. However, many people repeatedly reject the clear teachings of the Bible. Because they despise the truth, they think God's principles will fail and that His judgments will not come to pass. How wrong they are!

When a person goes to the doctor and is told he has cancer, rejecting the diagnosis does not prevent the condition from worsening. Denial of truth does not change reality. Instead, it only creates further trouble. Like it or not, when your sin is exposed through the reading or preaching of God's Word, the Lord expects you to change. Your unbelief does not render His precepts ineffective. So, whether you believe it or not, God's declarations will certainly come to pass.

What has God spoken to your heart about recently that you have been slow to believe? Have you failed to heed some of His warnings? Repent at once, or you will discover in the end that God was right. Your refusal to accept the truth about your condition doesn't spare you trouble.

Being justified freely by his grace through the redemption
that is in Christ Jesus... Romans 3:24

T oday's reading covers the glorious topic of salvation. Although the Scriptures remind us that we are sinners, they also provide encouragement when we face the guilt associated with frequent failures. Our text provides four tremendous words that describe our salvation.

First, *"justified"* reminds us that we have been given Christ's righteousness and are no longer guilty in the eyes of the Lord. We are not to be justified later—we are already justified. Praise God we are no longer condemned for our sin! Second, *"freely"* describes how we obtained this wonderful salvation. We did not have to do thousands of good works to be saved, and neither do we have to keep ourselves saved by our deeds. Salvation was freely given. Third, *"grace"* reinforces the fact that no merit of our own secured this deliverance. God gave us something we did not deserve. Remember also that we have already been given more than we are worthy of receiving. Therefore, never think that God owes you more or foolishly demand things of your heavenly Father. Fourth, *"redemption"* refers to the purchase of our souls by the Lord. Thankfully, He will never neglect or abandon His own.

He staggered not at the promise of God through unbelief; but was strong in faith, giving glory to God... Romans 4:20

When I think of the word *stagger*, I picture a drunkard who cannot walk straightly. He stumbles along and is unsure of each step he takes. This is typical of the lives of many believers in the area of faith. They move unsteadily throughout life, not knowing where they are going and unsure of what step to take next. Does that describe you?

Abraham had strong faith which gave him direction and enabled him to move forward for God. Lest we think things were easy for him, we are reminded that he *"against hope believed in hope."* He faced impossible circumstances but did not allow that to disturb his belief that God would keep His promise. He was *"strong in faith,"* which is described as *"being fully persuaded that, what he had promised, he was able also to perform."* Do you possess such confident faith?

Are you walking through life half-dazed and unsure of what will happen next? Faith in the Person and promises of God will straighten out your gait. Keep moving in the direction God has revealed through His Word, and you will surely find His blessing at the end of the path.

Therefore being justified by faith, we have peace with God through our Lord Jesus Christ... Romans 5:1

Once a person gets saved, he enjoys *"peace with God"* and is no longer at enmity with Him. This blessing results from being justified by faith in Christ alone. So many religious people attempt to appease God's anger at their sin by doing good works, but salvation is not obtained by such deeds. Therefore, they remain enemies of God, despite their best efforts to reconcile themselves. Remember that *"peace with God"* comes *"through our Lord Jesus Christ"*—not by your works.

Those of us who are saved have *"peace with God"* presently. That brings great privileges—we will never be treated as His detested enemy but as His beloved children. Do you ever fear that God hates or rejects you? Perhaps you have allowed sin into your life; and although sin may rob you of the peace *of* God, it cannot rob you of peace *with* God. Thankfully, sin only severs our fellowship, not our salvation. When you dabble in sin, your loving Father will withhold tranquility from your soul, but this is only an attempt to draw you back into fellowship. When you return to the Lord, you can enjoy the peace that Christ has already secured for your soul. God is your Father—not your enemy.

Being then made free from sin, ye became the servants of righteousness.
Romans 6:18

The moment you were saved, you were released from the power of sin. If you have any doubts about that, consider these clear statements throughout the entire chapter: *"freed from sin"* (v. 7), *"dead indeed unto sin"* (v. 11), *"sin shall not have dominion over you"* (v. 14), *"made free from sin"* (v. 18), *"ye were the servants of sin"* (v. 20), and *"now being made free from sin"* (v. 22). Are you convinced yet? Christ sets us free from being servants of sin!

Why is it then that we still sin? Although Jesus gives us freedom from sin, much depends on how we use that newfound liberty. In many cases, people abuse that freedom by returning to the very sin that once enslaved them. Paul said, *"to whom ye yield yourselves servants to obey, his servants ye are to whom ye obey."* Therefore, there is a choice to be made daily. Either we yield to sin, or we yield to righteousness. Simply put, we sin because we want to sin. However, when we yield to God, we will enjoy the freedom from sin that He promised. How have you used your freedom? Have you chosen to go back to sin or to serve the Lord?

For that which I do I allow not: for what I would, that do I not;
but what I hate, that do I. Romans 7:15

Oh, how terrible is the strife that rages within our hearts at times! We find ourselves doing things that we say we are against and failing to do what we know is right. Although we agree with the Law concerning the awfulness of sin, we indulge anyway. We are powerless, in ourselves to have victory over sin and are left in a most miserable state.

Paul testified that the law was good because it showed him what was right and wrong. Further he stated, *"For I delight in the law of God after the inward man."* However, he discovered there was another law, the law of sin, which brought his soul into captivity. He felt as if he was held as sin's prisoner. How do we escape the torment within?

First, admit like Paul, *"O wretched man that I am!"* There is no help and deliverance until we see our true, hopeless condition. Second, run to Jesus, and He will surely strengthen you through His Spirit. Paul said, *"who shall deliver me...? I thank God through Jesus Christ our Lord."* Although the law condemns us and our flesh is powerless to intervene, Christ promises His power. Therefore, we must wholly depend on the Lord to help us follow what is good and to refuse the evil.

Therefore, brethren, we are debtors, not to the flesh,
to live after the flesh. Romans 8:12

A debtor is one who owes something to another. Our text draws some clear distinctions. Notice, first, that *"we are debtors."* The previous verses explain how the Holy Spirit gives life, deliverance, and the promise of a future resurrection. Therefore, we owe God a debt that requires absolute surrender, self-denial, and dedication. Nothing should be withheld from our gracious Lord. Have you been paying your debt to Him, or are you holding onto some selfish desire?

Second, we are reminded that, although we are debtors, it is *"not to the flesh."* We owe our body nothing in regards to worldly pleasures. Advertisements entice us to their products with slogans such as, "Go ahead, you owe it to yourself!" Satan whispers the same lie to us in order to sidetrack our service for the Lord. When your flesh demands sin, simply reply, "I owe you nothing." Wouldn't it be foolish to pay someone a debt that you did not owe? You only have one life, and God advises not to *"live after the flesh."* Today, let's determine to find a way to pay our debt to the Lord and withhold all sinful demands of the flesh.

And we know that all things work together for good to them that love
God, to them who are the called according to his purpose. Romans 8:28

One of the most beloved promises in Scripture rests within today's reading. Many times we have sought to understand the meaning for some tragedy or looked for comfort from the words, *"all things work together for good."* Praise God that this promise never gets old!

However, another great truth cannot be ignored. We understand that *"all things"* are *"according to his purpose."* That means God has a plan in every event of life, whether it be a blessing or a burden. So, what is His purpose? The answer lies in the next verse—*"to be conformed to the image of his son."* When we put the two verses together, we see that God orchestrates the events of our lives to cause us to become more like Jesus. So, what if we fail to cooperate with the Lord when He tries to make us more like His Son? Does it stop His efforts? No. In fact, He often intensifies our trials to get us back on track.

The best thing any Christian can do when tribulation arises is to ask the Lord to have His way. At times we are so conformed to the world that God has to work one of His *"all things"* to get us back on track. So, what is the reason for your current trial? To make you more like Jesus.

...I have great heaviness and continual sorrow in my heart. Romans 9:2

The same man who wrote, *"Rejoice in the Lord alway"* also claimed that he had *"continual sorrow"* in his heart. Is this a contradiction? No. While reflecting on the Lord, we should greatly rejoice over the goodness He has extended to us. However, when we contemplate the plight of the unsaved, we cannot be filled with joy. True consideration of their situation will produce *"great heaviness and continual sorrow."*

Notice the first phrase, *"great heaviness."* Very few want to carry a burden for the Lord. Instead, Christians are consumed with seeking either levity or comfort. Although a *"merry heart doeth good like a medicine,"* at times it is necessary to be in *"great heaviness."* In fact, true gratitude and happiness over God's goodness in your own life will lead to a burden for others to enjoy that which you have experienced.

Observe the second phrase, *"continual sorrow."* God does not want us to lose our joy, but He is concerned that we may lose our burden for the unsaved. Paul was troubled over his *"kinsmen according to the flesh"* whom he knew to be without Christ. Have you lost your concern for those who do not know the Lord? Has your fervency in prayer for the salvation of souls waned? Perhaps you have lost a soulwinner's heart.

...who art thou that repliest against God? Shall the thing formed say to him that formed it, Why hast thou made me thus? Romans 9:20

God has made us all as unique individuals and has plans and designs for our lives to suit His purposes. Thus, we are all equipped with different talents, gifts, and opportunities. At times we are tempted to complain that others have it "better" than we do. However, it is not for us to question why the Lord has made us a certain way. Who are we to argue with God? Are we wiser than He?

We are reminded that the Potter can make whatever He pleases out of the clay. Therefore, never be discouraged by your station in life, mental capacity, or physical features. God has made you just the way He wants you and has placed you exactly where He knows is best! Faith accepts His sovereignty and finds satisfaction in fulfilling His plan.

Many of God's choicest servants faced undesirable handicaps but accomplished much for God. David was too small to face Goliath, Paul was too sick to travel, Peter was too uneducated to preach, Timothy was too young to lead, Sarah was too old to have children, and Joseph was too abused to have hope. However, God used them all just the way they were. So, cheer up! God's plan to use you is perfect.

How then shall they call on him in whom they have not believed? and
how shall they believe in him of whom they have not heard? and
how shall they hear without a preacher? Romans 10:14

Salvation is simple: a person only needs to call upon the name of the Lord Jesus in faith for the forgiveness of sins. Why then are not more saved? Our text reveals that some have not believed simply because they have not yet heard the true way of salvation.

Follow the reasoning that Paul presents to the Christians at Rome. People cannot call on the Lord without believing in Him; people cannot believe until they have heard the truth about Him; and people cannot hear the truth until someone goes and tells them.

In short, people are not being saved because Christians are not busy proclaiming the best news that has ever been given to mankind. Millions throughout the world are *"without a preacher."* We need men who will see the needy multitudes in foreign lands and become sensitive to the calling of God! Additionally, we must all be aware that people in our own communities are *"without a preacher."* Have you been indifferent about Christ's command to evangelize? Are you the reason people are not getting saved? In order to believe, they must first hear.

But what saith the answer of God unto him? I have reserved to myself
seven thousand men, who have not bowed the knee to the image of Baal.
Romans 11:4

The theme of this chapter is that God has not entirely cast away the nation of Israel. They were chastened and scattered as a result of their continual rebellion, but there was still a small remnant that was faithful to God just as there was in Elijah's day.

God's testimony to the prophet was that He reserved some *"who have not bowed the knee to the image of Baal."* Although it was a time of compromise and apostasy, some refused to follow the crowd. Are we not also tempted to bow the knee to worldliness in modern times? Unfortunately, many who once stood strong have *"bowed the knee"* to immodest dress, ungodly music, and a desire to be accepted by the world.

It is obvious that churches that once stood firm with strong convictions have forsaken Biblical principles. By God's grace, let us be like the faithful of Elijah's day! Moreover, never get discouraged as did Elijah when he said, *"I am left alone."* As the Lord had a remnant of Jews in the prophet's day, so He has a remnant of Christians in our day. Are you part of it? If so, act like it and refuse to bow to worldliness.

...thou wert cut out of the olive tree which is wild by nature, and wert graffed contrary to nature into a good olive tree... Romans 11:24

The process of grafting is amazing. A branch from one tree is cut off and joined to another tree in place of its own branch. Due to the unbelief of Israel, *"some of the branches"* were *"broken off,"* allowing a wonderful opportunity for even the Gentiles to be joined to Christ.

Before salvation, we possessed no righteousness but rather an unruly, wild nature that was against God. Although we were once *"wild by nature,"* God's grace changed everything. If there had been no break from the wild tree, we could not be joined to the good. Never forget what you were and where you came from before you were coupled with Christ.

While joined to a wild tree, the best we could produce before our union to Christ was wild fruit. Now that we are grafted into a good tree, we can produce fruit for the Lord. So, draw your strength from Jesus daily and you will bear much wholesome fruit. Do you ever think you can't do much for God? Think again—you are now part of a good tree. Consequently, when any good thing springs forth from your life, remember that it was the Lord Who produced it.

AUG. 3   OVERCOMING OR OVERCOME?   ROMANS 12

Be not overcome of evil, but overcome evil with good. Romans 12:21

Evil is a powerful force which is capable of overcoming you. Hence, God provides us with both a warning and a promise in our text to enable us to escape the power of sin.

First, we are prodded to realize that evil can overcome us. Many Christians do not fear sin but get dangerously close to it. We all recall how Samson, the strongest man alive, was overcome by a feeble woman. Evil has slain many mighty men of God who became careless. Further, our text says, *"Be not overcome."* This is a clear command not to allow ourselves to be tricked, enticed, or captured by sin. Thus, once again, God reminds us that sin is a choice and must be resisted.

Secondly, God gives us a liberating promise that we can *"overcome evil with good."* Praise God that we can indeed overcome evil! How? Remember there is more power in good than in evil, especially when the Source of our good is God. When mocked or ridiculed, we are tempted to retaliate; but that leaves us defeated, not victorious. How often are you overcome by reacting wrongly to mistreatment? Learn to maintain holiness and display an act of kindness instead of responding in a sinful manner. Are you currently overcoming, or have you been overcome?

*And that, knowing the time, that now it is high time to awake out of sleep:
for now is our salvation nearer than when we believed. Romans 13:11*

Satan has many tricks to render a Christian ineffective in the Lord's
service. If he cannot lure us into gross sin, he will try to lull us to
sleep. We must, therefore, remember that life is not about resting and
relaxing but about activity for God.

Many of God's people are presently asleep and doing little for the
cause of Christ. They are enchanted by worldly pleasures and have
forgotten that we are just pilgrims passing onward to our heavenly abode.
Soldiers of the Lord must remain alert at all times. A watchman who is
fast asleep is worthless for his appointed duty and is more vulnerable to
the attack of the enemy. We are to remain on guard, tending our post in
the Lord's army. Have you been lulled to sleep by one of Satan's
soothing lullabies? Has he not whispered convincingly that you have
worked hard for God and need a little rest? Beware, he's soon to pounce.

God has a task for each of us, and His exhortation should ring in our
ears, *"it is high time to awake out of sleep."* Time is expiring as our trip
to the Heavenly City is *"nearer than when we believed."* Our time to
complete our God-given duties is quickly drawing to an end. Wake up!

*Who art thou that judgest another man's servant?...he shall be
holden up: for God is able to make him stand. Romans 14:4*

The term nitpicking was familiar to me, but I never understood the
true meaning until one of my daughters unknowingly came into
contact with a girl that had every mother's nightmare—lice. Every night
my wife would tediously search for the little lice eggs called nits. The
nits were difficult to spot and equally stubborn to remove from long
strands of hair. Every nit had to be found or the "plague" would
continue. The term nitpicking took on an all new meaning to me after
watching the process. Although nitpicking is necessary in cases of lice
infestations, it is a bad practice for Christians to engage in when it comes
to being overly critical of one another.

Some people seem prone to examine and strain at the smallest
imperfections in others' lives. While it is true that we are to warn and
exhort one another, we are never told to nitpick. Today's verse asks a
good question, *"Who art thou that judgest another man's servant?"*
Don't over examine a person's life to decide if they are right or wrong in
every little matter. That is God's job. Our text suggests that God sides
with the one who is unjustly criticized. So, don't be a spiritual nitpicker.

*Now the God of hope fill you with all joy and peace in believing, that
ye may abound in hope, through the power of the Holy Ghost.
Romans 15:13*

As we look around at this evil, rebellious world, it is easy to become
discouraged. The practices we once thought unthinkable are now
commonplace in society. The "dirty old man" down the street of
yesteryear is a saint compared to the average young person. When we
look within and see our continual frailties and failures, we get further
disappointed. Instead of fretting, we must look to the *"God of hope."*
Because He gives hope, we can rise above our pitiful situation and be
victorious over sin and despondency.

Hope brings anticipation and expectation that God will intervene on
our behalf. What seems hopeless in our own strength becomes a glorious
possibility when we look to the *"God of hope."* Notice that His will is
that we *"may abound in hope."* A defeated attitude is never to linger in
the soul of a believer. God's hope will *"fill you with all joy and peace"*
and will renew your outlook on life. Have you grown despondent? It is
through *"the power of the Holy Ghost"* that we gain confidence that
there is still hope in our situation. Look to the *"God of hope"* today.

*Now I beseech you, brethren, for the Lord Jesus Christ's sake, and for
the love of the Spirit, that ye strive together with me
in your prayers to God for me... Romans 15:30*

As Paul closed the epistle to the church at Rome, he requested the
believers to form a partnership with him. Upon Paul's heart was the
evangelization of those who had not yet heard of Jesus, and he knew that
he was not able to complete such a task in his own strength. Thus, he
asked, *"strive together with me in your prayers."*

The more spiritual you are, the more you realize that you need God's
people interceding on your behalf. Requesting prayer should never be
seen as a sign of weakness, but on the contrary, a sign of strength. Paul
often requested prayer for the enablement to work more effectively.

The word *strive* means to struggle together with someone. Just as
Paul wrestled in prayer with God, he requested the brethren to do
likewise. Do you realize you are in a battle with the unseen forces of
darkness? Can you not see the evidence of Satan's activity around you?
Never hesitate to partner with others in prayer. When God's servants
request prayer, be sure to take it seriously. If Paul needed help, so do
pastors and missionaries whom you know. Will you partner with them?

...I would have you wise unto that which is good,
and simple concerning evil. Romans 16:19

Paul warned his beloved brethren of the infiltration of false teachers
into the church. He told them to *"mark them"* and *"avoid them"*
who *"by good words and fair speeches deceive the hearts of the simple."*
It is obvious that we are to steer clear of all who would try to deceive us
with their doctrine.

In context, today's verse speaks of being wise concerning pure
doctrine and simple regarding false doctrine.   Too many believers
needlessly fall into error because of curiosity over matters we are to
remain simple. It is better to study the truth more than error, allowing
you to recognize error when it comes along. Never become fascinated
with knowing much about false doctrine. Such a trap entices many to
their own peril as they become enchanted with knowing more about evil
matters. After a while, they become guilty of the very evil they were
only "investigating." Sin has a way of overcoming those who pursue it.

Although preachers need to know enough to warn people, they are to
remain simple in their knowledge of evil and error. It is more profitable
to study God's truth than the devil's deeds and doctrines.

God is faithful, by whom ye were called unto the fellowship of his Son
Jesus Christ our Lord. I Corinthians 1:9

Good friends are hard to find. Thankfully, we have a Friend in Jesus
whose faithful character prevents Him from ever failing us.
Whether a friend of yours has neglected or disappointed you, be assured
that Jesus will never do so. Because He is the best Friend one could ever
have, it makes sense to develop a stronger relationship with Him than
with any other person in the world. Let us consider His faithfulness.

God is faithful in *salvation*. The previous verse promises that He
"shall also confirm you unto the end."   Because we are not always
faithful to Him, we need One Who is more dependable than ourselves in
the matter of salvation. We cannot save ourselves or keep ourselves
saved; but because Jesus *"is faithful,"* He does both for us.

God is also faithful in *fellowship*. No matter how far you have
gotten away from God through sin and unbelief, the Father is willing to
accept you into close fellowship once again.   Do you miss those
heartwarming times? Confess your sins immediately and experience the
peace you once enjoyed. Remember that you are *"called unto the
fellowship of his Son."* Answer that call and return to Him today.

...But we have the mind of Christ. I Corinthians 2:16

How would you like to have all the wisdom you will ever need in life? Well, it is already at your disposal. Today's reading provides a wonderful contrast between the wisdom of man and the wisdom of God; and the chapter concludes with a powerful statement, *"But we have the mind of Christ."* Notice that we *"have"* it already.

While the world is left to rely on their own limited, fallible wisdom, God's children possess an advantage over even the educated elite. At salvation, we received the mind of Christ. You may say, "What does that mean?" God promises to give us good sense for any situation that we face. He will not leave us in the dark to wonder what we should do.

How is the mind of Christ revealed to us? Jesus said that the Holy Spirit *"shall receive of mine, and shall shew it unto you."* (John 16:14) Concerning the things the world cannot comprehend, *"God hath revealed them unto us by his Spirit."*

Parents often get frustrated when children don't use the brain that they have. Can you imagine how the Father feels when we fail to use the mind that Christ has bestowed upon us? With such unlimited wisdom, there is no excuse for misunderstanding God's will in any given matter.

Every man's work shall be made manifest: for the day shall declare it, because it shall be revealed by fire; and the fire shall try every man's work of what sort it is. I Corinthians 3:13

As Paul dealt with the carnal attitudes and divisions of the Corinthian believers, he gave them a compelling reason to change their ways— the coming judgment. One day, all of our works will be tested by the fires of God's judgment. Some of us *"shall receive a reward"* while others *"shall suffer loss."* What determines a reward or loss? The kind of materials we use to build our lives will decide the outcome.

The *"gold, silver, precious stones"* in the passage refer to our works that are of a spiritual nature, which have enduring qualities. On the other hand, *"wood, hay, stubble"* represent the temporary, carnal activities that we engage in. Thus, how we live our lives after being saved determines our treasures in heaven. Those who live selfishly and find little time to serve God will watch their works burn up, leaving a pile of ashes. Is that what you want to present to the Lord? Paul took this occasion to warn the Corinthians of the eternal consequences of their carnality. Should we not also take heed?

For who maketh thee to differ from another? and what hast thou that thou didst not receive? now if thou didst receive it, why dost thou glory, as if thou hadst not received it? I Corinthians 4:7

One of the foulest odors in the nostrils of God is the stench of pride. At times, pride raises its ugly head in each of us; and when it does so, our fellowship with God is severed. Peter tells us, *"God resisteth the proud."* (I Peter 5:5) As the Lord often uses questions to produce conviction in the hearts of men, here He poses three questions that will quickly humble those who consider them.

First, *"For who maketh thee to differ from another?"* If you have been elevated above your fellow man by way of opportunities or talent, who gave you those advantages? God did! He has given you all you have and made you all that you are. So, don't get puffed up about any superiority you may enjoy over another. Second, *"...what hast thou that thou didst not receive?"* Nothing! You entered this world empty-handed and have received all that you currently possess. Third, *"now if thou didst receive it, why dost thou glory, as if thou hadst not received it?"* How can you answer this last question with anything less than confession of your rotten pride? Let God's questions humble you.

It is reported commonly that there is fornication among you, and such fornication as is not so much as named among the Gentiles, that one should have his father's wife. I Corinthians 5:1

How horrible a sin! We may be tempted to ask, "How could a saved man commit such a wicked sin? Why did the people in the church tolerate it?" There is every indication that the man was saved (see v. 5), and the church was composed of *"saints."* Unfortunately, these believers were not spiritual. Paul said they were *"carnal"* and *"babes in Christ."* (I Corinthians 3:1) Let this be a warning to all of us. Carnality breeds further fleshly appetites, and even Christians can plunge to tremendous depths of sin when living carnally. When that happens, our sin will be *"reported commonly"* to the demise of our testimony.

Further, our sin can actually become worse than the unsaved who dwell around us. Paul said the evil found in the church was *"not so much as named among the Gentiles."* It is sad when Christians stoop lower than the unbelievers and provide the lost an excuse to blaspheme.

The problem is that *"a little leaven leaveneth the whole lump."* What is the solution? *"Purge out therefore the old leaven, that ye may be a new lump."* Deal with sin, or you may one day plunge to its depths.

And such were some of you: but ye are washed, but ye are sanctified, but
ye are justified in the name of the Lord Jesus, and by the
Spirit of our God. I Corinthians 6:11

What a glorious transformation salvation brings to our lives! Though once vile sinners, all that changed when Jesus saved us. Although the previous verses mention sins you may have been guilty of before salvation, such as fornication, adultery, thievery, covetousness, and drunkenness, those sins are no longer on your account. The Scripture says, *"...such were some of you."* Don't go back to such sins. Notice three wonderful events that transpired at the moment of salvation.

First, *"ye are washed."* Though your sin was dark as coal, God washed away every trace of guilt. Isn't it great to be clean? Second, *"ye are sanctified."* You are set apart from sin and consecrated to the Lord. This means that you are freed from the bondage of sin and no longer have to be enslaved to your former deeds. Paul said, *"I will not be brought under the power of any."* Sanctification liberates! Third, *"ye are justified."* Even though you were guilty of terrible sin, Jesus pronounced you righteous. In the Father's eyes, you are just as if you had never sinned. Why would you want to go back to what you *"were"*?

Now concerning the things whereof ye wrote unto me: It is good
for a man not to touch a woman. I Corinthians 7:1

Paul said, *"ye wrote unto me."* The people obviously had questions about what they were doing and sought godly counsel. There was a problem with fornication among many of the believers, and the Holy Spirit had been convicting them of their sin. They wondered what kind of physical contact was allowed between members of the opposite sex. Isn't it common that people want to see how much they get away with before it is considered sin? Paul made it clear that a man is *"not to touch a woman"* before marriage—no hugging, no kissing, *etc.* Those who engage in kindling a fire will soon be set ablaze with worse sin.

Along with the apparent lesson of maintaining moral purity, another truth can be gleaned from our text. When you have questions about a spiritual matter, get them cleared up as soon as possible. As the Holy Spirit works upon your heart, do you not begin to question certain activities in your life? It is wise to seek clarity from the Scriptures and get godly counsel from your pastor. Living in doubt could lead to further sin. Therefore, whatever the issue, get it settled in order to enjoy a clear conscience.

For he that is called in the Lord, being a servant, is the Lord's freeman:
likewise also he that is called, being free, is Christ's servant.
I Corinthians 7:22

The word *servant* literally means a slave, whether voluntarily or involuntarily. Though a man was a slave externally, if he received Christ as Savior, he was liberated internally, becoming *"the Lord's freeman."* What could be better than being a freed man? In a very real sense, all who have trusted Jesus have been unshackled from the bonds of sin. *"If the Son therefore shall make you free, ye shall be free indeed."* (John 8:36) Although free from sin, you have a new Master.

Are you one of the Lord's freemen? If so, how are you using your spiritual liberty? Though once compelled to serve a terrible ruler, shouldn't you now use your freedom to serve the One who liberated you? Our text continues, *"...he that is called, being free, is Christ's servant."* Those who are free should become a slave to Christ and follow His every command. Have you renounced all sinful habits? Rather than obey the passions of sin, yield yourself to Jesus today, obeying completely. Slaves to human masters serve out of dread and duty, but those serving a loving Lord do so with delight and desire. How do you serve the Lord?

But take heed lest by any means this liberty of yours become a
stumblingblock to them that are weak. I Corinthians 8:9

In Paul's day, the heathen were accustomed to eat meat sacrificed to idols. However, some Christians also partook of such sacrifices, but not in worship toward the idol. Knowing that eating meat was not a sin, they justified themselves saying, "I don't believe in this idol, but the food is good. So, I'll eat it." Although they were technically not committing idolatry, they were bad examples to other believers. Weaker brethren may have supposed that idolatry was not so bad after all, especially if a stronger brother was eating in the temple of an idol. Thus, the first brother's liberty became a stumbling block to others.

Be careful not to talk yourself into sin. Those who ate the meat thought they were okay because they did not believe in the idol. However, they had sinned. Paul said to them, *"...when ye sin so against the brethren, and wound their weak conscience, ye sin against Christ."* If you have to justify your actions through technicalities, you are probably venturing into sin and leading others to follow your bad example. How often do you sin against others through a reckless use of your liberty? Isn't it better to forgo some things for the sake of others?

Know ye not that they which run in a race run all, but one receiveth
the prize? So run, that ye may obtain. I Corinthians 9:24

The Apostle Paul used athletic terminology to motivate us to seek spiritual victories. Are you tired of losing the battle against sin? If you apply today's lessons, you are sure to gain many more victories.

A few guidelines for winning are given in this chapter. First, you need *determination—"one receiveth the prize...So run, that ye may obtain."* How should you run? Run like you want to win by giving it all you've got. Very few Christians will expend all their strength to conquer their sin, and that is why so many end up losing repeatedly. Second, winning requires *discipline—"every man that striveth for the mastery is temperate in all things."* In the fight against sin, you have to do more than just try to survive against the adversary. Instead, God wants us to strive. Striving requires hard work, self-denial, and self-control (temperance). Abstaining from anything that will hold you back from attaining your goal is a must. Third, you must have *desire—"...they do it to obtain a corruptible crown; but we an incorruptible."* They wanted to *"obtain"* the prize. Do you really want to conquer that besetting sin? With Jesus as our team Captain, we have no excuse to lose.

...but God is faithful, who will not suffer you to be tempted above that ye
are able; but will with the temptation also make a way to escape,
that ye may be able to bear it. I Corinthians 10:13

Temptation is inevitable—in fact, God said that it is *"common to man."* However, not all people face it the same way. Some go headlong into sin saying, "I had no choice because I was tempted." Yet, we are never forced to give in to temptation. Sin is always a choice.

Our text gives several wonderful promises that guarantee deliverance from Satan's allurements. First, notice that *"God is faithful."* The Lord will not leave you in your time of need. Furthermore, He is incapable of failure. Second, He *"will not suffer you to be tempted above that ye are able."* God knows your limits and frailties and has promised never to allow the pull of sin to be so strong that you cannot resist. Third, He *"will with the temptation also make a way to escape."* I like those last four words—*"a way to escape."* Instead of peering into the door of temptation, you must look for the escape route that God has promised! Last, the promise assures *"that ye may be able to bear it."* All temptation is bearable, and sin can be avoided by turning to the faithful God. Will you start looking for God's escape route?

Ye cannot drink the cup of the Lord, and the cup of devils: ye cannot be partakers of the Lord's table, and of the table of devils.
I Corinthians 10:21

The *"cup of the Lord"* and the *"Lord's table"* refer to the Lord's Supper. That precious ceremony allows us to reflect upon the sacrifice Christ made for our salvation, and it is a time of sweet fellowship with the Lord. However, something threatens all that.

Paul wrote these words to the carnal church of Corinth, whose members wanted fellowship with God without separating from idolatrous practices. His conclusion was that we *"cannot drink the cup of the Lord, and the cup of devils"* at the same time. No person can fellowship with God while closely associated with the enemies of God—the devil and his worldly influences.

Is there such a struggle within you today? Do you try to draw nigh to God through a devotional time but also feel a strong attraction towards the evil things in the world? You cannot partake of both God's ways and the devil's at the same time. Ungodly associations hinder close communion with the Lord. So, whose cup will you drink from today— the Lord's or the devil's?

Be ye followers of me, even as I also am of Christ. I Corinthians 11:1

Is it right to follow spiritual leaders? In religious circles, many have blindly followed preachers to their own destruction. Women have lost their purity with immoral pastors, children have been defiled by homosexual priests, and multitudes have lost fortunes to television evangelists. Certainly, God would never want a person to yield total allegiance to any individual. However, the Scriptures are clear that we should be in subjection to those in authority over us. Hebrews 13:17 states, *"Obey them that have the rule over you, and submit yourselves."* So, how do we know when we should follow and when we should not?

Our text provides wonderful clarity to this question. Without apology Paul said, *"Be ye followers of me."* However, he added a qualification to his demand, *"even as I also am* [a follower] *of Christ."* In other words, he only expected the believers to follow him as he followed Jesus. In any matter that a man deviates from the Scriptures, he should not be followed. For example, nobody should follow a preacher into immorality or false doctrine just because he is the "man of God." A true man of God only insists that people follow him to the extent he follows Jesus. However, don't look for his flaws to justify disobedience.

For if we would judge ourselves, we should not be judged.
I Corinthians 11:31

In context, our passage deals with the Lord's Supper service. It is a marvelous truth that we can draw near to God after strict self-examination. However, our text lays down a principle that should be applied to daily living also.

What a wonderful promise is given to us that, if we would judge ourselves of wrongdoing, we would be spared judgment by God. However, failure to condemn our sinful actions leads to God's judgment—*"we are chastened of the Lord."* I like the words *"not...judged"* better than *"chastened of the Lord."* Do you want to avoid God's stinging discipline? Do you not dread leanness of soul and trouble in the flesh that result from unconfessed sin?

Thankfully, your sin was already judged on the cross, and when you bring those acts of defilement to the Savior through confession, you are gloriously cleansed. Arise and judge your sinful ways at once. God, in His mercy, has provided a way for you to be clean. However, failure to exercise self-judgment will certainly lead to chastisement.

But the manifestation of the Spirit is given to every man to profit withal.
I Corinthians 12:7

Paul addressed the believers in Corinth concerning the working of the Holy Spirit among them. This was a church that was prone to divisions; and, therefore, it was vital that they understood how the Spirit worked differently between individuals. He reminded them that there were *"diversities of gifts"* and *"diversities of operations."* Simply put, God does not equip or use every Christian exactly the same.

However, divine assurance is given that the Spirit will be manifested *"to every man."* Therefore, there is no need for comparisons, jealousies, or divisions in the church. God has made us all differently and equipped us uniquely for His service *"to profit withal."*

More important than what gift we have is the realization that we must use what has been bestowed upon us for the glory of God. Never become envious at how God chooses to use another member of the body. Simply be a yielded vessel for the Spirit to use in the way He knows is best. Rejoice in the promise that the Spirit will manifest Himself through you in a profitable way; and refuse to be jealous of any other Christian's gifts, talents, or opportunities.

For the body is not one member, but many. I Corinthians 12:14

This chapter provides a comparison between a physical body and the local church. As many parts make up a body, many members compose a church. All parts of the body are vital and have their own unique function. For instance, although the nose cannot see, it can do what the eye cannot—it can smell. Likewise, every member of the church is necessary to keep the church running smoothly.

Unfortunately, there are individuals in every church who begin to think they are indispensable. They believe that they are the only ones who can perform any given task to perfection. Our text serves as a good reminder that *"the body is not one member, but many."* Have you begun to think you are one of the "faithful few" in your church? Don't be lifted up with pride. God wants us to realize that it takes all of the members to make up a church. Therefore, let us humbly fulfill our duties and strengthen others so they can perform theirs.

No person can say, *"I have no need of you"* to another member of the church because *"God hath tempered the body together."* In fact, He has *"given more abundant honour to that part which lacked."* When you begin to feel superior, remember that God doesn't see you as such.

And now abideth faith, hope, charity, these three; but the greatest of these is charity. I Corinthians 13:13

Three wonderful virtues are listed in today's passage: faith, hope, and charity. Concerning the importance of faith, Hebrews 11:6 says, *"...without faith it is impossible to please him."* Hope is a sign of being filled of the Spirit—*"...abound in hope, through the power of the Holy Ghost."* However, despite the value of faith and hope, *"the greatest...is charity."* Do you work as hard at showing love as you do trying to become a "better" Christian? Sadly, some who are very dedicated to their ministries display little charity to people they attempt to minister to.

Even if we possessed great spiritual gifts, understood deep Bible mysteries, and exercised mountain-moving faith, we are *"nothing"* if we do not possess love. We can give to the poor and die as a martyr; but without love, those things will bring no eternal reward. Although many of our best efforts in life only seem to crumble, *"Charity never faileth."* Rather than focusing on self-improvement, wouldn't it be better to strive for true spirituality? Let us be sure to follow after Christian virtues but always season them with love. Don't be distracted by good things to the neglect of the greatest—Christ-like love!

Brethren, be not children in understanding: howbeit in malice be ye children, but in understanding be men. I Corinthians 14:20

Many of the Corinthian believers were infatuated with speaking in tongues. They thought to speak in an unknown language was a mark of spiritual maturity. However, Paul pointed out that their desire to babble with no understanding of what they spoke was actually a mark of immaturity—*"be not children"* was his reprimand.

"Follow after charity" were the opening words of the chapter, which emphasized where the focus for a dedicated Christian should be. Unfortunately, the brethren in Corinth were so determined to speak in tongues that they did not seem to care if they even understood what they were saying. To them, it felt good—and that was all that mattered. They seemed to have forgotten that the purpose of tongues was to reveal the gospel to people in a known language. Our text provides a great truth—it is childish to put feelings above fruitfulness. Many things may make you feel good, but they are useless if they do not further God's kingdom. Focus on being a blessing to other people, rather than making yourself feel good. If coffee, donuts, and entertainment are the highlight of your church experience, it is time to grow up—*"be not children."*

AUG. 27   RESPECT AND ORDER   I COR. 14:21-40

Let all things be done decently and in order. I Corinthians 14:40

The spiritual gifts bestowed upon the church of Corinth were abused, and the worship services degenerated into chaos and confusion as people did as they pleased. Paul, in this chapter, laid down rules on how certain gifts were to be exercised in the church. He concluded with a wonderful principle, *"Let all things be done decently and in order."*

Our lives, as well as our church services, need to be conducted in a decent, respectable manner. As the world continues to degenerate, we should strive to live above reproach. We must not follow worldly trends that lead to indecency or loss of respect. Because we represent Christ, we must guard our dress and speech.

Our text also reminds us that *"all things"* must be done *"in order."* God is organized and expects our lives and church activities to be so, too. Oftentimes, we hear disorderliness excused by "spiritual" comments such as, "We just go with the flow as the Spirit moves." However, God should not be blamed for sloppiness. Where in the Bible does it teach to be out of control? Punctuality and schedules allow us to accomplish more in life with less chaos and distractions. So, whether in church or daily life, we must endeavor to maintain control and appropriateness.

But by the grace of God I am what I am: and his grace which was
bestowed upon me was not in vain... I Corinthians 15:10

The Apostle Paul believed in the power of God's grace. It had
transformed him from a persecutor to a trustworthy man of God.
The Lord made something special out of this man's life, and He can do
the same for you. Wouldn't it be exciting to be able to say, *"...by the
grace of God I am what I am"*?

God's grace is not only powerful, it is also humbling. All that we
are now or ever hope to be is not a result of self-improvement but is a
consequence of the Lord's grace. Never be too high-minded to think you
are what you are because of your own efforts. God made you and
blessed you with the talent, wisdom, and strength that you possess.

Furthermore, grace also involves stewardship. Paul said, *"...his
grace which was bestowed upon me was not in vain; but I laboured."*
We are to do something with what God has given to us! As Paul
"laboured more abundantly," so should we. Ask the Lord to make you a
fit vessel and, then, determine to work for Him. Have you asked for
grace today?

Awake to righteousness, and sin not; for some have not the knowledge
of God: I speak this to your shame. I Corinthians 15:34

After pointing out some problems in the believers' lives, Paul said, *"I
speak this to your shame."* The modern day equivalent of this
expression is, "Shame on you." Could that be God's message to you
today? Was there once a time in which you lived a more consistent,
godly life? Did you used to have a burden for lost souls that manifested
itself through fervent prayer and efforts to witness? Has your
soulwinning zeal cooled off? Can you sit with friends and listen to
inappropriate conversations? Shame on you!

Do you ignore the prompting of the Holy Spirit when tempted by
fleshly appetites? Can you watch filthy things on the television or videos
that are not pleasing to the Savior? Shame on you!

Christians are asleep when it comes to living a righteous life but
quite awake when it comes to enjoying sinful pleasures. Meanwhile, lost
souls lack someone to be a shining light and beacon of hope. We must
wake up, sin not, and evangelize those living in darkness. Are you
spiritually asleep today? Are you as busy for the Lord as He desires you
to be? If not, the Lord's message is, *"I speak this to your shame."*

In a moment, in the twinkling of an eye, at the last trump:
for the trumpet shall sound, and the dead shall be raised incorruptible,
and we shall be changed. I Corinthians 15:52

People long for change in their lives. It is difficult to be completely satisfied while living in a corrupt world with corruptible flesh. Even politicians sense the desire for change and promise much of it while campaigning. Let us be assured that no lasting, satisfying change is going to come at the hands of a politician! Neither will it come by looking inwardly. Our only hope for true transformation is found in the Person of Jesus.

Although we can experience significant inward changes in our lives, the ultimate alteration is yet to transpire. When Christ returns in the clouds and the trumpet sounds, we will be instantly, permanently changed! No more sin, sadness, sorrow, or struggles will plague us then. Don't be discouraged—things will be well in due time.

You may experience seasons of grief or sadness, but never forget the end of the story—*"we shall be changed."* No matter how bad things get in this life, one day it will be far better! Look up in anticipation for that glorious alteration. It will happen *"in the twinkling of an eye."*

AUG. 31   GO THROUGH THE DOOR   I COR. 16

For a great door and effectual is opened unto me, and
there are many adversaries. I Corinthians 16:9

God gives us open doors of opportunity to serve Him. He is the One who *"...openeth, and no man shutteth; and shutteth, and no man openeth."* (Revelation 3:7) Notice, however, that open doors are not always convenient doors. As a result of going through an open door, Paul had many adversaries. Hence, open doors do not promise ease.

Too many Christians are looking for comfortable avenues of service. When a thing appeals to them, they believe it must be an open door from the Lord. If things get a bit rough, they automatically conclude, "God closed the door." Just remember that the devil opens doors for you to exit the will of God and that not all open doors are from the Lord!

We must learn that God's open doors are for service, not self-satisfaction. The Lord has opened the doors to many mission fields where people are hungry for saving truth, but unfortunately, few of God's people are going through those doors. A *"great door"* with wonderful prospects may await you today. Don't allow the fear of a few adversaries hinder you from going through it! Be assured that Jesus will be your Guide and will enter the door with you. You are never alone.

...the God of all comfort; Who comforteth us in all our tribulation, that we may be able to comfort them which are in any trouble, by the comfort wherewith we ourselves are comforted of God. II Corinthians 1:3-4

Our culture is obsessed with comfort. From our shoes to our bedding, we seem to always be on the lookout for something more comfortable. In fact, what used to be considered a luxury item is now deemed a necessity. Further, huge amounts of our incomes go towards making life a little easier. The world has an insatiable appetite for comfort, but they will never find true comfort until they seek it from God. Nothing compares to the comfort that He brings to the soul.

We are promised a *heavenly comfort* in the words, *"the God of all comfort."* No one can cheer the heart like Jesus! It is also a *personal comfort*—*"Who comforteth us."* God's children can always expect their Father's consolation. Further, it is an *inclusive comfort.* Notice the words, *"all comfort... in all our tribulation."* You will never face a trial without corresponding comfort to get through it—what a promise! Lastly, it is a *purposeful comfort.* God's plan in comforting us is so that *"we may be able to comfort"* others who face the same trials we have endured. What are you seeking—physical or heavenly comfort?

Lest Satan should get an advantage of us: for we are not ignorant of his devices. II Corinthians 2:11

The devil wants to defeat every child of God. Typically, we think that he has an advantage over us because of his power, experience, and tenacity. However, the Scripture does not say that he already has it. It says, *"Lest Satan should get"* it. The wording implies that we already have the advantage and can only lose it by allowing sin into our lives. After all, *"If God be for us, who can be against us?"* (Romans 8:31) Rest assured that when close to Jesus, you already have the upper hand!

When a small boy is with his big brother, he is safe in the neighborhood. However, he becomes vulnerable to the local bully when he strays from his brother's side. Satan is like a bully and seeks those who have lost sight of the Savior by wandering into sin.

The devil's promise of a good time is not to satisfy you but to take away your advantage. Therefore, we must resist every dazzling temptation, knowing that it is only a trick to draw us away from our great Protector. Although *"we are not ignorant of his"* [Satan's] *devices,"* we sure are forgetful of them. Remember that God *"always causeth us to triumph in Christ."* Have you lost your advantage? Get close to God.

*But we all, with open face beholding as in a glass the glory of the Lord,
are changed into the same image from glory to glory, even as by
the Spirit of the Lord. II Corinthians 3:18*

Although the Jews were blinded by the veil of unbelief, the faithful
believer in Christ is promised a clear view of God. The phrase *"as
in a glass"* refers to a mirror. Just as a mirror reflects an image with
remarkable clarity, so we are able to see the glory of God clearly.

It is by seeing His glory that we can experience great changes. How
grand is the promise that we are *"changed into the same image."* It is of
utmost importance, therefore, that we focus on the glory of God. As we
behold His love, we can be changed into a loving person. Beholding His
holiness results in a life of righteousness. Oh, that we would be quick to
gaze upon the Lord's matchless attributes so such changes would begin
in our hearts today! How much time do you spend beholding Him?

The reason we fail to change is because we fail to behold. A casual
glance is not sufficient. The act of beholding needs to be ongoing—
"from glory to glory." As we continually seek the Lord, He repeatedly
changes us. However, beholding sin makes us more like this evil world.
What will you gaze upon today: sin or the Savior?

*For our light affliction, which is but for a moment, worketh for us a far
more exceeding and eternal weight of glory... II Corinthians 4:17*

How does your present affliction seem to you? Perhaps you have
bemoaned that the burden is too heavy or the trial is too lengthy.
Take heart and allow the promises in our text to provide a new outlook
on your afflictions. This verse is a wellspring of hope for troubled souls.

First, God boldly calls it a *"light affliction."* No matter how
crushing it may seem, we ought to look at it as God describes it. So, if it
is truly light, I can easily bear the burden! Should I find it becoming
tiresome, I can do what I should have done in the first place and cast my
burden upon the Lord. Did not Jesus say, *"For my yoke is easy, and my
burden is light"*? (Matthew 11:30)

Next, notice that the Lord's afflictions are not upon us forever. He
reassuringly says that they are *"but for a moment."* Trouble that lasts for
eternity is what the unsaved are called to bear, but God's children never
need to fear such treatment. Surely, you can endure *"for a moment."*

Lastly, we should glory in such an affliction because it *"worketh for
us."* We will be duly compensated with a larger reward than the burden
we were called to bear. Praise the Lord for a blessing at the trial's end!

(For we walk by faith, not by sight:) II Corinthians 5:7*

Typically, I would rather walk with my eyes open than closed. It is normal to rely heavily upon our natural sight. However, when it comes to walking with God, our natural eyes are of little worth. In fact, walking *"by sight"* hinders faith by looking on all the external circumstances before considering God's will.

When the car breaks down, sight says, "I don't have the time or the money to take it to the garage to get it fixed." Faith says, "God is in control and must have a purpose. I know He will work it all out." When the bills are more than your salary, sight says, "I can't afford to tithe right now." Faith says, "I can't afford not to tithe. God promised, *'Give, and it shall be given unto you,'* and I am going to prove it."

So, how do you walk? Are you looking at all the visible, earthly situations that you face? It's time to gaze upward and see your difficulty anew through the eye of faith, trusting that the all-wise God will take care of you. Walking by sight is not very exciting; but when you walk by faith, a sense of anticipation for God to work begins to reshape your entire outlook on life. It's your choice—how will you walk today? Just remember, how you see determines how you walk.

Wherefore come out from among them, and be ye separate, saith the Lord, and touch not the unclean thing; and I will receive you...
II Corinthians 6:17

When it comes to separating from sin, many Christians lament that they have to give up so much. They cringe at the thought of parting with worldly friends, styles, pastimes, or entertainment. In short, sin is so appealing that we tend to count our losses for separating from sin more than the rewards that result from it.

Our text should help make deciding simpler. The Lord promises that if we set aside our worldly ways, we will gain more than we lose—we gain Him with all His power and provision! He said, *"I will receive you."* Rejection of sin earns acceptance with God. The opposite is also true, acceptance of sin results in rejection by the Lord. Because sin cannot bring comfort, peace, love, joy, wisdom, eternal treasures, or a happy home, it is wiser to choose God over sin.

The truth is that you give up much more by failing to practice separation! Satan is a liar and will constantly try to turn your focus on what you lose rather than what you gain. Today, you will give up something—either sin or blessings. Which will you choose?

...our flesh had no rest, but we were troubled on every side; without were fightings, within were fears. Nevertheless God, that comforteth those that are cast down, comforted us... II Corinthians 7:5-6

Times of great distress will arise, and even God's choicest servants are not exempt from trouble. Paul testified, *"our flesh had no rest."* The words *"no rest"* are disheartening. When working hard, the anticipation of rest enables you to press on; but with no hope of respite, perseverance is difficult. Are you presently *"troubled on every side"* because of your service for Christ? If so, God knows your condition.

God recognizes your weaknesses; and rather than abandoning you for being weak, He is willing to run to your aid. After all, He desires that you stay in the battle for Him. Despite problems, our text lends hope— *"Nevertheless God..."* Those troubling difficulties which have caused you to bow are no match for the One *"that comforteth those that are cast down."* There is no need to collapse under the weight of your burden.

"Fightings" and *"fears"* arise because of natural weakness, but God's comfort delivers supernatural strength to endure. Regardless of your physical afflictions or emotional frailties, God's promise of comfort is good for every weakness. However, you must claim it. Will you?

Moreover, brethren, we do you to wit of the grace of God bestowed on the churches of Macedonia... II Corinthians 8:1

When we consider this chapter, normally we think of the subject of giving. Although many important lessons abound concerning giving, another truth is often overlooked. Notice that Paul started the chapter with *"we do you to wit of the grace of God."* It was God's grace that enabled the poor Macedonian believers to give so sacrificially. His desire for the Corinthians was not merely that they would give but that they would seek the same grace that could empower them to do likewise.

Grace is given by God to enable us to do what we cannot do by ourselves. If you lack a giving spirit, you really lack grace. Moreover, grace allows you to do what is naturally impossible! Too often, we look within to make changes, but God is not satisfied with our efforts of self-improvement. As the early believers were enabled to do things *"beyond their power,"* so can we; but we can only do so as we receive *"the same grace also."* Grace made the difference in the early Christians. Are you tired of continually forcing yourself to do things? As God bestowed grace on the early churches, He will do likewise to all who trust Him.

*But this I say, He which soweth sparingly shall reap also sparingly;
and he which soweth bountifully shall reap also bountifully.*
II Corinthians 9:6

The law of sowing and reaping is not only a natural law but also a spiritual one. God promises that we will reap what we have sown. In other words, you cannot expect to gather without some kind of investment. Further, our text indicates how much we can hope to reap.

Reaping is always in proportion to the amount sown. If you plant a few tomato seeds, you will grow only a few tomato plants, but if you sow many seeds the harvest will be much more bountiful. In God's economy, it is the same. When we give a little, we receive a little. Those who give much can expect a larger harvest of blessings from God. A person who witnesses more will see more souls saved than the one who rarely proclaims the gospel. Parents who devote much time to training their children will produce godlier children than those who do not make such a sacrifice. The results are dependent upon the one doing the sowing.

The question remains: how much do you want from God? After determining what size harvest you would like, begin to sow in the same proportion. How much you reap is up to you—so, go and sow.

*(For the weapons of our warfare are not carnal, but mighty through God
to the pulling down of strong holds;) II Corinthians 10:4*

With so much evil around us, we can be assured that the Christian life will be one of warfare. In many cases, Satan not only attacks daily but also establishes strongholds that are difficult to defend against. The devil assails us tirelessly with fiery darts designed to set us ablaze with sinful thoughts and attitudes. For this reason, we must run to God's arsenal and equip ourselves.

Because it is a spiritual war, only spiritual weaponry will suffice. Our defenses are *"not carnal."* Because the flesh is weak, even the best of our efforts, resources, and strategies will avail nothing. God's battles require His armament. We cannot contend for our marriages, children, or ministries in our own strength. Leaning upon human reasoning has led to the destruction of countless families and churches.

Thankfully, we are promised that God's munitions are *"mighty."* Through prayer and following Biblical principles, we can pull down Satan's strongholds. The devil's most powerful forces are no match for the Christian who relies upon God. Are you presently facing a battle? Use the right weapons and watch the enemy's defenses begin to crumble.

*For such are false apostles, deceitful workers, transforming themselves
into the apostles of Christ. II Corinthians 11:13*

L et's not forget that Satan is a master of deceit and that his ministers
follow his example. Clearly, false prophets taught a false gospel in
Paul's day, and we see the same thing happening in ours. It is amazing
that lies, heresy, and loose living are promoted in the name of Jesus and
are accepted by the masses. How could this be? False prophets
transform themselves *"into the apostles of Christ."*

Most false teachers look like good guys! They have big smiles and
can tell spellbinding stories. They speak about topics that people like to
hear, but they always depart from Scripture. Sadly, people of our day
desire experiences over the truth. They would rather feel good than be
convicted of their sinfulness. The promise of success, happiness, and
good health with no strings attached is an appealing message.

Preachers of today speak about blessings from God, but not about
repentance from sin. They boast about having a positive message, but
there is nothing positive about allowing people to feel comfortable in
their sin. Such negligent preachers are dangerous. Never follow charm
and charisma over the revealed truth found in Scripture.

*In weariness and painfulness, in watchings often, in hunger and thirst,
in fastings often, in cold and nakedness. II Corinthians 11:27*

P aul felt compelled to offer a defense of his ministry to the
Corinthians because they had begun to follow false teachers.
Although he had not previously boasted of his credentials, false prophets
had bragged of theirs. In an effort to show that he could have gained a
following the same way, he spoke *"as a fool."* His goal was not
sympathy, but rather to shame the Corinthians for receiving the false
apostles so readily. How could they ignore Paul's sacrifices for them?

What was a rebuke to the Corinthians turned out to be a blessing to
us. Paul's account of his sufferings has been a tremendous source of
hope and encouragement to many who have faced trying times. It is
highly unlikely that any of us would ever suffer all the hardships that
Paul did. However, we do face, on a lesser scale, some of them.

Our text describes weariness, pain, and sleeplessness. Realistically,
any of God's servants who experience such difficulties could be tempted
with discouragement. Perhaps you are tired or in pain today. Don't let it
stop you from serving the Lord. Enduring hardships is one of the marks
of true servanthood. As Paul received strength to endure, so will you.

And I will very gladly spend and be spent for you; though the more abundantly I love you, the less I be loved. II Corinthians 12:15

This chapter provides two great themes of the Christian life. The first is *suffering with strength*. Paul's afflictions caused him to cry out for deliverance; but God, in His wisdom, sent strength instead of removing the burden. Paul learned that God's *"strength is made perfect in weakness."* Therefore, he saw his sufferings in a new light—*"I take pleasure in infirmities, in reproaches, in necessities, in persecutions, in distresses for Christ's sake: for when I am weak, then am I strong."* Oh, that we would learn to accept God's provision. What could be better than His strength? Why would you beg for your strength above His?

The second truth exemplified by Paul is *sacrifice with satisfaction.* Notice he was willing to *"spend and be spent."* He took no money from these believers for his needs and endured great hardships to minister to them. All this he did *"very gladly"* because he knew that giving brings deep satisfaction. Sadly, his great display of selfless love was not even appreciated. The more he loved, the less they loved him! Do you ever feel that way? The source of your joy should not be the ones you serve, but God. Seek His approval. When He is happy, you can be, too.

The grace of the Lord Jesus Christ, and the love of God, and the communion of the Holy Ghost, be with you all... II Corinthians 13:14

It would be more than we deserve to have one member of the Trinity show a special interest in our lives. However, this verse assures us that every member of the Godhead is involved in blessing our lives.

Notice first that Jesus bestows *grace*, and this is fitting because He is *"full of grace and truth."* (John 1:14) Grace is favor, and Jesus loves to grant it to those who desire it. Do you need grace for your particular situation today? It is found in Jesus. Ask Him for it!

Second, the Father grants *love*. What need does a loving Father neglect in the life of one of His children? Will God fail to provide or protect? He loves you too much to abandon you! Right now, plead for His promised love and, then, rest in His mighty arms to protect and carry you. *"The eternal God is thy refuge, and underneath are the everlasting arms."* (Deuteronomy 33:27)

Last, the Holy Spirit provides *communion*, which means fellowship and participation. When we yield to His influence, He actively participates in all that we do, bringing us into close fellowship with God. What more could we ask? We have divine favor, love, and fellowship!

Who gave himself for our sins, that he might deliver us from this present evil world, according to the will of God and our Father... Galatians 1:4

Why did Jesus pay the ultimate price for our sins? The answer: *"that he might deliver us from this present evil world."* He knew all about the dangers that the world would pose for us and understood the evil influence it would have on our hearts and minds. Therefore, He entered the world to be hated, abused, rejected, and crucified by the ones He sought to rescue. He willingly suffered so we could be delivered from suffering. Have you shown appreciation for His sacrifice?

How sad it is to see Christians embracing the world after Christ came to deliver them from it! It is a slap in our Lord's face to desire what He wants us to escape—*"this present evil world."* How dare we be drawn to worldly conversation, entertainment, styles, and philosophies? Many believers are more comfortable in a house of pleasure than the house of worship. What are you attracted to: godliness or worldliness?

If you seek deliverance from the world, it is guaranteed. After all, Christ came *"that he might deliver us."* He gave Himself for all of our sins—even the sin of slapping Him in the face. Turn to Him anew and hate what He hates. Those who seek deliverance shall surely find it.

For he that wrought effectually in Peter...the same was mighty in me... Galatians 2:8

Here we see Paul's realization that the God of Peter was his God, too. Did the Lord work *"effectually"* in Peter? Oh, yes! Though often a self-willed man, once Peter yielded himself to God, great things transpired. In Acts chapters two and three, Peter preached two sermons, resulting in a total of eight thousand being saved. Paul said that the same God who used Peter was mighty in him also.

We would do well to glean a glorious truth from these two men: God works through people in tremendous ways. Paul did not seek the same results as Peter had or boast of the number of his converts. He was simply excited that God worked in his life to reach others with the message of salvation.

As I ask God to be *"mighty in me,"* I must be yielded to Him to use me as He sees fit. Be encouraged that the same God Who worked greatly in Peter and Paul is able to impart the same power to you, too. He has plenty of might to go around and is not the least bit weakened after lending strength to His many servants. Therefore, we can confidently return to Him for renewed strength for every heavenly-appointed task.

So then they which be of faith are blessed with faithful Abraham.
Galatians 3:9

Truly, Abraham was a blessed man! His first blessing was salvation. We are told, *"Abraham believed God, and it was accounted to him for righteousness."* This entire chapter argues that salvation is solely by faith. Before, during, and after the giving of the Law, justification was always solely by faith in Christ, without works. A man is most blessed when he stops trusting his good deeds to save himself, receiving Jesus' righteousness instead. Be sure you have this blessing first and foremost.

However, the blessings of Abraham extended far beyond his salvation, reaching into his daily life. His faith brought family blessings, too. Not only did his faith stir Sarah to trust in the Lord, it also resulted in the miraculous birth of Isaac. Further, his faith secured answers to prayer, peace with his enemies, and an inheritance for his posterity.

Because we *"are blessed with faithful Abraham,"* we can likewise obtain many blessings from the Lord. Is your faith any less effective than Abraham's? It is no less effective, but it may be less exercised. Start with being *"faithful"* like Abraham was, and soon the blessings will begin to overwhelm you.

Am I therefore become your enemy, because I tell you the truth?
Galatians 4:16

Let's face it, very few of us like to be told we are wrong. In many cases, the one being corrected gets angry, offended, and bitter. Because Paul cared about the believers in Galatia, he undertook the unpleasant task of rebuking them for error in their lives. Previously, the believers loved him and would have done nearly anything to help him; but after his rebuke, they changed their tune. They now counted Paul as an enemy! What changed their minds? Paul had told them *"the truth."*

When we are corrected, we would do well to first consider if what we have been told is, in fact, true. If so, we cannot fight against it without becoming the loser. A person who is willing to tell us the truth, no matter how painful it may seem, is a friend—not a foe! Instead of becoming defensive, let us humbly accept the truth, knowing that a friend has spoken it for our betterment. Count yourself happy if you have such a friend who would risk his friendship to help you!

Not only should you learn to swallow your pride and take correction, you should be courageous enough to tell the truth to an erring brother. After all, a silent friend is no friend at all.

But it is good to be zealously affected always in a good thing, and not only when I am present with you. Galatians 4:18

The believers in Galatia did well until a group of Jews persuaded them to go back under the bondage of the Law. In fact, they had become zealously affected, *"but not well."* Adherence to false doctrine caused them to turn against the beloved Paul. In short, the believers got excited about the wrong thing, and it led to the betrayal of godliness. Could that happen to you? It will if you fail to be *"zealously affected always in a good thing."*

Had the Galatians been as excited about the truth as they were about false teachings, the churches would have been full of blessings, not divisions. Unfortunately, Christians are too easily stirred about things that do not matter very much. Church members are more interested in programs, pageants, cantatas, and fellowships than they are about weightier matters. Perhaps you have lost your zeal for winning souls, teaching your Sunday school class, giving to missions, or living by faith.

What thrills you? If it is not *"a good thing,"* then it might be a bad thing. Let's focus on what is important to God and set aside frivolous activities and pursuits. It's time to get excited *"in a good thing."*

This I say then, Walk in the Spirit, and ye shall not fulfil the lust of the flesh. Galatians 5:16

Within every Christian, a battle rages between the Holy Spirit and the flesh. In fact, *"these are contrary the one to the other."* The Spirit opposes all the evil that the flesh would like to engage in, and the flesh seeks to undermine the Spirit's influence of producing righteousness. Both seek control of your life, but who wins is up to you.

The key to victory over the power of the flesh is to *"Walk in the Spirit."* You may ask, "What does that mean? How do you do that?" Well, walking is a term used to describe our movement through daily life. If you allow the Spirit of God to guide you throughout the day, you will not cater to the cravings of your wicked flesh. However, if you follow your sinful desires, you will quench the Spirit's control. As the flesh seeks to lure you to sin, the Spirit points you to walk God's way.

For every battle between the two, your will acts as the referee, deciding who wins. If you follow the flesh, it wins; but if you walk as the Spirit directs, *"ye shall not fulfil the lust of the flesh."* Although we are pulled this way and that by unruly desires, we do not have to yield to them. Is a battle raging within you today? Whom will you follow?

And let us not be weary in well doing: for in due season we shall reap, if we faint not. Galatians 6:9

Have you ever said, "What's the use of trying anymore?" Many times we attempt to do the right thing but seem to get nowhere despite our best efforts. That is the time Satan seeks to derail us with discouragement so that we quit our righteous endeavors. However, the time to relax is not when we face opposition.

Paul exhorts us, *"let us not be weary in well doing."* We must never get tired of doing right! Fatigue is a natural result of toil, but it should not break our resolve. Hard work is always rewarded in the end. The lumberjack may be exhausted from swinging his axe repeatedly, but he knows the tree will eventually fall if he keeps at it. Let us keep swinging until the rewards fall! The promise is that *"in due season we shall reap, if we faint not."* I like those words, *"we shall."* There is no doubt that we will reap! However, there is no reward promised to those who quit.

Are you tired of fighting what seems to be a losing battle? Have you thought of quitting? Banish all such thoughts. It is time to get busy, knowing that one day you *"shall reap"* if you determine not to faint.

Blessed be the God and Father of our Lord Jesus Christ, who hath blessed us with all spiritual blessings... Ephesians 1:3

I heard a ringtone one day in which a Pentecostal preacher shouted, "God is going to bless you in your body! God is going to bless you in your finances!" Unfortunately, like many others, this man had placed his attention on physical blessings rather than spiritual ones.

Our text clearly states that God has indeed *"blessed us."* However, the blessings mentioned are *"spiritual blessings."* I would never deny that the Lord graciously promises to meet our earthly needs. After all, He instructed us to ask for our *"daily bread."* Nevertheless, there is a huge difference between needs and wants. The Lord promises bread, but many people demand cars, houses, and luxuries. Sadly, some mistakenly think happiness results from acquiring more material blessings.

Living in Africa for several years allowed me to witness Christians who were happy without an abundance of material blessings. How could they be happy? They were *"blessed...with all spiritual blessings."* Forgiveness of sins, peace within, a happy marriage, godly children, and answers to prayer are far better than all the possessions in the world. What kind of blessings have you been seeking most?

But God, who is rich in mercy, for his great love wherewith he loved us...
Ephesians 2:4

E very Christian stumbles and becomes ashamed at how low they have stooped by committing some transgression. At times, we feel worthless and completely undeserving of God's forgiveness, even wondering if God would pardon us one more time for the same foolish sin. It is under such anguish of soul that Satan gains many victories. He tries his best to keep you from going to God with your heavy load of sin.

If you have lost hope, allow our text to encourage you. Our God *"is rich in mercy."* When God exercises mercy, He withholds judgment. So, if you feel guilty today, you are a prime candidate to receive mercy! How can the Lord be so gracious to those who have repeatedly failed Him? Notice the words, *"for his great love wherewith he loved us."* His great love produces great mercy. As you would never doubt His love, never doubt His mercy. Neither can fail.

Do you need some mercy today? Go with the promissory note of God's great love, and you shall cash it in for a windfall of mercy. You will never be able to bankrupt the account of God's mercy—He is rich!

Now unto him that is able to do exceeding abundantly above all that we ask or think, according to the power that worketh in us... Ephesians 3:20

H ow could we possibly undertake a careful consideration of God's power in the space allotted? It is impossible. However, our text provides a few gems to ponder as we pose some questions.

First, who has this power? It is *"him that is able."* It should be reassuring that God is able to do anything. Although your abilities are limited, God's are not. How often have you thought a thing to be impossible? Never forget *"him that is able."*

Second, what can this power do? This almighty power *"is able to do exceeding abundantly above all that we ask or think."* I am sure that Solomon was surprised when God not only gave him wisdom but also loaded him with many material blessings he had never requested. When you seek the kingdom of God first, God often gives a heap of benefits you never even thought about requesting.

Third, where does this power work? Amazingly, it is called *"the power that worketh in us."* If you are saved, you can include yourself in the word, *"us."* The Lord is *"not a God afar off."* He wants to be active in your life each day, giving you strength and victory through His Spirit.

That we henceforth be no more children, tossed to and fro, and carried about with every wind of doctrine, by the sleight of men, and cunning craftiness, whereby they lie in wait to deceive... Ephesians 4:14

Few want to be told that they are acting childish. However, this is precisely what Paul told the believers in Ephesus. Perhaps they thought, as many do today, that they had reached a level of spiritual maturity. Let's check our own life to see if we are spiritually immature.

First, we must be open to the *suggestion of childishness*. When Paul told the Ephesians, *"be no more children"* it meant that they were acting like little kids in some ways. What is your reaction when someone implies that you are acting like a child? Immature people get offended.

Second, notice the *signs of childishness*. Two characteristics of spiritual immaturity are mentioned: *"tossed"* and *"carried."* It is easy to toss or carry children, and those who are easily swayed with new doctrines prove to be juvenile in their walk with God. People run from one church to another, following the latest craze or teaching touted by up-and-coming "gifted" pastors. How stable are you in Bible doctrine?

Last, the *solution to childishness* is, *"grow up into him in all things."* We must grow in the Lord in every area. Christlikeness is true maturity.

That ye put off concerning the former conversation the old man, which is corrupt according to the deceitful lusts...And that ye put on the new man...created in righteousness and true holiness. Ephesians 4:22, 24

When the oil in your car is old and worn out, what do you do? You replace it. We do the same thing with our shoes, clothes, and phones. When something is useless or injurious, it is always best to replace it. The same is true in your spiritual life.

The principle of replacement is one of the most important lessons you can ever learn. It's not enough to get bad things out of your life— you must put some good things in their place. Our text begins a detailed lesson on replacing bad things with good things. It starts by saying, *"put off...the old man"* and adds, *"put on the new man."* The works of the flesh need to be replaced by the deeds of the Spirit.

The passage continues with many examples: replace lying with speaking the truth (v. 25), anger with peace (v. 26-27), stealing with working and giving (v. 28), corrupt words with good words (v. 29), and bitterness with kindness and forgiveness (v. 31-32). Perhaps it is time to replace your friends, music, reading material, entertainment, or attitude. What bad things has God been convicting you about replacing?

Wherefore be ye not unwise, but understanding
what the will of the Lord is. Ephesians 5:17

The phrase, *"be ye not unwise"* is a nice way of saying, "Don't be foolish." The Lord is very concerned that we do not make senseless decisions. Unfortunately, we often forge ahead in matters, not knowing God's will. In many cases, we want our will so badly that we don't even dare consult with God for fear that He may tell us, "No."

Notice that it is *"unwise"* to reject counsel from God. After all, He knows everything! Only a fool thinks he can avoid judgment for following his own ways. How wise is the thief sitting in jail or the teen girl who is pregnant out of wedlock? Even "good" Christians refuse godly counsel, but their families, ministries and finances suffer terribly.

Observe also the clear command to understand *"what the will of the Lord is."* Understanding only comes after careful consideration of a matter. In the previous verses, the Lord gave clear instructions such as, *"walk in love," "walk as children of light," "have no fellowship with...darkness,"* and *"walk circumspectly* [uprightly]*."* It is as if God said, "I told you what to do. Now don't be foolish and ignore My will." To understand God's will, you must consult the Bible. Then, follow it.

And be not drunk with wine, wherein is excess;
but be filled with the Spirit... Ephesians 5:18

Yesterday, we learned of the importance of knowing the will of God. Today, we discover that part of His will is to *"be filled with the Spirit."* That sounds good, but how do you know if you are? In the immediate verses that follow our text, the Lord provides three signs that indicate what a Spirit-filled life should be like.

First, the Spirit produces *singing—"Speaking to yourselves in psalms and hymns and spiritual songs, singing and making melody in your heart to the Lord."* The Lord puts a song in the heart of those who are filled with Him. How often do you have a hymn of praise in your heart or on your lips? Having a worldly song or no song at all is telling.

Second, the Holy Spirit will bring *satisfaction—"Giving thanks always for all things."* Those who murmur and complain are not satisfied with the situation God has allowed to come into their lives, but the Spirit-filled Christian is grateful *"for all things."*

Last, a sign of the Spirit's control is *submission—"Submitting yourselves one to another in the fear of God."* God expects us to submit to the authority He has placed over us. The Spirit produces no rebels.

Put on the whole armour of God, that ye may be able to stand against
the wiles of the devil. Ephesians 6:11

Every day is a battle with the unseen forces of darkness, and it is imperative that you prepare for it. We are sure to face *"the wiles of the devil."* Wiles refer to Satan's trickery in attacking the soul of man. You are no match for the evil one, who has sharpened his skills over the centuries, knowing the most effective assault to launch against your soul. Thankfully, you do not have to fear—God has prepared a strategy that will succeed every time you follow His battle plan. So, how do we win?

First, God demands that we *get ready*. The command is, *"Put on the whole armour of God."* This chapter lists the entire suit of protection: honesty, righteousness, soulwinning, faith, salvation, the Word of God, and prayer. Disregarding any piece will leave you vulnerable. That's why you must maintain a vibrant, consistent devotional life.

Second, the Lord expects us to *fight back*—*"stand against the wiles of the devil."* What is a soldier expected to do in battle? Fight! Satan wants to destroy our families, and it is our job to stand up and resist all of his attempts to spread his venomous evil. This is not a time for tolerance, but action. Put on the gloves, stand your ground, and fight.

But I would ye should understand, brethren, that the things which
happened unto me have fallen out rather unto the furtherance
of the gospel... Philippians 1:12

While detained as a prisoner, Paul wrote to comfort the Philippian believers. Despite unfavorable circumstances, he could see with the eye of faith that God was using his predicament as a means to further the gospel. Faith enables the Christian to envision the good that results from a bad situation. Do you have that kind of faith? Can you see that God will, one day, use your trouble to glorify His name?

Unfortunately, we often see the storm clouds of life without anticipating the showers of blessing that accompany them. Our vision becomes faulty when we focus on what we currently see instead of what God will soon do. Faith in an all-wise, all-powerful God is the eye salve that cures despondency. It is hard to be sad, knowing God is at work.

Paul could say, *"the* [bad] *things which happened unto me"* worked out to be good things! This should encourage us to see the good in every unfavorable situation. Rather than looking for pity, Paul pointed others to the wonders God intended them to see. Oh, for faith that sees negative circumstances in a positive way! Lord, increase my faith.

And in nothing terrified by your adversaries... Philippians 1:28

Those who stand for righteousness often have many adversaries. The name *devil* means adversary, and we know that he leads the charge against the godly. To make matters worse, Satan's followers far outnumber us in the world. Oh, it would be easy to despair! However, our gracious Lord provides comforting words, *"in nothing terrified by your adversaries."*

Terror brings fear to a heart, crippling the walk of faith. Do you ever feel terrorized within? Many Christians have been maligned and relentlessly opposed by co-workers on the job. Perhaps a humble, submissive wife currently faces an oppressive, churlish husband. A teen may be standing alone for Christ in his school with constant resistance. What is the solution to all of these situations? Paul said, *"in nothing terrified."* You may not be able to control the attacks of the enemy, but you can determine your response. To exhibit fear is always a choice.

Satan may be the terrorist of your soul, but God is the Guardian of it! With the Lord by your side, you never have to accept terror within. Exercising faith in an all-powerful God, you can face every foe *"with all boldness."* God may call you *"to suffer"* but not to be terrorized.

For it is God which worketh in you both to will and to do
of his good pleasure. Philippians 2:13

In every church, there are people who are willing to work for the Lord but feel inadequate. The opposite is also true. Many are able but not willing. Has either attitude hindered you? Just imagine how the work of God would thrive if every Christian was both willing and able!

Today's text provides a remedy for both stubbornness and laziness. Do you often find yourself in either the "I don't want to" or "I can't" category? As you know, such attitudes leave you discouraged and defeated. However, today's promise brings hope and victory.

Notice whose job it is to make us willing and able—*"it is God which worketh in you both to will and to do..."* Although you may feel helpless to change your desires, God can alter them. Have you been unwilling to do a job that God has chosen for you? Confess it at once and ask Him to change your heart. I have found He does so every time I honestly ask.

Do you feel unfit for a task? Remember that God will enable you to do what He calls you to do. Therefore, you can boldly request the necessary strength for the job. If you struggle with either willingness or ability, look to the One Who *"worketh in you both to will and to do."*

Because for the work of Christ he was nigh unto death, not regarding his life, to supply your lack of service toward me. Philippians 2:30

In our reading today, Paul lamented the fact that so many *"seek their own, not the things which are Jesus Christ's."* However, a few faithful servants broke from the ranks of selfishness. Epaphroditus was one such hero. Notice his *ordeal.* The record reveals that *"he was nigh unto death."* While some sought their own interests, he risked his life *"for the work of Christ."* As we consider the labors that brought a man to the brink of death, let us contemplate the value of our own efforts.

Next, consider his *offering—"not regarding his life."* How is it that he so willingly endangered his life? He had given his life to Jesus instead of selfish pursuits. His regard was to follow God's will rather than his own. Do you have too much regard for your own interests? Perhaps more souls would be reached at home and abroad if we unconditionally offered ourselves to the Lord's service.

Last, we see the *occasion* of his great sacrifice. He engaged in the work because of the *"lack of service"* of others. When one fails to perform his duties, another has to arise and fill the gap. Are you a gap-filler or a gap-creator?

Finally, my brethren, rejoice in the Lord. To write the same things to you, to me indeed is not grievous, but for you it is safe. Philippians 3:1

Repetition is a key to learning. Too often, however, people are wearied by the "drudgery" involved and think it is a waste of time to listen to the same lesson again. In some cases, when the preacher announces his sermon title, people in the audience say to themselves, "I know this already," or, "We just heard a message on that topic recently."

To be frequently reminded of a truth only reinforces it in our lives. In fact, Paul said, *"for you it is safe."* As error dominates and prevails in so many around us, hearing *"the same things"* bolsters our faith and protects our walk with God. Never begrudge being taught a lesson more than once. After all, the Lord knows that you have not mastered as many subjects as you think you have. So, don't let pride hinder your growth.

Furthermore, it was *"not grievous"* to Paul to reiterate *"the same things"* to his hearers. Why should it be to us? Sadly, pastors tire of preaching the same truths, and parents become frustrated with teaching their children *"the same things"* repeatedly. We should patiently instruct those under our care, knowing that the safety of their souls depends upon our cheerful, persistent efforts. Try not to be annoyed with slow learners.

I can do all things through Christ which strengtheneth me.
Philippians 4:13

We are often faced with situations that seem impossible to us, but how we react determines the outcome. Far too many Christians are prone to blurt out, "I can't." Is such negativity ingrained in your heart? A defeated attitude is not only futile but also faithless. It alleges that God has either abandoned you or refuses to assist you.

When facing overwhelming trials, Paul learned to say, *"I can do all things."* Was he superhuman? No. He told us how we can overcome impossible situations, too. The key to being able to *"do all things"* is found in the words that follow—*"through Christ which strengtheneth me."* The only ones who need to be strengthened are those who are weak. As Paul realized his own natural weakness, it made way for Christ to empower him. Victory begins with humility—"I may not be able to do this in my own strength, but Jesus will enable me!" Faith prevails.

To those of us who have children, we do them a great disservice by allowing them to say, "I can't." Wouldn't it be better to teach them to look to Jesus as the Source of their help and strength? As they watch your life, are they learning "I can't" or *"I can...through Christ"*?

Strengthened with all might, according to his glorious power, unto
all patience and longsuffering with joyfulness... Colossians 1:11

As we learned yesterday, God promises strength for His children to face what seems impossible. While it is true that God will empower you to conquer and overcome sin, He never promised to enable you to avoid every problem or adversity. It is time to gain a higher view of Christ's *"glorious power."*

Our text tells of the purpose these believers were strengthened *"with all might."* It was so that they could endure hardships and trials— *"Strengthened...unto all patience and longsuffering."* Consider the Lord Jesus as He hung upon the cross. It was a greater display of power to refrain from destroying His persecutors than to annihilate them. He could have spoken a word and consumed them in an instant, but *"his glorious power"* was magnified more through His patient endurance.

Has God called you to endure a challenging trial? If so, *"his glorious power"* is available. Ask Him to enable you to exercise *"patience and longsuffering"* when it seems humanly impossible to do so. Perhaps the greatest display of God's power is that it enables us to endure *"with joyfulness."* God gives joy even in times of difficulty.

For I would that ye knew what great conflict I have for you...
Colossians 2:1

The church in Colosse began to be affected by doctrinal error. Some were led into such practices as the *"worshipping of angels,"* while others believed their spirituality consisted of following strict rules such as, *"Touch not; taste not; handle not."* Paul's great burden for the Colossian believers drove him to address the errors that had begun to infiltrate the church. Although they had not seen the serious dangers involved, the preacher had; and he wished they understood what motivated him. Therefore, he began the chapter saying, *"I would that ye knew what great conflict I have for you."*

Unfortunately, many who begin to backslide not only fail to see their departure from the Lord; but they also become annoyed with the preacher for pointing out their sin. Have you ever gotten angry at the pastor for exposing your sin? If so, please remember why he does what he does. A true man of God gets no pleasure in scolding the flock. On the contrary, he wishes you would understand the burden he has for you and your family. Like Paul, he says, "I wish you knew the great agony of soul I have for you." Why not thank your preacher for his concern?

Set your affection on things above, not on things on the earth.
Colossians 3:2

Today's reading challenges us to live a holy life and to beware the carnal appetites of fornication, covetousness, anger, and bitterness. Further, we are instructed to be merciful, kind, humble, forgiving, and loving. How can we possibly avoid giving in to the lusts of the flesh and, instead, live a life of righteousness? Our text provides the answer.

Adherence to this one command sets the stage for victorious living. After all, most of our failures come because our affections are *"on things on the earth."* Looking *"on things above"* is the cure for covetousness, lust, and unbridled tempers. As we look heavenward, we do not focus on the temptations of the world. Our problems begin when we stop looking up and begin looking around.

Where has your focus been lately? Do you find yourself easily distracted by earthly causes? Although we must live in an imperfect world, we do not have to set our affections on it. When you find yourself preoccupied with the world, redirect your thoughts toward heaven. A quick prayer will often help you to adjust your disposition and change your perspective on things. Where will you set your affection today?

Continue in prayer, and watch in the same with thanksgiving...
Colossians 4:2

Has your prayer-life become dull and lifeless? Is it a mere ritual that you observe to maintain a sense of spirituality? If so, it's time to get a fresh view of what God says about the power of prayer.

First, we see an *exhortation* to pray—*"Continue in prayer."* Because prayer has worked in the past, continue with it now. Don't be discouraged because you have to wait for an answer to come. Gardeners understand that it takes time for their vegetables to grow. As they continue to tend to their garden while awaiting the harvest, so you should continue to cultivate your prayer life.

Prayer also requires *expectation*. Notice the charge to *"watch."* As children often gather at the window, looking earnestly for the arrival of expected guests, we must watch for the Lord. He is on His way with blessings and, in due time, will arrive with an answer to our prayers.

Lastly, rekindle the *excitement* you once expressed in prayer. True supplication not only delights when the answer arrives but also rejoices in anticipation of the answer. Prayer that is offered *"with thanksgiving"* demonstrates faith that God will soon grant your request.

...ye turned to God from idols to serve the living and true God...
I Thessalonians 1:9

Many people become troubled by their circumstances and regret the consequences of their sin. Being tired of misery and sorrow, they attempt to alter their life, hoping that sadness and guilt will soon pass. Although they honestly desire a dramatic change, they often fall short of complete repentance.

Consider the *requirement* of repentance. The Thessalonians *"turned to God from idols."* True repentance includes both turning to God and turning from sin. Unfortunately, many people only work half of the equation. Some may try to get back to God but refuse to turn from their sin. Others, knowing the destructive nature of their evil deeds, attempt to give them up; but they fail to turn to God in the process. Both are doomed for failure! Our turning must be *"to God"* and *"from"* sin.

A noticeable *result* always follows true repentance. One who sincerely repents will *"serve the living and true God."* If you continue in your sinful ways, don't deceive yourself into thinking you repented. Turn to the Lord right now and turn your back on the sin that haunts you.

Wherefore we would have come unto you, even I Paul, once and again; but Satan hindered us. I Thessalonians 2:18

Our text reminds us of the spiritual warfare that we face while serving our Lord. The believers in Thessalonica were young in the faith and faced tremendous persecution. Because the brethren needed strength and encouragement, Paul sought to visit them to bolster their faith; but Satan hindered him. It seems that the devil intensifies his efforts when we are on the verge of a great victory for God. Be on guard for such hindering efforts of the enemy, and don't be surprised when they come.

Perhaps the threat of Satan's attack strikes fear in your heart. Don't miss the good news found within our text! A great difference exists between being hindered and being halted. Satan may temporarily slow down the work of God, but he cannot stop it! With that in mind, we are guaranteed victory in the end. Too many Christians accept defeat before entering into the battle. Thus, instead of hindering the work, Satan stops it completely. So, take our text as a promise of victory rather than a warning of defeat. Christians should never expect or accept defeat. Determine not to become fearful or discouraged by Satan's attacks. If anything, muster courage and valiantly engage in the battle for the Lord.

Therefore, brethren, we were comforted over you in all our affliction and distress by your faith... I Thessalonians 3:7

While enduring *"affliction"* and *"distress,"* Paul received help from an unlikely source—new believers. The Thessalonian church encountered persecution from its inception, but they remained strong in faith. Their steadfast spirit uplifted Paul in his time of distress. He said, *"...we were comforted...by your faith."*

You never know who is watching your life. Someone in the heat of the battle may draw encouragement from your faith as they observe your perseverance in sore trials. Although Paul was a more experienced saint, he was aided by the testimony of new believers, proving that God can use anyone and any situation. Maybe the purpose of your current trial is to motivate others to endure their own afflictions.

Are there not times that you draw strength from the faith of others? One dear to you may depend on your testimony and example today. Perhaps your spouse, child, friend, or neighbor will consider your life in his/her time of distress. Don't let that one down. Be a source of inspiration that compels others to keep fighting the good fight of faith. Beware, however, that a lapse in faith could hurt the very ones you love.

...we beseech you, brethren, that ye increase more and more...
I Thessalonians 4:10

The meaning of the word *more* is learned at an early age. When a little child finishes eating something he likes, he says, "More!" Whether it is food, money, clothing, or other possessions, our cry throughout life is often the same—"More!" A great spiritual awakening would result if we had the same desire for an increase of righteousness. Shouldn't we plead with God, "Please give me more patience, more love, more kindness, more grace, and more victory"?

The believers at Thessalonica were commended for demonstrating brotherly love towards one another, but then they were encouraged to *"increase more and more."* Perhaps, by God's grace, you abound in a particular virtue. Do not allow yourself to become content with your current level of spirituality. Even if you outshine all others around you, God expects *"more and more."*

Because the Lord desires that you *"increase more,"* rest assured that more is not only available but also attainable. Therefore, in addition to examining our lives for shortcomings, let us also consider which of our strong points can be further strengthened. After all, God craves *"more."*

Quench not the Spirit. I Thessalonians 5:19

The Holy Spirit is likened to a fire. As flames cleanse, purify, refine, and illuminate, so the Holy Spirit works within the heart of each believer. However, just as a fire can be extinguished, so the Spirit's influence in your life can be dampened.

In nature, a fire can be put out several ways: it can be doused with water, smothered with dirt, or starved of the fuel that keeps it going. Have you quenched the Holy Spirit in similar ways? Disobedience, stubbornness, and neglect are like buckets of water to burning coals. Perhaps, the fire of God has been snuffed by worldly pleasures as a campfire is smothered by a shovelful of earth. It may be that you have lost your glow simply because you have neglected to feed the fire with the Word of God. Flames quickly dissipate when neglected and unfed.

When your devotional life wanes, don't be surprised that your heart becomes dark and cold. How can you expect warmth, comfort, security, and light when the fire goes out? Arise at once and tend the fire by protecting it from floods of disobedience and the dirt of the world! Then feed it furiously with prayer and the Word of God—*"Pray without ceasing...Despise not prophesyings."* Don't let the fire go out!

...your faith groweth exceedingly... II Thessalonians 1:3

Have you ever been shocked after seeing a child whom you have not seen for a couple of years? It is surprising how rapidly some children grow! In similar fashion, the faith of the believers in Thessalonica had grown beyond expectation. Paul said, *"your faith groweth exceedingly."* Can that be said of your faith?

Our text brings assurance that, even if your faith is presently small, it can grow—*"your faith groweth."* When Gideon was called to lead the Israelites against Midian, he was hiding from the enemy; but he did not continue living in fear. In a matter of days his faith budded and flourished, defeating an entire army with only three hundred men. What changed him? His faith grew exceedingly. Thankfully, yours can, too.

Notice what sparked the Thessalonians' growth—*"persecutions and tribulations."* Was that not true of Gideon? As the enemy oppressed, he was challenged to trust in the might of Jehovah. When a great need to rely upon God arises, your faith can increase; but with no trials to test you, your growth may be stunted. Those who are challenged the most tend to grow the most. So, never despise the afflictions that you suffer as a Christian, knowing that trials are steppingstones to greater faith.

II Thess. 2   THE COMING ANTICHRIST   OCT. 16

Who opposeth and exalteth himself above all that is called God, or that is worshipped; so that he as God sitteth in the temple of God, shewing himself that he is God. II Thessalonians 2:4

In context, today's Scripture speaks of the Antichrist who will come to power during the time of the Great Tribulation. Sometime after the temple is rebuilt in Jerusalem, the Antichrist will enter it, *"shewing himself that he is God."* Although, he is not the true God, many will worship him because Satan will energize him *"with all power and signs and lying wonders."* With his tremendous power, Satan has already convinced multitudes to follow him; and we know it will only get worse.

Despite all of the looming darkness to come and the threat of judgment upon the earth, God's words to His people were *"be not soon shaken in mind, or be troubled."* Those who are saved will not face the terror of the Lord when He comes to take *"vengeance on them that know not God, and that obey not the gospel of our Lord Jesus Christ."*

Rather than fearing the rise of the Antichrist and Satan's power, allow Jesus to, *"Comfort your hearts, and stablish you in every good word and work."* Although the Antichrist will take a seat in the temple, you do not have to allow Satan's influence to move into your temple.

But the Lord is faithful, who shall stablish you, and keep you from evil.
II Thessalonians 3:3

Every believer will experience times of uncertainty. During those difficult periods, God is trying your faith to see *"of what sort it is."* Are you unsure what the Lord is doing in your present situation? Take solace in the wonderful promises of our text.

First, remember that *"the Lord is faithful."* What more consolation do you need than that? Has God ever failed you before? No, and He shall not do so now. The Lord is many things, but He is not a failure.

Next, we are promised that He *"shall stablish you."* This has the idea of being rooted and settled. Everything in life may seem "up in the air," but you have assurance that God will settle your heart. Not every problem will disappear, but your heart can be at rest, firmly trusting God.

Last, observe that God will *"keep you from evil."* The word *keep* means to guard. Much trouble surrounded the believers in Thessalonica, but God made it clear that He would protect them from it. Though the three young men were thrown into the fiery furnace in Daniel's day, they were spared from the heat of the flames. It's time to believe that God will do likewise for you! Jesus offers peace when Satan promotes panic.

Oct. 18   Avoid Shipwreck   I Timothy 1

Holding faith, and a good conscience; which some having put away
concerning faith have made shipwreck... I Timothy 1:19

The word *shipwreck* is every sailor's nightmare, and it ought to be the same for each Christian. Just as ships suffer great damage and loss when dashed by jagged rocks, so the lives of wayward Christians will experience disastrous results by the effects of sin. You cannot navigate through the dark waters of temptation carelessly without running aground spiritually. Many stately vessels have confidently sailed through tempestuous waters only to lose their splendor in a moment of careless navigation. Far too many of God's people have done likewise, living victoriously until a brief lapse of faith runs them aground.

As a captain firmly holds onto the helm of a ship, so a child of God must cling to some things. First, you must hold tightly to faith because failure to live by faith runs the risk of shipwreck. When dark clouds arise and you cannot see how God will deliver you from the storm, find a promise in God's Word and grasp the wheel of faith. Second, always maintain a *"good conscience."* Ignoring the guilt that you feel in your conscience can also lead to a shipwreck. Don't fail to deal with your sin, or the smooth-sailing journey you now enjoy will soon come to an end.

*I will therefore that men pray every where, lifting up holy hands,
without wrath and doubting. I Timothy 2:8*

S ome take this passage as an exhortation to raise their hands toward
heaven while praying. Such an action would be dangerous if you
prayed like that while driving a car! This verse should be taken
symbolically rather than literally. It is similar to another passage of
Scripture that cannot possibly be interpreted literally, *"Let us lift up our
heart with our hands unto God in the heavens."* (Lamentations 3:41)

The Bible records many other postures of prayer: kneeling, standing,
bowing, falling with the face to the ground, and looking upward. It is not
feasible to be in all of those positions at the same time. Therefore, the
attitude in which we pray is far more important than the position. For
instance, God is far more interested in the submission of our heart than
the outward action of bowing.

The symbolic meaning of *"lifting up holy hands"* is two-fold. First,
it demonstrates a life of holiness. How can you lift up a prayer with
known sin in your life? Hands and hearts that are stained with sin are
unacceptable to God. Second, it shows expectation of an answer. With
clean hands, we "reach" toward heaven, anticipating God's assistance.

*These things write I unto thee, hoping to come unto thee shortly: But if
I tarry long, that thou mayest know... I Timothy 3:14-15*

P aul had plans to visit the church of Ephesus and to provide Timothy
with practical guidelines for church leadership.   Although he was
"hoping to come...shortly," Paul did not want to delay giving the
instructions they needed. He could have reasoned, "I'll deal with those
things when I get there." However, the message was so important that he
did not dare wait to deliver it. So, despite his plans to visit Timothy, he
wrote to him immediately. Great leaders are people of action.

It is very easy to put off something, especially when you have
tentative plans to do it in the near future; but before you know it, you
have put it off again and again. Unfortunately, procrastination becomes a
way of life, and it often affects others. For example, if you continue to
delay witnessing to someone who has been on your heart for a while, it
may be too late one day. Imagine the guilt and shame you will feel when
you receive a phone call notifying you of the person's unexpected death.
So, whether it is witnessing to a lost soul, fulfilling responsibilities as a
parent, or warning a wayward friend, don't put it off. When you know
God wants you to do something, get busy and do it.

...exercise thyself rather unto godliness. For bodily exercise profiteth little: but godliness is profitable unto all things... I Timothy 4:7-8

S ome people wrongly believe that our text teaches we should not bother with physical exercise. The language used does not condemn such exercise in any way. The word *little* refers to time—bodily exercise only profits for a short time. However, some twist the verse to say that exercise is of little worth. On the contrary, we observe that physical inactivity leads to a loss of stamina and vitality—it must be maintained.

The reason Paul used the illustration of bodily exercise was to draw a sharp contrast with the lasting results of spiritual exercise. Unlike physical fitness, godliness helps in *"the life that now is"* and in the one *"which is to come."* Because of the temporal and eternal benefits of godliness, we should spend much time getting in good spiritual condition. Although strenuous physical activity can lead to injury, no such risk exists for the soul! Therefore, we have no excuse for failing to get our spiritual life in shape. After all, *"godliness is profitable."*

Some similarities also exist between both types of exercise. Each requires hard work, becomes difficult to resume after stopping for a while, and makes you feel better if sustained. Are you out of shape?

OCT. 22　　　　　PROVIDE FOR YOUR OWN　　　　I TIMOTHY 5

But if any provide not for his own, and specially for those of his own house, he hath denied the faith, and is worse than an infidel.
I Timothy 5:8

T his chapter details the treatment of widows. Certain widows should be relieved by the church, but those with children should be cared for by them. If a man will not provide for his widowed mother, he is worse than an unbeliever. Hence, a great principal is established: provide for the needs of your family. Truly, this applies to our children also because the verse adds, *"...specially for those of his own house."*

Failure to provide for your family is considered a denial of the faith. Therefore, it is a serious offence to neglect the needs of those in your home. I have seen parents foolishly squander money on themselves, disregarding the needs of their children. Our duty is to provide for those in our home, and this includes both material and spiritual provision. In addition to food, shelter, and clothing, we must provide love, security, instruction, and correction. Family Bible reading and prayer time, church attendance, a Christian education, and discipline are all important to the development of your children. Have you failed to provide for any of their spiritual needs? Ponder these words, *"...worse than an infidel."*

...men of corrupt minds, and destitute of the truth, supposing that gain is godliness: from such withdraw thyself. I Timothy 6:5

A "prosperity" gospel is on the rise among people professing Christianity. It is nothing new and was around even in Paul's day. In Galatians 1:6, he warned of *"another gospel"* that would *"trouble"* those who received it. Unfortunately, several other gospels have arisen. The prosperity gospel, being one of them, promotes that godly people will become wealthy. However, Paul taught that *"men of corrupt minds"* suppose that *"gain is godliness."*

Never seek wealth as a reward for holy living. Plenty of godly believers currently live in poverty around the world, and the Bible is filled with accounts of poor saints. Furthermore, Jesus had few earthly possessions. He said, *"Foxes have holes, and birds of the air have nests; but the Son of man hath not where to lay his head."* (Luke 9:58) Jesus, the holiest Person in history, had no permanent home or fluffy pillow.

The prosperity gospel actually promotes covetousness by teaching people to constantly look for and expect wealth. Those who have followed this false gospel *"have erred from the faith, and pierced themselves through with many sorrows."* Beware! Gain is not godliness.

For God hath not given us the spirit of fear; but of power, and of love, and of a sound mind. II Timothy 1:7

Timothy appears to have had a timid disposition or been prone to fear. Perhaps your constitution is similar. Let us consider how this paralyzing emotion robs its victims of many blessings from God.

Fear says, "I can't do it," but God has given you the *"spirit...of power"* to enable you to accomplish anything He asks of you. Fear replies, "I don't want to do it," but the Lord has given you the *"spirit...of love"* to move you to sacrifice your own comfort for the sake of others. Fear insists, "I don't know what to do," but God has equipped you with the *"spirit...of a sound mind,"* which enables you to think clearly in any situation. God has provided you with everything you need to defeat fear.

Remember that God has *"not given us the spirit of fear."* Because He is not the Author of this crippling disposition, we can be certain that He wants to liberate us from it. Just as fear displaces faith, so faith can remove fear. Trusting God for victory is the key. However, faith requires action—*"faith without works is dead."* As you get busy for God, you will get the power to conquer your fear; but if you retreat and hide, your fear will conquer you. What spirit will you display today?

If a man therefore purge himself from these, he shall be a vessel unto honour, sanctified, and meet for the master's use, and prepared unto every good work. II Timothy 2:21

The Lord is searching for people who are fit for His service. However, *"...many are called, but few are chosen."* (Matthew 22:14) Not every vessel is worthy of the King's selection. In order to be used of God, a person must *"purge himself"* from evil influences.

Do you desire to be chosen by God for a special task? If so, you must first be thoroughly cleansed because the Lord seeks clean vessels to use. When entertaining an important dinner guest, how do you prepare your table? Do you use spotted glasses and dishes that are crusted over with last week's mashed potatoes? No! You choose your best dinnerware. Likewise, God seeks clean lives to fill with His goodness.

Once you have been cleansed by confession of sin and separation from it, then you *"shall be a vessel unto honour, sanctified, and meet for the master's use."* God wants to use you; and when you are clean, you will be able to do anything God calls you to do. Consider the promise, *"prepared unto every good work."* I stress again—we can do every work that God calls us to do. So, get clean and you'll be ready to serve.

But continue thou in the things which thou hast learned and hast been assured of, knowing of whom thou hast learned them... II Timothy 3:14

Times will get difficult, opposition will become fierce, and evil men shall increase. All indications are that things will get much worse as the last days approach. Certainly, our present time is more ungodly than it was a generation ago, and we can expect resistance from those who despise our Lord. *"Yea, and all that will live godly in Christ Jesus shall suffer persecution."* These words are not meant to discourage the child of God but rather to prepare him for what lies ahead.

Some would be tempted to retreat, hide, and quit in such perilous times. However, Paul's exhortation to Timothy was just the opposite— *"continue thou."* He was to push forward in his service for God, despite persecution and affliction.

If there was ever a time that the world needed bright shining lights, it is now. As darkness grows, beams of light become stronger. Therefore, when more evil is present in the world, you become a brighter beacon to those without hope. If we fail to *"continue"* to let our lights shine, souls will perish. Rather than be frightened by how bad things are, it is better to focus on the increased possibilities to bring the lost to the Light.

At my first answer no man stood with me, but all men forsook me: I pray
God that it may not be laid to their charge. Notwithstanding the
Lord stood with me, and strengthened me... II Timothy 4:16-17

This chapter records the final known words of Paul before he was executed for his faith. As these words were penned in prison, he displayed no signs of regret for having lived a life of hardship and deprivation for Christ. He was not vindictive towards his oppressors or those who had forsaken him in his hour of difficulty. What a testimony!

True spirituality accepts that God is not only in control of our circumstances but also present to carry us through them. Although *"all men forsook"* him, *"the Lord stood"* with him. When you are called to stand alone at work, in your home, or at school, be assured that as God strengthened Paul, He will do the same for you. Paul's deliverance was so great that he was *"delivered out of the mouth of the lion."* It seems that he was spared from being thrown into the amphitheater with a ferocious lion. We also face one who is similar to a lion—*"the devil, as a roaring lion, walketh about, seeking whom he may devour."* When Satan threatens to pounce, trust your Deliverer, and you will say like Paul, *"the Lord stood with me, and strengthened me."*

...not selfwilled... Titus 1:7

Paul had charged Titus to ordain pastors for the churches on the island of Crete. He then provided a detailed list of spiritual qualifications that must be met to hold such a sacred office. Near the top of the list, we read, *"not selfwilled."* Because the man of God is to be an example to others, we can be assured that the Lord desires all of His people to follow His guidelines for holy living. Therefore, let us consider those words on a personal level. Can your character be described as self-willed?

Stubbornness has brought multitudes of people into terrible trouble. A couple of examples should serve as a warning to us. Ananias and Sapphira were killed because they were self-willed concerning their possessions. Gehazi, the servant of Elisha, was plagued with leprosy after willfully disobeying the words of the man of God. A backslider is self-willed, being *"filled with his own ways."* (Proverbs 14:14)

The servant of God must be willing to set aside his will for God's will. Perhaps you need to pray as Christ did, *"...not my will, but thine, be done."* Those who yield to the Lord spare themselves much grief and turmoil. Unfortunately, some people live most of their lives pursuing their goals with little regard to the Lord's will. Are you one of them?

For the grace of God that bringeth salvation hath appeared to all men,
Teaching us that, denying ungodliness and worldly lusts, we should live
soberly, righteously, and godly, in this present world... Titus 2:11-12

A stark difference exists between the Law and grace. The Law brings bondage while grace offers liberty. However, self-proclaimed theologians have fabricated a distorted view of grace. Their new "grace" has few demands for holy living. Further, it provides a license to do what feels comfortable, rather than what is right; and those of us who insist on strict standards of holiness are accused of being legalists, living under bondage. However, nothing could be further from the truth. A legalist observes the Law to gain salvation, but we believe that salvation is by faith. Therefore, by the Biblical definition, we are not legalists.

Those who redefine liberty to justify sin claim to be "under grace," but that notion is false because grace produces holiness, not compromise. They have it all backwards! Grace teaches us to deny *"ungodliness and worldly lusts"* and that *"we should live soberly, righteously, and godly, in this present world."* Those who are truly under grace have freedom from the bondage of sin, allowing them to live a life that is pleasing to God. Grace was never intended to provide liberty to be worldly.

...be ready to every good work...be careful to maintain good works...
learn to maintain good works... Titus 3:1, 8, 14

A lthough we are not saved by good works, we are expected to do them once we are saved. Thereby, our lives provide wonderful billboards for our gracious Lord Who has transformed us. However, a saint without good works is like ice cream with no sweetness—he is missing a main ingredient. Three times in one chapter we are called to good works, and each instance sheds light on how we can perform them.

First, we must have a *desire—"ready to every good work."* Much of the time we have to be pushed and prodded to do what is right, but few have a deep yearning for it naturally. Sadly, we are often more attracted to evil than righteousness; but once our hearts are set on God's ways, doing right becomes simpler. Second, we must have *devotion—"careful to maintain good works."* It is always easier to start something than to finish it. Have you quit something you started for the Lord? If so, you must learn to persevere, despite hindrances. Last, we must have *determination—"learn to maintain good works."* Learning is a life-long process which entails failures; but with determination, you dust yourself off and rise to the challenge. Don't look for excuses to quit.

But withal prepare me also a lodging: for I trust that through your
prayers I shall be given unto you. Philemon 22

How pitiful our prayers are at times! We often pray but expect little or nothing to happen. Truly, this is dishonoring to the One we petition. Is He really that unwilling or unable to meet our present need as we imply by our lack of faith in Him? Certainly not!

Paul had what we must acquire—real faith. He possessed confidence that his release from prison was soon to come because of the prayers of God's people. He believed it so much that he said, *"prepare me also a lodging."* The evidence of his faith is seen in his preparation for the answer. He knew that if the believers did their part by furnishing a room, God would do His part by supplying Paul to fill it. Oh, that we might learn to *"prepare"* for the reception of God's blessings!

It is difficult to imagine that something as mundane as getting a room ready is a display of faith. We tend to focus on the sensational, while God emphasizes the ordinary—preparation. For example, David prepared for victory against Goliath by merely gathering stones. Prayer is good, but living with an eye toward heaven, anticipating help, is better! Real prayer believes something is going to happen. Try it today.

Are they not all ministering spirits, sent forth to minister for them
who shall be heirs of salvation? Hebrews 1:14

People are intrigued with the thought that angels visit mankind. In fact, the interest has been so great at times that television series and movies have been created to capitalize on this fascination. Not only has the entertainment industry distorted the true nature of angels, it has cleverly turned man's attention to created beings rather than to the Creator. Unfortunately, some believers have misplaced their focus, too.

The writer of Hebrews never sought to glorify angels. Although angels are *"sent forth to minister,"* we must remember that they are merely servants of God. Christ is *"much better than the angels"* because He is the Creator (v. 2) and God (v. 8).

Rather than be intrigued by a visit from a guardian angel, we ought to be excited about the presence of Christ in our lives. One much better than any created being is ready to assist us—the Creator Himself! Think about it. Jesus has all power, whereas an angel only has limited power. The same God that strengthens angels for their service has promised to empower us, too. So, look for a visit from the Son and enjoy *"the brightness of his glory"* today. He is much better than an angel.

For in that he himself hath suffered being tempted, he is able to succour them that are tempted. Hebrews 2:18

The word *succour* is not commonly used today and is often skipped over by the average reader. However, proper understanding of the word brings great hope and encouragement to those who are troubled. *Succour* means to help, relieve, or aid. Who would want to miss help?

Let's notice first what Christ can do—*"he is able to succour."* Despite the difficulty of your present trial, Jesus is able to help you. No burden is too heavy for Him to lift and no heartache is too crushing for Him to relieve. Others may be willing to help, but only One *"is able."*

Next, consider why Jesus is able to help—*"he himself hath suffered being tempted."* The Lord has already experienced the power, pain, and pressure involved in temptation. He willingly suffered so that He could identify with our sorrows. No trial or temptation that you face will ever be greater than what Jesus endured.   Therefore, His experience as a sufferer equips Him as a succourer. It is comforting to know that Jesus understands by experience how it feels to be tested and tried. Further, He is willing to run to your side and help you. Do you need some relief or assistance today? Look to your Heavenly Helper!

Take heed, brethren, lest there be in any of you an evil heart of unbelief, in departing from the living God. Hebrews 3:12

God is very concerned about His children and knows the sad results that await those who turn from Him. Observe three thoughts.

First, consider the *caution against departure—"Take heed, brethren."* God wants us to learn from the examples of others. He was grieved with a previous generation and did not wish that the current one would follow in their wayward footsteps. When the man of God warns you, take no offence, knowing that God has sent him to prevent your fall.

Second, notice the *cause for departure—"an evil heart of unbelief."* We tend to rate unbelief as a lesser sin—perhaps as a mere lapse of faith. However, God considers it evil. What leads to an evil heart? God's testimony was, *"they have not known my ways."* Failure to read and heed the truths of the Bible will inevitably lead to an evil heart, which eventually departs from the living God. Never let your Bible-time slip!

Last, realize the *consequences for departing—"they could not enter"* the land of Canaan. Those who leave the paths of God fail to enter a life of joy and victory. Do you want to miss out on God's blessings and remain in the barren wilderness? If not, stay close to the Lord.

Let us therefore come boldly unto the throne of grace, that we may obtain mercy, and find grace to help in time of need. Hebrews 4:16

How marvelous a text! Before us today is one of the greatest motivations we have to pray.

We begin by noticing our *direction—"come...unto the throne of grace."* Not only do we have direct access to the King of the universe, we are encouraged to *"come."* Thankfully, this is a throne of grace, not of merit because none of us are deserving of such a privilege. Since Jesus was *"tempted like as we are,"* it touches His heart when we tell Him our troubles and sorrows. At this throne, we *"obtain mercy,"* implying that we acknowledge our shortcomings.

Next, observe the *demeanor* of our approach to the throne—*"come boldly."* Boldness refers to confidence. However this is not confidence in our own worthiness but rather in the goodness of the One upon the throne! We can go to God with full assurance that He will hear and grant our requests for His name's sake, even though we are undeserving.

Last, consider our *discovery.* What shall we find at the throne? *"...grace to help in time of need."* We are assured of help when we need it. Are you in a *"time of need"*? Why do you linger? Get to the throne!

Of whom we have many things to say, and hard to be uttered, seeing ye are dull of hearing. Hebrews 5:11

The author of Hebrews appears to have been frustrated with the spiritual development of the Jewish believers. They should have matured enough to become teachers but, instead, were still spiritual babies. How much have you developed? Are you as useful to God as He wishes? If not, the problem could be that you *"are dull of hearing."*

Notice the great *potential.* God has *"many things to say"* to us. Have you ever noticed that some people seem to grow more quickly than others? The reason is that those who act upon the truths they have heard are given more knowledge. In fact, God has much wisdom to impart to you if you will heed what He has already spoken.

However, a great *problem* exists which prevents many from learning more—they are *"dull of hearing."* The word *dull* refers to being sluggish. Those who are slow to listen and respond to what God has spoken limit their growth and usefulness for the Lord. Dull hearing leads to dull living. Are you tired of living a dull, unproductive life? Sharpen your hearing by being quick to receive and obey God's instructions. Have you refused to listen to the Lord in some area? Don't be dull.

For God is not unrighteous to forget your work and labour of love, which ye have shewed toward his name, in that ye have ministered to the saints, and do minister. Hebrews 6:10

At times, we will suffer for our labor in the Lord's work, and in our weakness we are tempted to say, "Lord, I've done so much for you. Why are you allowing this to happen to me? Have you forgotten about me?" Sadly, many of us have expressed such a faithless attitude at one time or another. Perhaps one reading these lines has fallen to such depths today.

To think God would forget your work, sacrifice, and suffering for His name's sake is to accuse Him of being unrighteous. However, we are reminded that *"God is not unrighteous to forget."* Two facts remain constant despite our unbelief: God is not unrighteous, and He does not forget one of His faithful servants. Did He forget Joseph while in the pit? Did He forget Paul in the Philippian jail? Did He disregard Job's pain or severe losses? No, no, no! He blessed them all in due time, and He will do the same for you. Don't lose faith in God's promise—*"God is not unrighteous to forget your work and labour of love."* Those who labor for Him will soon be rewarded. Anticipate His intervention!

Wherefore he is able also to save them to the uttermost that come unto God by him, seeing he ever liveth to make intercession for them. Hebrews 7:25

The Levitical priesthood, through the sons of Aaron, was incomplete because *"the law maketh nothing perfect."* Furthermore, the priests were mere mortals who had their *"own sins"* that needed to be forgiven. Thus, a better Priest was necessary *"to save"* mankind. Thankfully, Jesus came to provide *"a better hope"* and *"a better testament."*

Notice two duties of priests: make atonement for sin and intercede for the sinner. Only Jesus can fully perform both of these responsibilities. Because of His great sacrifice, He *"is able also to save."* No human priest can forgive sin or save a sinner! Moreover, Jesus saves *"to the uttermost"*—completely. Confidence in a man or in the works of the Law could never lead to anyone's salvation.

Next, consider that Jesus *"ever liveth to make intercession"* for you. Even now, He talks to the Father on your behalf. No other priest grants continual, unhindered access to the Father. Further, His *"unchangeable priesthood"* ensures that He is always available. So, whatever your need, go to Jesus, knowing that He is willing to intercede and help!

...I took them by the hand to lead them out of the land of Egypt...
Hebrews 8:9

Egypt is a picture of bondage, and the Jews had been enslaved in that land and forced to endure great hardships. However, God, in His kindness, came to the aid of His people. His testimony reads, *"I took them by the hand."* What reassuring words! When a father clasps the hand of his little child, he provides comfort, safety, and guidance to the one he loves. What kind of father would ignore the outstretched hand of his helpless child who longs for his help? If you are in need of direction, your loving Father will not neglect your extended hand.

Consider God's *power*—*"I took them by the hand."* When holding the hand of Omnipotence, the powers of darkness are rendered ineffective. Is there not solace in Jesus' words, *"My Father...is greater than all; and no man is able to pluck them out of my Father's hand."* (John 10:29) What have we to fear when held by God?

Next, observe God's *purpose*—*"to lead them out of the land of Egypt."* It is never God's will for you to be enslaved to any sin, and He longs to lead all who are currently bound out of bondage. Will you reach heavenward to grasp the Father's hand today? He is ready to lead you!

How much more shall the blood of Christ...purge your conscience
from dead works to serve the living God? Hebrews 9:14

The sacrifice of animals under the Law had limited effect. The blood shed was only sufficient to purify the flesh in a ceremonial manner, but it could never cleanse the inner man of his sin. The *"blood of bulls and of goats"* was continually offered for each new offence, implying that such sacrifices were incomplete. Thus, a better sacrifice was necessary, and Jesus provided it when He shed His blood.

Notice that His blood *purges*. The entire stain of sin is completely removed from our conscience when we look to Jesus. Sin clouds our minds and robs us of heavenly wisdom. Consequently, a defiled conscience leads to foolish decisions and unholy living. The only thing that can purge out the filth and rubbish in our minds is the blood. Has your conscience been darkened by the presence of sin? Seek Christ's cleansing and you will have such peace that you can sing, "Amazing grace! 'tis Heav'n below to feel the blood applied..."

Next, consider the *purpose* of being cleansed—*"to serve the living God."* You cannot serve the Lord effectively until you are clean; and once the blood is applied, your service will be revived and blessed.

And their sins and iniquities will I remember no more. Hebrews 10:17

Memory can either help or haunt a person. Although God wants you to have peace of mind, the devil schemes to ruin your effectiveness for the Lord by bringing up past failures to discourage, dishearten, and defeat you. Thankfully, Jesus not only cleanses and forgives the most hideous offences, He also promises to remember them *"no more."* He will never bring up such matters again to upbraid you—even the worst sins are miraculously cast out of His memory! His sacrifice was *"once for all"* and it *"perfected for ever them that are sanctified."* Therefore, forgiveness is complete through Jesus.

You can rest assured that God has already forgotten what you have already confessed. Therefore, if He chooses to forget, so should you. Dwelling on past failures spoils present peace and future usefulness. Learn to enjoy the cleansing that Jesus has provided and allow it to motivate you to steer clear of further excursions to the land of sin.

Furthermore, always remember that forgiveness involves forgetfulness. If God has forgotten your offences, you should be quick to forget the transgressions of others against you. To say, "I can forgive, but I cannot forget," is not Christ-like. Make your memory like God's.

For ye have need of patience, that, after ye have done the will of God, ye might receive the promise. Hebrews 10:36

What is your pressing need? It may be something different than you suppose. Let's consider what's involved in obtaining our needs.

First, consider the *reality*—*"ye have need of patience."* Our society has rapidly changed to a culture of instant gratification. Rather than write a letter and await a reply, people send emails or instant messages using their portable electronic devices. We have the power to make many things happen in the palm of our hands. However, you must remember that God is not in the palm of your hands! You may say, "I need this thing right now," but God often sees it differently. Notice what He says your great need is—*"ye have need of patience."* Your true need is patience, not the thing you so earnestly desire. That is reality.

Next, see God's *requirement*—*"the will of God."* Before we can expect God to move for us, we must move for Him. Only after doing His will can we expect to receive His blessings.

Last, notice the *reward*—*"the promise."* After patiently enduring your present trial and faithfully performing the will of God, you will be rewarded. Once you realize that your need is God, He can bless.

By faith Abraham, when he was called to go out into a place which he should after receive for an inheritance, obeyed; and he went out, not knowing whither he went. Hebrews 11:8

Is blind faith Biblical? Although many suggest that it is, we see no such teaching in Scripture. What about our text? Someone might say, "Abraham could not see where he was going, and God considered it faith." Although he *"went out, not knowing whither he went,"* it was not blind faith. Let's remember something important about faith, *"...faith cometh by hearing, and hearing by the word of God."* (Romans 10:17) Abraham was called by God to journey to an unknown land, and his faith that he would find such a land was based upon God's promise to him. So, in reality, his faith had a basis—God's Word.

It may be that God will lead you in a direction that is not comfortable as He did Abraham. Humanly speaking, it may not make sense, and you see no way things can work out. However, you must put God's Word first and set aside your feelings. Faith oftentimes requires us to obey *"not knowing."* It is not that we do not know what God wants us to do but that we do not know how it will work out. However, as you obey God's clear command, He will reward you as He did Abraham.

By faith the walls of Jericho fell down, after they were compassed about seven days. Hebrews 11:30

Joshua had led Israel over the Jordan River and into the Promised Land, expecting a great victory. However, something stood between God's people and their goal—*"the walls of Jericho."* Have you ever felt like some obstacle hindered the blessings of God? At times, barriers to God's blessings seem insurmountable, but God has provided a way to overcome them. Notice two requirements for victory.

First, we read that the walls fell *"by faith."* The Lord had chosen an unconventional method to level the walls of Jericho, commanding Israel to march around the city seven days and, then, shout. This required faith that God's way would, in fact, be successful. Perhaps some of the valiant men of war thought this to be a ridiculous plan. After all, no army had ever won a war by merely marching and shouting. Although God's methods are often different from your own, never question Him.

Second, success requires obedience. Jericho's mighty walls only fell *"after"* the people had followed God's instructions, proving that faith leads to obedience. Perhaps the walls that you face refuse to crumble because you have failed to obey the Lord in some area. Yield today!

And ye have forgotten the exhortation which speaketh unto you as unto children, My son, despise not thou the chastening of the Lord, nor faint when thou art rebuked of him... Hebrews 12:5

We often like to forget the unpleasant things in life. However, we must never forget God's warning of chastisement. Have you forgotten that the Lord will correct your wrongdoing?

Remember the *reason* that God disciplines His children—*"the Lord loveth."* God knows the misery and destruction that await those who wander down the path of sin, and His great love causes Him to try to prevent it. Our hearts should be filled with gratitude that God would lightly afflict us in order to spare us greater heartache and hardship.

Consider also the proper *response* to chastening—*"despise not...nor faint."* Never disregard God's efforts to turn you back to Himself. Could it be that your current troubles are the result of your Father's hand of correction? Rather than plunge to the depths of discouragement, yield your stubborn will to the Lord.

Last, notice the *result* of God's correction—*"the peaceable fruit of righteousness."* Living right brings peace within! When you amend your ways, God will bring rest to your troubled heart. Happiness awaits.

Let your conversation be without covetousness; and be content with such things as ye have: for he hath said, I will never leave thee, nor forsake thee. So that we may boldly say, The Lord is my helper... Hebrews 13:5-6

The greatest threat to contentment is covetousness. Thus, God provides a *caution* against materialism—*"be without covetousness."* Has Satan convinced you, as he has many others, that happiness comes from gaining more earthly possessions? You must remember that it is impossible to be satisfied as long as you are covetous. In fact, Solomon warned, *"...the eyes of man are never satisfied."* (Proverbs 27:20) Therefore, refuse to fill your eyes with the things of this world.

The Lord also issues a solemn *command*—*"be content with such things as ye have."* Have you ever tried to be content but found it difficult? Contentment is more than a state of mind—it is a decision to rest upon the Lord for all your needs. Rather than focus on what you don't have, remember Who you do have.

Notice the *consolation* that God gives—*"I will never leave thee."* As long as you have the Lord, you have everything you need. Leaning upon Him brings *confidence*, enabling you to say, *"The Lord is my helper."* Thus, contentment is a choice to trust God to meet your needs.

But whoso looketh into the perfect law of liberty, and continueth therein,
he being not a forgetful hearer, but a doer of the work,
this man shall be blessed in his deed. James 1:25

Do you long to be happy and blessed? James tells us of three simple requirements to obtain God's blessings, along with a guarantee that the one who fulfills them *"shall be blessed in his deed."*

You must first learn to *look.* The word *looketh* in our text has the idea of leaning over and peering into something. God wants us to get our eyes in position to daily look into His Word, which is *"the perfect law of liberty."* The Bible promises liberty to those who take the time to absorb its truths. While sin enslaves, the Scriptures liberate. One will never be happy until he is freed from the shackles of sin through the Word.

The second condition of happiness is to *continue.* It is one thing to occasionally glance at the Scriptures and quite another to continue in them. Freedom and blessings are tied to faithfulness. As continued exercise keeps the body fit, persistent Bible study renews the soul.

Last, in order to be blessed, you must *do.* God warns not to be *"a forgetful hearer."* The happiest people in life are those who obey God. Today, you will either be a *"forgetful hearer"* or a *"doer."* Which one?

Hearken, my beloved brethren, Hath not God chosen the poor of this
world rich in faith, and heirs of the kingdom which he hath promised
to them that love him? James 2:5

We tend to look at poverty as a condition to be dreaded. However, such a state can open doors of spiritual prosperity to those who seek the Lord. Let us consider God's grace extended to the needy.

Notice their *condition—"poor."* They have been deprived of many of life's luxuries; and at times, they struggle just to gain basic necessities. This is not as much of a curse as one might think. Because they need much, they can trust much. Consider their *consolation—"rich in faith."* Faith obtains promises, sees the hand of God at work, and encourages the soul. Whatever sorrow comes by poverty is replaced by joy when God rewards a person's faith. Further, we observe their *communion—"heirs of the kingdom."* Here they may reside in a tent among beggars, but in Heaven they will dwell in a mansion close to Jesus.

What is worse than being poor in this life is to be so in the next life. You may be blessed above measure here below, but do not allow those blessings to rob you of treasure above. Regardless of your station in life, be *"rich in faith."*

But the tongue can no man tame; it is an unruly evil,
full of deadly poison. James 3:8

The expression, "Good things come in small packages," is not always true. Although the tongue is little in size, it can be large in mischief. In fact, it often gets us into more trouble than any other part of our body.

The tongue is *wild*—*"the tongue can no man tame."* Man can tame lions, tigers, and snakes from the jungle; but he has limited power over the tongue in his own mouth. That is why David cried, *"Set a watch, O LORD, before my mouth; keep the door of my lips."* (Psalm 141:3) Only supernatural help from God can enable you to control your speech.

Additionally, the tongue is *wicked*—*"it is an unruly evil."* Its destructive character is so out of control that it is likened to a fire, consuming everything in its path. We also see that the tongue has tremendous power to *wound*—*"full of deadly poison."* A large enough dose of poison can kill, but even a small amount can cause great injury. Let us beware of the little weapon that is concealed within our mouth! Have we forgotten how prone we are to utter slurs and slanders that cut others to the heart? A minor slip of the tongue can result in hurt feelings, severed friendships, and ruined testimonies. Beware!

Ye ask, and receive not, because ye ask amiss, that ye may
consume it upon your lusts. James 4:3

Knowing that God answers prayer, have you ever wondered why He has not responded to some of your requests? After all, Jesus promised, *"...ask, and ye shall receive, that your joy may be full."* (John 16:24) If no answer comes, either the Lord has a good reason to make you wait for an answer or something is wrong with your prayer.

In our text, the people had prayed without receiving. Thankfully, we have the Lord's reason for their failure recorded, too—He said, *"...ye ask amiss."* The word *amiss* means in a faulty manner or contrary to truth. The explanation for many unanswered prayers is simply that they are bad prayers! How do we know if a prayer is faulty?

First, a bad prayer is *selfish*—*"that ye may consume it."* What is the motive behind your prayer? Is it to devour all that you can get from God or to share some of His blessings with others? When Jesus told us to ask for our daily bread, He instructed us to say, *"Give us,"* not *"Give me."* Self-centered prayers are often denied. Second, bad prayers are *carnal*, involving *"your lusts."* Wrong prayers seek to gratify fleshly desires rather than spiritual needs. When prayers are right, answers will come!

Behold, we count them happy which endure. Ye have heard of the patience of Job, and have seen the end of the Lord; that the Lord is very pitiful, and of tender mercy. James 5:11

When reading a book, most people enjoy a happy ending. When God writes the story of His faithful servants, it always ends well for them. Although Job endured tremendous deprivations and hardships at one point in his life, we *"have seen the end"* of the story—*"the LORD gave Job twice as much as he had before."* (Job 42:10)

How are things with you today? Have you suffered great loss or heartache? Never forget *"that the Lord is very pitiful, and of tender mercy."* Although you may think that God has forgotten you, be quick to renew your confidence in His goodness. He will soon have pity and show His tenderness. The Lord allows trials to see if we will trust Him, not only when things go well but in times of darkness also.

What is your present duty in this season of affliction? Patiently endure. A wonderful promise is given to all who continue to trust the Lord without sinking in self-pity—*"we count them happy which endure."* In due time, God will write the end of your story, too. If you faithfully trust Him, the closing line will read, "happily ever after."

To an inheritance incorruptible, and undefiled, and that fadeth not away, reserved in heaven for you...Wherein ye greatly rejoice, though now for a season, if need be, ye are in heaviness... I Peter 1:4, 6

Consider what we have to look forward to! We may not have much in this life, but in the next life we have an inheritance that is *"incorruptible"* and *"undefiled."* On earth, our treasures are temporary and tainted. Things break, wear out, or get stolen. However, our heavenly inheritance is enduring—it *"fadeth not away."* Because God's blessings last forever, we ought to spend more time securing eternal treasures than earthly ones.

If your present situation is gloomy, remember the blessings that await you. Times of affliction will arise, but the Lord provides encouragement for that, too. Although you will be *"in heaviness"* of heart, you can *"greatly rejoice,"* knowing that your trial is only *"for a season."* Like any season, your trouble will one day come to an end. Furthermore, such afflictions are not random chance. Note the words, *"if need be."* God only allows trouble when He has a purpose for it. Therefore, enjoy the promise of incorruptible treasures in heaven and relief from present difficulties. This provides hope for today's journey!

Dearly beloved, I beseech you as strangers and pilgrims, abstain from
fleshly lusts, which war against the soul... I Peter 2:11

It is one thing to be injured by an enemy and quite another to inflict pain on yourself. Knowing that Satan is out to hurt you, it would be foolish to help him reach his goal. Consider the *concern* that Peter had—*"Dearly beloved."* He cared so much for the saints that he wanted them to avoid injury to their walk with God. A stern warning from the man of God should be understood as a compassionate plea to protect you.

Also, notice the *command*—*"abstain from fleshly lusts."* Because we are *"strangers and pilgrims,"* we must remember that our citizenship is in heaven, not on earth. We serve a different King and must refrain from the activities of Satan's followers.

Finally, observe a *cause* for abstinence from carnal pursuits—*"fleshly lusts...war against the soul."* Although such lusts please the body, they wound the soul. How much damage have you done to your relationship with God by pursuing worldliness? Each indulgence grieves the Holy Spirit Who dwells within. Could this be the reason you have lost that inner peace you once enjoyed? While trying to please self, you actually hurt yourself. Stop inflicting so much trouble upon your soul!

Not rendering evil for evil, or railing for railing:
but contrariwise blessing; knowing that ye are thereunto called,
that ye should inherit a blessing. I Peter 3:9

Nobody enjoys being mistreated, and it is human nature to want to get back at those who have caused you grief. Perhaps one who is reading this today has been harboring evil feelings toward another. Rather than plot revenge, learn to follow God's plan for your dilemma.

The Lord wants us to exercise *control*—*"Not rendering evil for evil, or railing for railing."* Isn't it easy to insult those who have insulted you? When your blood seems to boil, remember that God commands you not to retaliate with evil. When treated wrongly, do you find yourself wanting to get even in some way? Learn to refrain.

Also, remember your *calling*—*"ye are thereunto called."* We are expected to endure hardships and, at the same time, render a blessing to those who treat us cruelly. Demonstrating such restraint and compassion may be too much to expect from the natural man but not from a Spirit-filled believer. Thankfully, a *consolation* awaits all who react properly to abuse—*"ye should inherit a blessing."* God can turn evil into a blessing, especially when the situation is handled in a Christ-like manner.

Beloved, think it not strange concerning the fiery trial which is to try you,
as though some strange thing happened unto you: But rejoice...
I Peter 4:12-13

Every believer experiences times of testing, but the *"fiery trial"* is on a grander scale. Few things hurt more than the pain inflicted by fire, and scorching heat seems to accompany some trials. However, God does not intend for us to dread these afflictions. So, what is involved?

God provides *reassurance—"Beloved."* When facing the fiery trial, you must remember that God's love has not failed. In fact, because of His love, He seeks to make you a better person through afflictions. As fire refines gold, so trials purify the believer. The Lord just wants you to shine a little brighter for Him. Despite troubles, His love is constant.

Face *reality—"the fiery trial...is to try you."* One day, such a trial will happen. Rather than fear it, prepare for it. Fix your heart upon God and determine to trust Him, regardless of how hot the trial becomes. Job said, *"Though he slay me, yet will I trust in him."* (Job 13:15)

Finally, learn to *rejoice—"think it not strange...But rejoice."* Resist every temptation to complain, knowing that God's goodness will enable you to endure any hardship and secure the Lord's intended blessing.

...God resisteth the proud...Humble yourselves therefore under the
mighty hand of God, that he may exalt you in due time... I Peter 5:5-6

Many people aspire to greatness. Unfortunately, pride is often the means used to attain their goal. The idea of elevating self is nothing new. Satan tried to exalt himself above the throne of God, but it led to his fall. That is why we are told to be *"clothed with humility."*

When you push yourself upward, the Lord will push you back down—*"God resisteth the proud."* You must remember that it is God's job to exalt a person. Wouldn't you rather trust the *"the mighty hand of God"* to lift you up instead of your own feeble abilities? Beware also of setting goals that are too lofty. As dangers increase the higher a child climbs a tree, so destruction is more likely for those who venture to heights that God had never intended for them to reach. However, when God exalts you, His *"mighty hand"* will safely uphold you.

Our main focus should be humility, not exaltation. It is far better to humble ourselves than to be humbled. In God's economy, promotion works much differently than it does in the world's system. With God, the way up is down. As you humble yourself, God will *"exalt you in due time."* Have you been trying to advance God's way?

Whereby are given unto us exceeding great and precious promises: that by these ye might be partakers of the divine nature, having escaped the corruption that is in the world through lust. II Peter 1:4

Throughout history, people have searched for mines of gold, hoping to strike it rich. However, the promises of God are better than gold!

Notice that the promises of God are *plentiful—"exceeding great."* The word *exceeding* means more than enough! For every problem you face, there is a promise to help. A gold mine has limited amount of treasure, but the Word of God is inexhaustible! So, dig into the Bible.

The promises are also *precious—"precious promises."* This reminds us that God's Word is highly valuable. Although more hours at work may bring more pay, the money will not last long. However, more time in the Bible will change your life, your family, and your future. What is your priority: worldly possessions or heavenly promises?

Thankfully, the promises are *personal—"given unto us."* If you are saved, you are part of *"us."* These blessings are not reserved for an elite few. They are for you as much as they were for David, Peter, and Paul.

Finally, theses promises are *powerful—"partakers of the divine nature."* God's Word gives us power to become more like the Master.

For that righteous man dwelling among them, in seeing and hearing, vexed his righteous soul from day to day with their unlawful deeds...
II Peter 2:8

John Bunyan, in his classic *The Holy War*, wrote of the enemy's assaults on the city of Mansoul. Two of the gates that led into the heart of the city were Eye-gate and Ear-gate. The allegory teaches that Satan seeks avenues to penetrate our lives with his evil influences.

Lot provides a perfect example of how the devil topples a believer. Although he did not live a godly life, Lot was a saved man as seen in the words, *"that righteous man."* His demise began by *"dwelling among"* the wicked. Failing to separate from the ungodly crowd, he left the Eye-gate and Ear-gate exposed to continual assaults by Satan. It was the constant *"seeing and hearing"* that *"vexed his righteous soul."*

As many of us argue, so did Lot, "I can handle being around these influences. I'm strong enough to resist." However, as the enemy travelled into his soul through the gates *"day to day,"* he was weakened. You, too, will be overwhelmed by the devil if you fail to guard your eyes and ears. The television, Internet, and radio are used *"day to day"* to destroy righteous men. Beware of the attacks on Mansoul!

But, beloved, be not ignorant of this one thing, that one day is with the Lord as a thousand years, and a thousand years as one day. II Peter 3:8

Oh, how often our feeble faith doubts the dependable promises of our faithful Creator! When God says He will do something, it will surely come to pass. However, it will only be performed when, in His wisdom, He deems best.

We must remember how infinite God truly is and that He sees things on a much grander scale than we do. As a day seems short to us, so a thousand years is seen only as one day to the Lord. That He is even mindful of us is a miracle in itself. Therefore, let us remember that God's timing is always right; and, then, our faith will be renewed. Surely, the Lord has always delivered those who have sought His refuge.

When you have to wait upon the Lord, remember the words, *"The Lord is not slack concerning his promise."* In His timing your need will be met. What may seem long to you is short in light of eternity. Can you not trust the One Who created time? In context, the passage tells us that Christ has delayed His return to give people more time to repent. From this we see that His tarrying often leads to bigger blessings. So, *"be not ignorant of this one thing."* God will one day fulfill His promise to you.

And these things write we unto you, that your joy may be full. I John 1:4

If joy were measured by a gauge as on a fuel tank, how full would your tank be today? Perhaps your estimate would be about half of a tank. Some might find themselves running on fumes, while others would be completely empty. What is the solution if you are not full of joy?

All too often, we confuse happiness with joy. Happiness is dependent upon favorable circumstances, whereas joy relies upon God Who arranges the circumstances. Happiness comes and goes, but joy should not. Therefore, a believer can rejoice in his God whether sailing on smooth seas or through the storm. Regardless of your situation, you can have real, lasting joy.

So, why does your level of joy fluctuate so much and how do you remain full of joy? Our text holds the answer—*"these things write we unto you, that your joy may be full."* The Word of God is the key to joy. As you read it and heed it, your joy will be full. A sick person who focuses on his aches and pains will not get any better until he turns his attention to the cure. Likewise, a Christian who is void of joy must center on the remedy, which is the Word of God. Get in the Bible, and you will be refueled. Then, you can rejoice whether in sunshine or rain.

He that loveth his brother abideth in the light, and there is
none occasion of stumbling in him. I John 2:10

God is light, and those who dwell in His presence enjoy great
benefits. The first blessing is that we will be of greater use to
others. The one abiding in the light *"loveth his brother."* As the sun
warms and cheers hearts after a cold, dark night, so the Son radiates
energizing warmth within His servants. With hearts renewed, we find it
much easier to be a blessing to others.

Abiding also helps us. The light enables us to see more clearly.
Darkness dulls our vision and prevents us from discerning the pathway
ahead. Many evils lurk in the night, and Satan has set obstacles in shady
places to cause us to stumble. However, abiding in God's glorious light
brightens every step of our journey so that *"there is none occasion of
stumbling."* Staying close to Jesus will prevent you from falling into sin.

How do we know if we are abiding *"in the light"*? Take a look at
your relationship with the brethren. Do you love them as you should, or
are you at odds with a fellow believer? Perhaps you need to get back
into the light! Ask God to forgive you, receive His strength, and settle
any conflict that hinders the light from shining into your soul.

...little children, abide in him; that, when he shall appear, we may have
confidence, and not be ashamed before him at his coming. I John 2:28

Little children often become distracted by their surroundings and
forget to focus on the duty at hand. For instance, years ago, my son
was told to put his toys away; and when I left the room, he began doing
as he was told. However, a few moments later, I returned to check on his
progress, only to find him playing with a toy that had captured his
attention. When he saw me, his joyful countenance changed, knowing
that he had disappointed his father. Sadly, many Christians are often as
"little children" who are prone to stray from their Father's instructions.

To avoid disappointing the Lord, we must *"abide in him."* If we
remain in fellowship with God, faithfully doing as we have been
instructed, we will *"have confidence"* when Christ returns. However,
those who are playing instead of working will *"be ashamed before him."*
If Jesus returned today, would you have to hang your head in shame due
to your actions? God commands, *"Love not the world, neither the things
that are in the world."* Have you been so focused on the world that you
have forgotten what the Lord has told you to do? Don't get distracted.
What will the Lord find you doing when He returns? Be watchful.

Behold, what manner of love the Father hath bestowed upon us,
that we should be called the sons of God... I John 3:1

Those who have not been blessed with a wonderful earthly family can enjoy the blessings of a heavenly one. Consider our *family label—* *"the sons of God."* How can we comprehend *"what manner of love the Father hath bestowed upon us"*? When we were vile, rebellious sinners, He lovingly adopted us into His own family and calls us *"sons."*

As children of God, we share a *family likeness—"Whosoever is born of God doth not commit sin; for his seed remaineth in him."* The phrase, *"doth not commit sin"* does not mean that you will never sin again. The tense of the verb indicates that you will not habitually practice it as before. God's Holy Spirit dwells within every saved person, and no child of God can go on sinning without being convicted and corrected by the Lord. True salvation does not bring sinlessness, but it does produce a new attitude towards sin. Notice our *family love—"we ought to lay down our lives for the brethren."* Because Christ gave His life for us, we should demonstrate sacrificial love for one another. As believers, we also have a *family language*, which is prayer. When we follow the Lord, *"whatsoever we ask, we receive of him."*

If a man say, I love God, and hateth his brother, he is a liar: for he that loveth not his brother whom he hath seen, how can he love God whom he hath not seen? I John 4:20

No man loves God if he does not love his brother. It is a lot easier to love someone you can see than it is to love someone you cannot see. Therefore, one who claims to love God but hates his brother is a liar.

Satan is very clever. Knowing that he cannot sever God's love from you, he seeks to cause your love for the Lord to falter by attempting to create strife in your heart toward another believer. Never underestimate Satan's knowledge of the Scriptures. He knows that if he can get you at odds with God's people, you will immediately be at variance with the Lord. Has he been stirring up trouble between you and another? If so, do not yield to the temptation for even a minute!

Remember that God loves all of His children equally—even the one you may currently have a quarrel against. Therefore, never allow bitterness towards another to spoil your relationship with the Lord. You cannot be at peace with God when at war with a brother! Why not just love them both? It is impossible to love God when you don't love those He loves. So, get right with others and you can be right with the Lord.

For this is the love of God, that we keep his commandments:
and his commandments are not grievous. I John 5:3

Have you ever found it difficult to obey the Lord? At times, we are tempted to think that God's ways are hard or oppressive. However, to the one who loves the Lord, *"his commandments are not grievous."* Therefore, if following God has become burdensome to you, realize that the problem rests with you and not with His command.

Surely, if anyone had been asked of God to do something seemingly too difficult, it would have been Abraham. The Lord had directed him to offer his son, Isaac, as a burnt sacrifice. Instead of arguing with God or resisting His will, Abraham proceeded to obey without hesitation. His love for the Lord enabled him to *"keep his commandments."* Love for God produces obedience, not grief. We all know that the happiest people are those who follow God, not those who live in disobedience to His will.

Are you presently sad? It is not a commandment from God which has produced your sorrow—it might be your stubbornness. So, if you are feeling down, obey the Lord! Soon, peace and joy will begin to flood your soul. God's commandments are not meant to bring sadness. On the contrary, Jesus said, *"...happy are ye if ye do them."* (John 13:17)

DEC. 5　　　　　WHAT IS LOVE?　　　　　II JOHN

And this is love, that we walk after his commandments... II John 6

Love is defined differently by many; and, unfortunately, most hold a very superficial view of love. Someone might say, "I love pizza," but love is more than merely liking something. People who are attracted to one another often confuse lust with love. However, God defines love differently: *"And this is love, that we walk after his commandments."*

The Lord's definition of love includes obedience. Our love for God is seen by our adherence to His commands. Jesus put it this way, *"If ye love me, keep my commandments."* (John 14:15) It is a person's walk, not his talk, that truly reveals his dedication to the Lord. Many claim to love God, but their reckless, ungodly living proves otherwise. What about you? Are you living in disobedience to the Lord today? If so, can you honestly say that you love Him? Whether we like to admit it or not, lack of obedience reveals a lack of love.

Love is also based on your hearing—*"as ye have heard...walk in it."* It is difficult to obey a commandment that you have not heard. Therefore, if you truly love God, you will faithfully study His Word to learn what is important to Him. Love is about hearing and doing! What has God been speaking to you about lately? If you love Him, do it.

I have no greater joy than to hear that my children walk in truth.
III John 4

What could warrant such a bold expression as *"no greater joy"*? Many things bring joy, but to see our children walking in truth is the grandest of them. The apostle John penned these words regarding his children in the faith, but this truth applies to our physical children as well as our spiritual ones.

What could bring greater joy to parents than to see their children growing up to be kind, loving, faithful servants of God? Just as wayward children bring heartache, godly ones produce a wellspring of joy. However, no child walks in truth accidentally. In order to walk in the truth, a child must first be taught the truth. Our greatest challenge and responsibility as parents is the daily instruction of God's Word.

Since our joy as parents depends upon how well we guide our children, let's refocus our efforts. Although it is easy to blame our children for going astray, perhaps much of the blame rests in our failure to consistently point them in the right direction. Are you faithfully instructing your children from the Bible? If so, you, too, will one day say, *"I have no greater joy than to hear that my children walk in truth."*

Mercy unto you, and peace, and love, be multiplied. Jude 2

The book of Jude describes the apostasy and ungodliness that will exist in the end times. Although the world may cause you tribulation, God will more than compensate for it with His blessings.

First, the Lord grants *mercy*. As the world becomes more wicked, it is unfortunate that some of God's people allow themselves to be influenced by its evil. Thankfully, God is merciful and will withhold judgment upon His own when repentance is found. Have you gone astray? If you confess it and return to the Lord, He will extend His unfailing mercy to you. Second, God adds *peace*. As assaults on our faith become more prevalent, it is easy to fear what will become of us; but the peace of God is able to alleviate any pangs of fear. Thirdly, God adds *love*. Not only does He continue to prove His love to us, He also fills our hearts with love towards others, enabling us to *"have compassion, making a difference."*

God's math begins with addition but continues with multiplication— mercy, peace, and love are to *"be multiplied"* to each of His faithful servants. Though the world is getting worse, God gives more help than the world can render trouble. Ask for His multiplied blessings today.

*And he had in his right hand seven stars: and out of his mouth went a
sharp twoedged sword: and his countenance was as the sun shineth
in his strength. Revelation 1:16*

Today's text provides a partial glimpse of Christ's present glory. His holiness shines as the sun, and His voice thunders like many waters. The Words which proceed from His mouth are likened to *"a sharp twoedged sword."* In this day of spiritual compromise, many Christians have forgotten the true nature of the Word. In an attempt to either gain or maintain a crowd, preachers have worked hard to soften the message of the Bible to make it more acceptable. However, on the battlefield, we need a sharp sword, not a dull one!

The Sword of the Lord is not meant to tickle but to deal a lethal blow to the sin that is in our lives. Of necessity, it must be sharp and heavy to do its job. While it is true that God's Word brings comfort, it also produces conviction. Churches that steer clear of strong preaching against sin, stressing only positive messages, are not true to the Word.

Swords pierce, cut, and divide. Why should we expect God's Word to do any less? Have you ever heard of someone using a soft sword in battle? Be thankful that God's Word cuts to the heart of your sin.

*...These things saith he that holdeth the seven stars in his right hand, who
walketh in the midst of the seven golden candlesticks... Revelation 2:1*

The seven golden candlesticks refer to seven churches that existed in the days of the apostle John. Jesus walks in the midst of every true church; and as He walks, He is not idle. Notice some of the activities He is currently engaged in.

He *sees—"I know thy works."* Our labor for the Lord may go unnoticed by men, but God observes every action. Additionally, He maintains a detailed record of each deed, whether it is bad or good. Christ also *examines—"thou hast left thy first love."* Perhaps your zeal was once fervent in days gone by, but now you serve God out of duty rather than love. If so, He *instructs—"repent, and do the first works."* Repentance is more than an attitude. It involves action—*"do."* You must get back to the basics of the Christian life, known as *"the first works."* Jesus also *warns—"repent...or else."* Consequences always exist for those who refuse to humble themselves and amend their ways.

As Jesus walks in the midst of your church, what does He see? Does He find you in attendance each service? Are you faithfully serving Him with vibrant love or by mere habit? Make Jesus your *"first love."*

And I gave her space to repent of her fornication; and she repented not.
Revelation 2:21

The church in Thyatira had some very good works, but it also had some terrible ones. A prophetess had seduced members of the congregation to commit fornication and practice idolatry; and God, in His mercy, *"gave her space to repent."* Although she had an opportunity to change, *"she repented not."* Thus, the severity of judgment fell—*"I will kill her children with death."*

No matter how many noble deeds and godly qualities are found in a church, God does not overlook sin. He mercifully gives *"space to repent,"* but failure to do so results in judgment. Have you been granted such a space to consider your wayward steps? If so, repent at once! The Lord *"searcheth the reins and hearts,"* promising to *"give unto every one of you according to your works."* Unfortunately, many use the space that God provides for repentance to go farther down the path of sin.

In Thyatira, some in the church were godly, but evil people thought they were safe because of the righteousness of others. Those practicing coattail Christianity could not escape God's all-seeing eye, and neither will you if you are also guilty of the same sin. Repent while there's time.

...I know thy works, that thou hast a name that thou livest, and art dead.
Revelation 3:1

People are often more worried about their reputation than their character and work feverishly to maintain their image. Have you become overly concerned about how you are perceived by others? Just remember that a good name is only respected if it is backed up by good living. No matter how well you cover up your true nature, it will come to light one day.

Notice the Lord's *consideration*—*"I know thy works."* Regardless of how you appear to others, God knows your true condition. If you are dead and backslidden, stop putting on a front. Your service to God will be shallow and powerless as long as you live on past blessings. What counts with God is your present spirituality, not your previous activity.

It is time to heed God's *command*—*"Remember...and hold fast, and repent."* Remember the peace that formerly flooded your soul, and long for nearness to God once again. Before the Lord will restore you to fellowship, you must admit your backslidden state. Then, *"strengthen the things which remain,"* letting nothing else in your life slip! Finally, *"repent."* Return to the Lord, refusing to live on yesterday's spirituality.

*And he that sat was to look upon like a jasper and a sardine stone: and
there was a rainbow round about the throne, in sight
like unto an emerald. Revelation 4:3*

In this chapter, the Lord began to reveal to John the *"things which must
be hereafter."* Prophecies concerning heaven, end-time troubles, the
millennial reign of Christ, and future judgment would soon be unveiled
to the apostle; but first, God revealed something special about Himself.
As John gazed upon the throne, he saw *"a rainbow round about"* it.

The significance of the rainbow should not be forgotten. It reminds
us that God is One Who keeps His promises. All of the revelations that
the apostle would soon receive were guaranteed to come to pass because
God had set His seal of the covenant rainbow to them.

Notice that the rainbow is *"round about the throne."* As a circle is
never ending, so are the promises of God. They last throughout eternity.
There will be no fear of being cast out of heaven because the heavenly
rainbow will be a constant reminder of God's promise of eternal life.

Let us lay hold upon some needed promise today, knowing that it is
empowered by the One Who has faithfully kept all of His promises.
Every rainbow in the sky should inspire us to trust the Lord more.

*...the four beasts and four and twenty elders fell down before the Lamb,
having every one of them harps, and golden vials full of odours,
which are the prayers of saints. Revelation 5:8*

Our view of the splendors of paradise is limited, but glimpses of
heavenly activity are revealed. So, what goes on in heaven?

First, we see worship—the heavenly beings *"fell down before the
Lamb."* To be overwhelmed by the majesty of God is a demonstration of
true submission to Him. If it is a preoccupation of those in heaven,
shouldn't it be practiced by all who claim to love the Lord here below?

Second, music of praise and adoration abounds at the throne—
"having every one of them harps." This is not modern-day dance music
but spiritual melodies. Only songs that elevate our heart toward heaven
are acceptable at the throne of grace. Is your music heavenly or
energized by fleshly passions?

Last, we observe the *"the prayers of saints."* Our prayers are sweet-
smelling incense to God and are so precious that they must be kept in
vials of gold! We can be engaged in heavenly activity right now by
making our petitions to the One upon the throne. Why not bring a little
heaven into your life here below by mirroring heaven's activities?

For the great day of his wrath is come; and who shall be able to stand?
Revelation 6:17

The seven seals refer to judgments that will come upon the earth during the time of the Great Tribulation. The first six seals are opened in this chapter, describing the chaos that will be unleashed upon the earth. Peace will be taken away, famine will follow, multitudes will die, and an earthquake unlike anything the world has ever seen will strike terror in the hearts of many.

Those who were once bold in their blasphemies will witness the power of the Lord. Many will cry, *"...hide us from the face of him that sitteth on the throne, and from the wrath of the Lamb."* People who have lived carelessly with no fear of God will one day be shaken to the core.

Although many in this world are currently bold to speak against our Savior, they will one day acknowledge His power. Notice that *"kings of the earth...rich men...and the mighty men"* will hide from the Lord Jesus. Neither position, prosperity, or power will avail anything in *"the great day of his wrath."* You may ask, "What can I learn from this passage?" Never assume that position or prominence in this life will spare you from judgment. *"...those that walk in pride he is able to abase."* (Daniel 4:37)

And I heard the number of them which were sealed: and there were sealed an hundred and forty and four thousand of all the tribes of the children of Israel. Revelation 7:4

Most of us have heard that the Jehovah's Witnesses' religion teaches that only 144,000 people will go to heaven. However, this is not only false doctrine but willful ignorance of the passage they claim as support of their argument.

First of all, the 144,000 mentioned in this verse are Jews who will be saved during the Tribulation period, following the rapture. Additionally, just a few verses later, we are told of another group of people who will be saved during that time—*"...a great multitude, which no man could number, of all nations, and kindreds, and people, and tongues, stood before the throne, and before the Lamb...These are they which came out of great tribulation."* (v. 9, 14) So, the 144,000 just happen to be part of a greater multitude who will be in heaven!

Never be alarmed when confronted with a passage of Scripture taken out of context by false teachers. Simply learn to look at the verses surrounding the passage and allow the truth to speak for itself. Studying the Bible brings great satisfaction and confidence in what you believe.

And when he had opened the seventh seal, there was silence in heaven
about the space of half an hour. Revelation 8:1

Earlier, the scene in heaven was full of praise, adoration, and singing. Here, we read that *"there was silence in heaven."* What could warrant such a hush to come across the entire realm of paradise?

The opening of the seventh seal marks the beginning of the seven trumpet judgments, which pronounce terrible woes upon those who reject the Creator. The consideration of weighty matters often creates silence and a somber mood. Because judgment is serious business, I can only imagine that the silence in heaven reveals the severity of the Lord's treatment of His rejecters. It is so dreadful that none can speak.

Is there not a lesson for us to consider personally? Although we will not experience the judgments of the Tribulation, God does correct our waywardness. *"The Lord shall judge his people. It is a fearful thing to fall into the hands of the living God."* (Hebrews 10:30-31) Truly, the fear of God should strike terror in the heart of us all.

Have you sensed that God has been silent towards you? Although it is not necessarily a sign of pending judgment, it could be. If you have strayed from His ways, return to Him before the "trumpet" sounds.

Neither repented they of their murders, nor of their sorceries, nor of their
fornication, nor of their thefts. Revelation 9:21

The fifth trumpet, known as the first woe, will open the bottomless pit from which fierce locusts shall arise, *"and their torment was as the torment of a scorpion, when he striketh a man."* Power will be given to the locusts to inflict pain for five months, being so terrible that *"in those days shall men seek death, and shall not find it."* Surprisingly, the anguish will not be enough to cause men to repent. Things will get worse when the sixth trumpet sounds, which unleashes an army that will slay one third of the inhabitants of the earth.

You would think that people would want to avoid experiencing more of God's wrath! But despite the pain and suffering they will endure, they still will not repent. How foolish! Their love for sin will harden their hearts, preventing them from exercising common sense.

Sin will harden your heart, too. God warns us not to be *"hardened through the deceitfulness of sin."* (Hebrews 3:13) Sin promises a good time but delivers miseries; and the longer you refuse correction concerning your sin, the harder your heart will become. What sin are you holding onto? Have you become so hardened that you won't repent?

*...there should be time no longer...the mystery of God should be finished,
as he hath declared to his servants the prophets. Revelation 10:6-7*

Some suggest that this passage marks the end of time as we know it. Although time may end one day, this proclamation does not indicate such a turning point. As proof, we only need to consider that the thousand-year reign of Christ upon the earth is yet to come. How would we know when the thousand years were fulfilled if there were no time?

So, what does *"time no longer"* refer to? The word *time* can mean *delay* or *season* depending upon its usage. Here, it seems obvious that God speaks of a delay that would soon come to an end concerning when *"the mystery of God should be finished."* So, God is not speaking about the end of time but the end of a delay.

Are you becoming frustrated because a present need seems to be neglected by the Lord? God does not work on your timetable. He has a master plan for your life and follows His own schedule to get things done. Be assured that the Lord does send help, but sometimes only after a delay. By faith you can look forward to when *"there should be time* [delay] *no longer."* Rather than get upset at God's timing, be excited that His delay will soon end!

*And after three days and an half the Spirit of life from God entered into
them, and they stood upon their feet; and great fear fell upon
them which saw them. Revelation 11:11*

The two witnesses will have a powerful ministry during the Tribulation period. They will preach and perform miracles, yet people's hearts will still be hardened against God. After the beast kills both of the witnesses, the world will rejoice and celebrate. However, the defeat of God's servants is only temporary—God will revive them.

What a wonderful reminder we have before us today. Those who labor long in the battle against unrighteousness may be despised and suffer loss, but that is never the end of the story for one of God's warriors. Perhaps you are discouraged from a spiritual battle that has pressed heavy upon your body, soul, or mind. Look for a visit from the *"Spirit of life"* and soon you will be upon your feet as were the two witnesses. We may be cast down but are never deserted by our great King. He will always give new strength to stand for the next battle!

Notice also that God used the defeat for His glory. Once the men were revived, *"great fear fell upon them which saw them."* Perhaps a great victory awaits you today!

*And they overcame him by the blood of the Lamb, and by the word of
their testimony; and they loved not their lives unto the death.
Revelation 12:11*

A great spiritual battle rages upon earth and is led by Satan, our
adversary. His character is described in verse nine. As a dragon he
seeks to destroy, as a serpent he is subtle, as the devil he falsely accuses,
and as Satan he deceives the whole world. Who can overcome such a
powerful, sly, and vicious foe? When we look at the world today with its
violence and perversion, we conclude that multitudes have already been
conquered by the devil. How can we possibly be victorious?

Our text brings great hope! Notice that the brethren *"overcame him
by the blood of the Lamb."* As the song reminds us, "There's power in
the blood!" To overcome the devil in your daily life, you need to ask the
Lord to cleanse you of sin by the power in His blood. Next, they
overcame Satan through *"the word of their testimony."* Being faithful to
the Word of God will give us a powerful testimony against the devil's
accusations against us. Finally, we observe their self-denial—*"they
loved not their lives unto the death."* If we are cleansed by the blood,
faithful to the Word, and denying self, we will overcome our foe. Amen!

*And he doeth great wonders...And deceiveth them that dwell on the earth
by the means of those miracles which he had power to do in the sight of
the beast... Revelation 13:13-14*

The Tribulation period will be a time of great blasphemy in which
people will openly worship Satan and the world leader, the beast.
(See verse four.) Furthermore, notable miracles will be performed by the
Antichrist who will deceive those living on the earth.

The devil has always had great power and offers it to those willing to
follow him. People living in areas where witchcraft and voodoo are
practiced can attest to the reality of satanic forces. Such power is always
associated with oppression and darkness because the devil has no power
to produce anything wholesome or edifying.

Never be fascinated with demonic powers. They may be real, but
they always make the partakers pay a tremendous price. This day's
reading provides a perfect example of this. After the Antichrist secures
allegiance through signs and wonders, he will threaten his subjects with
death and financial ruin. Satan always uses his power to enslave his
followers while Christ uses His to liberate. Whose power do you want?

*...Blessed are the dead which die in the Lord from henceforth: Yea, saith
the Spirit, that they may rest from their labours; and their works
do follow them. Revelation 14:13*

Those who receive the mark of the beast during the Tribulation will ultimately be punished with eternal torment. They will have their satisfaction of serving the devil on earth, but they will receive no blessing in eternity. However, the opposite is true for all of God's children—*"Blessed are the dead which die in the Lord."* Blessed in heaven is a never-ending state of happiness. Everlasting contentment far outweighs the temporary pleasure offered by Satan.

In heaven, God's people *"may rest from their labours."* Oh, how we long for rest when toiling in the fields! However, God did not promise rest in this life but in the one that follows. No Christian should seek a life of ease but, instead, labor diligently for the Master, knowing that *"the night cometh, when no man can work."*

Thankfully, our efforts will be rewarded once our heavenly rest begins. Our treasures above will be based upon our labors below— *"their works do follow them."* Therefore, we must work now and rest later.

*And they sing the song of Moses the servant of God, and the song of the
Lamb, saying, Great and marvellous are thy works, Lord God Almighty;
just and true are thy ways, thou King of saints. Revelation 15:3*

Those saved during the Tribulation period will have to endure great hardships as they resist the power of the beast. Ultimately, their death will usher them into the splendors of heaven, giving them *"victory over the beast."* As they stand on the sea of glass, they will express no sorrow or regret for the torments they suffered while on earth. Instead, songs of praise to the *"King of saints"* shall proceed from their lips.

When we realize that Jesus is truly our King, we will gladly endure anything for His name; and we will do so with a song of adoration. Can we not proclaim, *"Great and marvelous are thy works,"* even in our present distress? God's ways are always perfect! The Tribulation saints will boldly declare to God, *"...just and true are thy ways."* To be just means to be fair and equal. Do you always consider God's ways to be fair? Oftentimes we are tempted to cry out, "It's just not fair that I have to go through this!" This sort of clamor is never heard from the lips of any of the redeemed in heaven. Rather than complain, let us learn to sing, "Take my life and let it be consecrated, Lord, to Thee."

And I heard the angel of the waters say, Thou art righteous, O Lord,
which art, and wast, and shalt be, because thou hast judged thus.
Revelation 16:5

A fter the third angel turns the waters to blood, he will proclaim, *"Thou art righteous, O Lord."* In this judgment we see that God will repay blood for blood. The wicked men upon the earth will take great delight in killing God's people and prophets; and as they shed the blood of man, God will give them *"blood to drink; for they are worthy."* Retribution will be meted out to those He deems worthy.

Be assured that God is righteous to give to sinners what they deserve to receive. His judgment may seem long in coming, but it will come! Perhaps we have suffered ill treatment at the hands of the wicked and wonder why God has not defended us as we had hoped. In such a case, we may even be tempted to take matters into our own hands. However, the Lord says, *"Dearly beloved, avenge not yourselves...Vengeance is mine; I will repay, saith the Lord."* (Romans 12:19)

Not only is there a payday for the lost sinner, God will judge the saved, too. He takes account of our deeds and knows what judgment we are worthy to receive. Repent of your waywardness to avoid His wrath.

And the angel said unto them, Fear not: for, behold, I bring you good
tidings of great joy, which shall be to all people. Luke 2:10

T he job of the shepherds was to stay alert and watch for any danger that might threaten the sheep. Certainly, unexpected sights and sounds would have grabbed their attention. Therefore, it is no wonder that they were *"sore afraid"* at the presence of the angel.

Darkness brings fear, and if there were ever a day that the earth was filled with spiritual darkness, it is now. Multitudes are overtaken by common fears: financial instability, an uncertain future, violent criminals, and global unrest. The message to us is the same given to the shepherds—*"Fear not."* Jesus came to deliver us from all fear. What a Christmas present! Fear is so terrible because it causes us to take our eyes off of Jesus and robs us of the *"great joy"* that He wants us to have. While it is easy to remember Jesus today, be sure to do so every day.

Despite the darkness and evil in the world, we have *"good tidings of great joy."* Rejoice that Christ came to save you from the bondage of sin. Then, renew your efforts to tell others about the good news that has cheered your heart and changed your life. After all, these tidings are *"to all people."*

*These have one mind, and shall give their power and strength
unto the beast. Revelation 17:13*

Ten men will pledge their loyalty to the beast in return for promotion. This is nothing new. Men have always been willing to give their best to Satan in return for earthly glory. However, as in every case, the promised blessing is short-lived. These men will *"receive power as kings one hour with the beast."* How long? Only one hour!

What a terrible master the devil is! He demands one's mind, abilities, and strength but gives nothing worthy in return. It is terrible to freely give to Satan what rightly belongs to God. Have you given too much attention to the things of the world, neglecting your duty to the one true God? Although the devil promises wonderful blessings, *"every perfect gift is from above, and cometh down from the Father."* (James 1:17) Only the Lord delivers on His promises!

Can we not learn a valuable lesson from our text today? Rather than give our best to Satan for temporary pleasure, let us give our all to the true King Who promises eternal rewards. Shouldn't we show as much dedication to the Lamb as evil men do toward the devil? God's people must have *"one mind"* and *"give their power and strength"* unto Jesus.

*And I heard another voice from heaven, saying, Come out of her,
my people, that ye be not partakers of her sins, and that
ye receive not of her plagues. Revelation 18:4*

Today's reading speaks of the judgment of Babylon near the end of the Tribulation period. It must be remembered that Babylon refers to both a political and ecclesiastical power that will be known as *"the habitation of devils."* The city will flourish in wealth and materialism; but because of its wickedness, it will suffer utter devastation.

Throughout all ages, God has commanded His people to separate from worldliness and apostasy. His instruction to us is the same as to the saints of the Tribulation, *"Come out of her, my people, that ye be not partakers of her sins."* Failure to depart from ungodly influences around us will surely lead to our participation in their evil deeds. Is this a warning to you today? Are you too involved in "Babylonian" associations?

To partake in the world's sins leads you to partake in its judgment. God warns His people to *"Come out"* so they will *"receive not of her plagues."* If you play in the dirt, you will get dirty; and if you play with sin, you will reap judgment. *"Come out"* to be spared certain misery!

And I heard as it were the voice of a great multitude, and as the voice of many waters, and as the voice of mighty thunderings, saying, Alleluia: for the Lord God omnipotent reigneth. Revelation 19:6

A t times we become discouraged when we witness so much evil going on about us. We recall that the devil is the god of this world, but we should also realize that he is not God! Our text reminds us that *"the Lord God omnipotent reigneth."* This should cheer our hearts.

The noise of evil can never rise above the sound of praise for the true King. Jesus will return to the earth one day to execute judgment on all of Satan's forces. The beast and false prophet will be *"cast alive into a lake of fire burning with brimstone."* Furthermore, all of the armies gathered together against our Lord at the battle of Armageddon will be destroyed.

God's people must never live in fear of Satan because they are on the winning side! Oh, it is true that the devil has power, but it is limited and regulated by the One Who has all power. Dwell on the omnipotence of God for a while, and your faith will be bolstered once again.

It is not just that the Lord will reign—He reigns presently. Therefore, let us sing, *"Alleluia,"* to our King and look for His deliverance from our present trial of affliction.

Blessed and holy is he that hath part in the first resurrection: on such the second death hath no power, but they shall be priests of God and of Christ, and shall reign with him a thousand years. Revelation 20:6

M any fear the end of the world. We have been warned by scientists and politicians that everything from nuclear war to global warming will destroy the earth. However, they are all wrong! You do not have to be afraid of doomsday predictions, regardless of how credible you think the theory or source may be. God has already written the end of the story—the earth will last at least another one thousand and seven years.

Consider the order of prophetic events. Jesus will return in the clouds for the saved at the rapture. The next seven years will include the rise and fall of the Antichrist during the Great Tribulation. Next, Christ will return to the earth and rule for a period of one thousand years. Satan will be bound during Christ's earthly kingdom but will be released at its conclusion for one final battle. Upon his defeat, he will be *"cast into the lake of fire"* forever. Then, the lost souls of every age will be judged by Jesus at the Great White Throne and *"cast into the lake of fire."* Finally, God will destroy the earth, making new heavens and a new earth. Man won't destroy the world. So, don't fear doomsday—fear God!

And God shall wipe away all tears from their eyes; and there shall be no more death, neither sorrow, nor crying, neither shall there be any more pain: for the former things are passed away. Revelation 21:4

Although many Christians talk about going to heaven, I believe that few actually spend much time thinking about it. Today's reading gives us the opportunity to focus on our eternal home for a few moments. As a man in a strange country may comfort himself with thoughts of home, so Christians can find relief by reflecting on their heavenly abode.

When thinking of your earthly home, you tend to recall the blessings that are there—your own bed, a comfortable chair, and especially your beloved family. When thinking of heaven today, let's focus on some things that will not be there rather than those we know await us.

Consider that *"there shall be no more death."* The fear and dread of dying are nonexistent in heaven. The loss and heartache associated with parting loved ones will be forever gone. Next on the list is, *"neither sorrow."* Oh, to get to the land where nothing will discourage or sadden the heart! There will be no *"crying."* Every tear shall be wiped away, leaving only joy and bliss. Can you imagine no *"more pain"*? All aches and pains will vanish. Just be sure that you are not missing in heaven!

He which testifieth these things saith, Surely I come quickly. Amen. Even so, come, Lord Jesus. Revelation 22:20

Throughout the year, we have considered many of God's precious promises. It is fitting, therefore, that we draw our attention to the closing words of the Bible, which contain one final promise and a corresponding prayer.

Let us first consider the last *promise—"Surely I come quickly."* Whether you are presently on a mountaintop or in a deep valley, the reminder of Christ's return brings hope. When He comes, your struggles with sin and sorrow will finally conclude. Although your present trials may seem overwhelming, Jesus has not forgotten you. In due time, He will deliver you from this present evil world. In His kingdom, every injustice will be punished, and all of the faithful shall be rewarded. Earlier in the chapter Jesus promised, *"...my reward is with me."*

Next, notice the final *prayer* of Scripture—*"Even so, come, Lord Jesus."* The last promise prompted the concluding prayer. This serves as a reminder to pray over every promise we find in the Bible. On the eve of a New Year, determine that you will diligently search for promises to plead, knowing that God delights to keep His promises.

CONCLUDING THOUGHTS

We have completed our journey through the New Testament! Hopefully, you have gleaned some helpful guidance for your daily life. I encourage you, as Paul charged Timothy, to *"continue thou in the things which thou hast learned."* (II Timothy 3:14) The Lord has many more wonderful lessons to teach you as you study His Word. Daily light from the Bible will surely brighten your path.

May the Lord bless you as you continue to strengthen your faith through a time in His Word each day. If you choose to read through *Daily Light* again, I trust that you will find the truths just as appropriate as you did the previous year. To anyone looking for a similar book to use while reading through the Old Testament, I recommend another of my devotionals, *Morning Light*.

DAILY BIBLE READING SCHEDULE

		JANUARY	
DAY	NEW TESTAMENT	OLD TESTAMENT (A.M.)	OLD TESTAMENT (P.M.)
1	Matthew 1	Genesis 1-2	Job 1:1-12
2	Matthew 2	Genesis 3-4	Job 1:13-22
3	Matthew 3	Genesis 5-6	Job 2
4	Matthew 4	Genesis 7-8	Job 3
5	Matthew 5:1-20	Genesis 9-10	Job 4
6	Matthew 5:21-48	Genesis 11-12	Job 5
7	Matthew 6	Genesis 13-15	Job 6
8	Matthew 7	Genesis 16-17	Job 7
9	Matthew 8	Genesis 18-19	Job 8
10	Matthew 9:1-17	Genesis 20-21	Job 9
11	Matthew 9:18-38	Genesis 22-23	Job 10
12	Matthew 10:1-20	Genesis 24	Job 11
13	Matthew 10:21-42	Genesis 25-26	Job 12
14	Matthew 11	Genesis 27	Job 13
15	Matthew 12:1-21	Genesis 28-29	Job 14
16	Matthew 12:22-50	Genesis 30	Job 15
17	Matthew 13:1-30	Genesis 31	Job 16
18	Matthew 13:31-58	Genesis 32-33	Job 17
19	Matthew 14	Genesis 34-35	Job 18
20	Matthew 15:1-20	Genesis 36	Job 19
21	Matthew 15:21-39	Genesis 37-38	Job 20
22	Matthew 16	Genesis 39-40	Job 21
23	Matthew 17	Genesis 41	Job 22
24	Matthew 18:1-19	Genesis 42-43	Job 23
25	Matthew 18:20-35	Genesis 44-45	Job 24
26	Matthew 19	Genesis 46-47	Job 25
27	Matthew 20:1-16	Genesis 48-49	Job 26
28	Matthew 20:17-34	Genesis 50	Job 27
29	Matthew 21:1-22	Exodus 1-2	Job 28
30	Matthew 21:23-46	Exodus 3	Job 29
31	Matthew 22:1-22	Exodus 4-5	Job 30

DAILY BIBLE READING SCHEDULE

		FEBRUARY	
DAY	**NEW TESTAMENT**	**OLD TESTAMENT (A.M.)**	**OLD TESTAMENT (P.M.)**
1	Matthew 22:23-46	Exodus 6-7	Job 31
2	Matthew 23:1-22	Exodus 8-9	Job 32
3	Matthew 23:23-39	Exodus 10-11	Job 33
4	Matthew 24:1-25	Exodus 12	Job 34
5	Matthew 24:26-51	Exodus 13-14	Job 35
6	Matthew 25:1-30	Exodus 15-16	Job 36
7	Matthew 25:31-46	Exodus 17-18	Job 37
8	Matthew 26:1-30	Exodus 19-20	Job 38
9	Matthew 26:31-56	Exodus 21-22	Job 39
10	Matthew 26:57-75	Exodus 23-24	Job 40
11	Matthew 27:1-25	Exodus 25-26	Job 41
12	Matthew 27:26-44	Exodus 27-28	Job 42
13	Matthew 27:45-66	Exodus 29	Psalm 1
14	Matthew 28	Exodus 30-31	Psalm 2
15	Mark 1:1-20	Exodus 32-33	Psalm 3
16	Mark 1:21-45	Exodus 34-35	Psalm 4
17	Mark 2	Exodus 36	Psalm 5
18	Mark 3	Exodus 37-38	Psalm 6
19	Mark 4:1-20	Exodus 39	Psalm 7
20	Mark 4:21-41	Exodus 40	Psalm 8
21	Mark 5:1-20	Leviticus 1-2	Psalm 9
22	Mark 5:21-43	Leviticus 3-4	Psalm 10
23	Mark 6:1-29	Leviticus 5-6	Psalm 11
24	Mark 6:30-56	Leviticus 7	Psalm 12
25	Mark 7:1-19	Leviticus 8	Psalm 13
26	Mark 7:20-37	Leviticus 9-10	Psalm 14
27	Mark 8:1-21	Leviticus 11-12	Psalm 15
28	Mark 8:22-38	Leviticus 13	Psalm 16
29	Read Favorite Chapters		

Daily Bible Reading Schedule

Day	New Testament	Old Testament (A.M.)	Old Testament (P.M.)
March			
1	Mark 9:1-29	Leviticus 14	Psalm 17
2	Mark 9:30-50	Leviticus 15-16	Psalm 18:1-26
3	Mark 10:1-27	Leviticus 17-18	Psalm 18:27-50
4	Mark 10:28-52	Leviticus 19-20	Psalm 19
5	Mark 11	Leviticus 21-22	Psalm 20
6	Mark 12:1-27	Leviticus 23-24	Psalm 21
7	Mark 12:28-44	Leviticus 25	Psalm 22:1-21
8	Mark 13	Leviticus 26	Psalm 22:22-31
9	Mark 14:1-26	Leviticus 27	Psalm 23
10	Mark 14:27-50	Numbers 1	Psalm 24
11	Mark 14:51-72	Numbers 2	Psalm 25
12	Mark 15:1-24	Numbers 3	Psalm 26
13	Mark 15:25-47	Numbers 4	Psalm 27
14	Mark 16	Numbers 5-6	Psalm 28
15	Luke 1:1-25	Numbers 7	Psalm 29
16	Luke 1:26-56	Numbers 8-9	Psalm 30
17	Luke 1:57-80	Numbers 10	Psalm 31:1-13
18	Luke 2:1-24	Numbers 11	Psalm 31:14-24
19	Luke 2:25-52	Numbers 12-13	Psalm 32
20	Luke 3	Numbers 14	Psalm 33:1-11
21	Luke 4:1-30	Numbers 15	Psalm 33:12-22
22	Luke 4:31-44	Numbers 16	Psalm 34:1-10
23	Luke 5	Numbers 17-18	Psalm 34:11-22
24	Luke 6:1-26	Numbers 19-20	Psalm 35:1-16
25	Luke 6:27-49	Numbers 21	Psalm 35:17-28
26	Luke 7:1-23	Numbers 22	Psalm 36
27	Luke 7:24-50	Numbers 23-25	Psalm 37:1-20
28	Luke 8:1-25	Numbers 26	Psalm 37:21-40
29	Luke 8:26-56	Numbers 27-28	Psalm 38:1-12
30	Luke 9:1-36	Numbers 29-30	Psalm 38:13-22
31	Luke 9:37-62	Numbers 31	Psalm 39

DAILY BIBLE READING SCHEDULE

APRIL			
DAY	NEW TESTAMENT	OLD TESTAMENT (A.M.)	OLD TESTAMENT (P.M.)
1	Luke 10:1-22	Numbers 32	Psalm 40
2	Luke 10:23-42	Numbers 33-34	Psalm 41
3	Luke 11:1-28	Numbers 35-36	Psalm 42
4	Luke 11:29-54	Deuteronomy 1	Psalm 43
5	Luke 12:1-34	Deuteronomy 2-3	Psalm 44:1-14
6	Luke 12:35-59	Deuteronomy 4	Psalm 44:15-26
7	Luke 13	Deuteronomy 5-6	Psalm 45
8	Luke 14	Deuteronomy 7-8	Psalm 46
9	Luke 15	Deuteronomy 9-10	Psalm 47
10	Luke 16	Deuteronomy 11-12	Psalm 48
11	Luke 17	Deuteronomy 13-14	Psalm 49
12	Luke 18:1-17	Deuteronomy 15-16	Psalm 50
13	Luke 18:18-43	Deuteronomy 17-18	Psalm 51
14	Luke 19:1-27	Deuteronomy 19-21	Psalm 52
15	Luke 19:28-48	Deuteronomy 22-23	Psalm 53
16	Luke 20:1-26	Deuteronomy 24-25	Psalm 54
17	Luke 20:27-47	Deuteronomy 26-27	Psalm 55:1-11
18	Luke 21	Deuteronomy 28	Psalm 55:12-23
19	Luke 22:1-23	Deuteronomy 29-30	Psalm 56
20	Luke 22:24-46	Deuteronomy 31	Psalm 57
21	Luke 22:47-71	Deuteronomy 32	Psalm 58
22	Luke 23:1-26	Deuteronomy 33-34	Psalm 59
23	Luke 23:27-56	Joshua 1-2	Psalm 60
24	Luke 24:1-27	Joshua 3-5	Psalm 61
25	Luke 24:28-53	Joshua 6-7	Psalm 62
26	John 1:1-27	Joshua 8-9	Psalm 63
27	John 1:28-51	Joshua 10	Psalm 64
28	John 2	Joshua 11-12	Psalm 65
29	John 3	Joshua 13-14	Psalm 66
30	John 4:1-26	Joshua 15	Psalm 67

DAILY BIBLE READING SCHEDULE

	MAY		
DAY	**NEW TESTAMENT**	**OLD TESTAMENT (A.M.)**	**OLD TESTAMENT (P.M.)**
1	John 4:27-54	Joshua 16-18	Psalm 68:1-18
2	John 5:1-23	Joshua 19	Psalm 68:19-35
3	John 5:24-47	Joshua 20-21	Psalm 69:1-18
4	John 6:1-21	Joshua 22-23	Psalm 69:19-36
5	John 6:22-48	Joshua 24	Psalm 70
6	John 6:49-71	Judges 1-2	Psalm 71:1-13
7	John 7:1-27	Judges 3-4	Psalm 71:14-24
8	John 7:28-53	Judges 5-6	Psalm 72
9	John 8:1-20	Judges 7-8	Psalm 73:1-15
10	John 8:21-40	Judges 9	Psalm 73:16-28
11	John 8:41-59	Judges 10-11	Psalm 74
12	John 9:1-23	Judges 12-14	Psalm 75
13	John 9:24-41	Judges 15-16	Psalm 76
14	John 10:1-21	Judges 17-18	Psalm 77
15	John 10:22-42	Judges 19	Psalm 78:1-18
16	John 11:1-29	Judges 20	Psalm 78:19-36
17	John 11:30-57	Judges 21	Psalm 78:37-54
18	John 12:1-26	Ruth 1-2	Psalm 78:55-72
19	John 12:27-50	Ruth 3-4	Psalm 79
20	John 13:1-20	I Samuel 1-2	Psalm 80
21	John 13:21-38	I Samuel 3-4	Psalm 81
22	John 14	I Samuel 5-7	Psalm 82
23	John 15	I Samuel 8-9	Psalm 83
24	John 16:1-16	I Samuel 10-11	Psalm 84
25	John 16:17-33	I Samuel 12-13	Psalm 85
26	John 17	I Samuel 14	Psalm 86
27	John 18:1-18	I Samuel 15-16	Psalm 87
28	John 18:19-40	I Samuel 17	Psalm 88
29	John 19:1-22	I Samuel 18-19	Psalm 89:1-17
30	John 19:23-42	I Samuel 20-21	Psalm 89:18-34
31	John 20	I Samuel 22-23	Psalm 89:35-52

DAILY BIBLE READING SCHEDULE

		JUNE	
DAY	NEW TESTAMENT	OLD TESTAMENT (A.M.)	OLD TESTAMENT (P.M.)
1	John 21	I Samuel 24-25	Psalm 90
2	Acts 1	I Samuel 26-27	Psalm 91
3	Acts 2:1-21	I Samuel 28-29	Psalm 92
4	Acts 2:22-47	I Samuel 30-31	Psalm 93
5	Acts 3	II Samuel 1-2	Psalm 94:1-11
6	Acts 4:1-20	II Samuel 3-4	Psalm 94:12-23
7	Acts 4:21-37	II Samuel 5-6	Psalm 95
8	Acts 5:1-20	II Samuel 7-9	Psalm 96
9	Acts 5:21-42	II Samuel 10-11	Psalm 97
10	Acts 6	II Samuel 12-13	Psalm 98
11	Acts 7:1-19	II Samuel 14-15	Psalm 99
12	Acts 7:20-40	II Samuel 16-17	Psalm 100
13	Acts 7:41-60	II Samuel 18	Psalm 101
14	Acts 8:1-25	II Samuel 19	Psalm 102:1-11
15	Acts 8:26-40	II Samuel 20-21	Psalm 102:12-28
16	Acts 9:1-21	II Samuel 22	Psalm 103:1-12
17	Acts 9:22-43	II Samuel 23-24	Psalm 103:13-22
18	Acts 10:1-22	I Kings 1	Psalm 104:1-18
19	Acts 10:23-48	I Kings 2	Psalm 104:19-35
20	Acts 11	I Kings 3-4	Psalm 105:1-15
21	Acts 12	I Kings 5-6	Psalm 105:16-30
22	Acts 13:1-25	I Kings 7	Psalm 105:31-45
23	Acts 13:26-52	I Kings 8	Psalm 106:1-15
24	Acts 14	I Kings 9-10	Psalm 106:16-31
25	Acts 15:1-21	I Kings 11	Psalm 106:32-48
26	Acts 15:22-41	I Kings 12-13	Psalm 107:1-16
27	Acts 16:1-21	I Kings 14-15	Psalm 107:17-30
28	Acts 16:22-40	I Kings 16-17	Psalm 107:31-43
29	Acts 17:1-17	I Kings 18	Psalm 108
30	Acts 17:18-34	I Kings 19-20	Psalm 109:1-16

DAILY BIBLE READING SCHEDULE

JULY			
DAY	**NEW TESTAMENT**	**OLD TESTAMENT (A.M.)**	**OLD TESTAMENT (P.M.)**
1	Acts 18:1-17	I Kings 21	Psalm 109:17-31
2	Acts 18:18-28	I Kings 22	Psalm 110
3	Acts 19:1-20	II Kings 1-2	Psalm 111
4	Acts 19:21-41	II Kings 3-4	Psalm 112
5	Acts 20:1-16	II Kings 5-6	Psalm 113
6	Acts 20:17-38	II Kings 7-8	Psalm 114
7	Acts 21:1-17	II Kings 9	Psalm 115
8	Acts 21:18-40	II Kings 10	Psalm 116
9	Acts 22	II Kings 11-12	Psalm 117
10	Acts 23	II Kings 13-14	Psalm 118:1-14
11	Acts 24	II Kings 15	Psalm 118:15-29
12	Acts 25	II Kings 16-17	Psalm 119:1-8
13	Acts 26	II Kings 18	Psalm 119:9-16
14	Acts 27:1-25	II Kings 19-20	Psalm 119:17-24
15	Acts 27:26-44	II Kings 21-22	Psalm 119:25-32
16	Acts 28:1-16	II Kings 23	Psalm 119:33-40
17	Acts 28:17-31	II Kings 24-25	Psalm 119:41-48
18	Romans 1:1-17	I Chronicles 1-2	Psalm 119:49-56
19	Romans 1:18-32	I Chronicles 3-4	Psalm 119:57-64
20	Romans 2	I Chronicles 5	Psalm 119:65-72
21	Romans 3:1-18	I Chronicles 6	Psalm 119:73-80
22	Romans 3:19-31	I Chronicles 7-8	Psalm 119:81-88
23	Romans 4	I Chronicles 9-10	Psalm 119:89-96
24	Romans 5	I Chronicles 11	Psalm 119:97-104
25	Romans 6	I Chronicles 12-13	Psalm 119:105-112
26	Romans 7	I Chronicles 14-15	Psalm 119:113-120
27	Romans 8:1-18	I Chronicles 16	Psalm 119:121-128
28	Romans 8:19-39	I Chronicles 17-18	Psalm 119:129-136
29	Romans 9:1-16	I Chronicles 19-21	Psalm 119:137-144
30	Romans 9:17-33	I Chronicles 22-23	Psalm 119:145-152
31	Romans 10	I Chronicles 24-25	Psalm 119:153-160

DAILY BIBLE READING SCHEDULE

AUGUST			
DAY	NEW TESTAMENT	OLD TESTAMENT (A.M.)	OLD TESTAMENT (P.M.)
1	Romans 11:1-16	I Chronicles 26-27	Psalm 119:161-168
2	Romans 11:17-36	I Chronicles 28-29	Psalm 119:169-176
3	Romans 12	II Chronicles 1-2	Psalm 120
4	Romans 13	II Chronicles 3-5	Psalm 121
5	Romans 14	II Chronicles 6	Psalm 122
6	Romans 15:1-16	II Chronicles 7-8	Psalm 123
7	Romans 15:17-33	II Chronicles 9-10	Psalm 124
8	Romans 16	II Chronicles 11-12	Psalm 125
9	I Corinthians 1	II Chronicles 13-14	Psalm 126
10	I Corinthians 2	II Chronicles 15-17	Psalm 127
11	I Corinthians 3	II Chronicles 18-19	Psalm 128
12	I Corinthians 4	II Chronicles 20	Psalm 129
13	I Corinthians 5	II Chronicles 21-22	Psalm 130
14	I Corinthians 6	II Chronicles 23-24	Psalm 131
15	I Corinthians 7:1-20	II Chronicles 25-26	Psalm 132
16	I Corinthians 7:21-40	II Chronicles 27-28	Psalm 133
17	I Corinthians 8	II Chronicles 29	Psalm 134
18	I Corinthians 9	II Chronicles 30-31	Psalm 135
19	I Corinthians 10:1-17	II Chronicles 32	Psalm 136
20	I Corinthians 10:18-33	II Chronicles 33-34	Psalm 137
21	I Corinthians 11:1-16	II Chronicles 35-36	Psalm 138
22	I Corinthians 11:17-34	Ezra 1-2	Psalm 139:1-13
23	I Corinthians 12:1-13	Ezra 3-5	Psalm 139:14-24
24	I Corinthians 12:14-31	Ezra 6-7	Psalm 140
25	I Corinthians 13	Ezra 8-9	Psalm 141
26	I Corinthians 14:1-20	Ezra 10	Psalm 142
27	I Corinthians 14:21-40	Nehemiah 1-2	Psalm 143
28	I Corinthians 15:1-20	Nehemiah 3-4	Psalm 144
29	I Corinthians 15:21-40	Nehemiah 5-6	Psalm 145
30	I Corinthians 15:41-58	Nehemiah 7-8	Psalm 146
31	I Corinthians 16	Nehemiah 9	Psalm 147:1-11

DAILY BIBLE READING SCHEDULE

		SEPTEMBER	
DAY	**NEW TESTAMENT**	**OLD TESTAMENT (A.M.)**	**OLD TESTAMENT (P.M.)**
1	II Corinthians 1	Nehemiah 10-11	Psalm 147:12-20
2	II Corinthians 2	Nehemiah 12	Psalm 148
3	II Corinthians 3	Nehemiah 13	Psalm 149
4	II Corinthians 4	Esther 1-3	Psalm 150
5	II Corinthians 5	Esther 4-7	Proverbs 1:1-9
6	II Corinthians 6	Esther 8-10	Proverbs 1:10-19
7	II Corinthians 7	Isaiah 1-2	Proverbs 1:20-33
8	II Corinthians 8	Isaiah 3-5	Proverbs 2:1-11
9	II Corinthians 9	Isaiah 6-8	Proverbs 2:12-22
10	II Corinthians 10	Isaiah 9-10	Proverbs 3:1-10
11	II Corinthians 11:1-15	Isaiah 11-13	Proverbs 3:11-24
12	II Corinthians 11:16-33	Isaiah 14-16	Proverbs 3:25-35
13	II Corinthians 12	Isaiah 17-20	Proverbs 4:1-13
14	II Corinthians 13	Isaiah 21-23	Proverbs 4:14-27
15	Galatians 1	Isaiah 24-26	Proverbs 5:1-14
16	Galatians 2	Isaiah 27-29	Proverbs 5:15-23
17	Galatians 3	Isaiah 30-32	Proverbs 6:1-11
18	Galatians 4:1-16	Isaiah 33-35	Proverbs 6:12-22
19	Galatians 4:17-31	Isaiah 36-37	Proverbs 6:23-35
20	Galatians 5	Isaiah 38-40	Proverbs 7:1-12
21	Galatians 6	Isaiah 41-42	Proverbs 7:13-27
22	Ephesians 1	Isaiah 43-44	Proverbs 8:1-18
23	Ephesians 2	Isaiah 45-47	Proverbs 8:19-36
24	Ephesians 3	Isaiah 48-49	Proverbs 9:1-9
25	Ephesians 4:1-16	Isaiah 50-52	Proverbs 9:10-18
26	Ephesians 4:17-32	Isaiah 53-56	Proverbs 10:1-11
27	Ephesians 5:1-17	Isaiah 57-59	Proverbs 10:12-22
28	Ephesians 5:18-33	Isaiah 60-62	Proverbs 10:23-32
29	Ephesians 6	Isaiah 63-64	Proverbs 11:1-10
30	Philippians 1:1-14	Isaiah 65-66	Proverbs 11:11-20

DAILY BIBLE READING SCHEDULE

		OCTOBER	
DAY	NEW TESTAMENT	OLD TESTAMENT (A.M.)	OLD TESTAMENT (P.M.)
1	Philippians 1:15-30	Jeremiah 1-2	Proverbs 11:21-31
2	Philippians 2:1-16	Jeremiah 3-4	Proverbs 12:1-10
3	Philippians 2:17-30	Jeremiah 5-6	Proverbs 12:11-19
4	Philippians 3	Jeremiah 7-8	Proverbs 12:20-28
5	Philippians 4	Jeremiah 9-10	Proverbs 13:1-8
6	Colossians 1	Jeremiah 11-12	Proverbs 13:9-17
7	Colossians 2	Jeremiah 13-14	Proverbs 13:18-25
8	Colossians 3	Jeremiah 15-16	Proverbs 14:1-11
9	Colossians 4	Jeremiah 17-18	Proverbs 14:12-23
10	I Thessalonians 1	Jeremiah 19-20	Proverbs 14:24-35
11	I Thessalonians 2	Jeremiah 21-22	Proverbs 15:1-11
12	I Thessalonians 3	Jeremiah 23	Proverbs 15:12-22
13	I Thessalonians 4	Jeremiah 24-25	Proverbs 15:23-33
14	I Thessalonians 5	Jeremiah 26-27	Proverbs 16:1-11
15	II Thessalonians 1	Jeremiah 28-29	Proverbs 16:12-22
16	II Thessalonians 2	Jeremiah 30-31	Proverbs 16:23-33
17	II Thessalonians 3	Jeremiah 32	Proverbs 17:1-9
18	I Timothy 1	Jeremiah 33-34	Proverbs 17:10-18
19	I Timothy 2	Jeremiah 35-36	Proverbs 17:19-28
20	I Timothy 3	Jeremiah 37-38	Proverbs 18:1-8
21	I Timothy 4	Jeremiah 39-40	Proverbs 18:9-16
22	I Timothy 5	Jeremiah 41-42	Proverbs 18:17-24
23	I Timothy 6	Jeremiah 43-44	Proverbs 19:1-9
24	II Timothy 1	Jeremiah 45-47	Proverbs 19:10-19
25	II Timothy 2	Jeremiah 48	Proverbs 19:20-29
26	II Timothy 3	Jeremiah 49	Proverbs 20:1-10
27	II Timothy 4	Jeremiah 50	Proverbs 20:11-20
28	Titus 1	Jeremiah 51	Proverbs 20:21-30
29	Titus 2	Jeremiah 52	Proverbs 21:1-10
30	Titus 3	Lamentations 1-2	Proverbs 21:11-20
31	Philemon	Lamentations 3	Proverbs 21:21-31

DAILY BIBLE READING SCHEDULE

DAY	NEW TESTAMENT	OLD TESTAMENT (A.M.)	OLD TESTAMENT (P.M.)
		NOVEMBER	
1	Hebrews 1	Lamentations 4-5	Proverbs 22:1-9
2	Hebrews 2	Ezekiel 1-2	Proverbs 22:10-19
3	Hebrews 3	Ezekiel 3-4	Proverbs 22:20-29
4	Hebrews 4	Ezekiel 5-6	Proverbs 23:1-12
5	Hebrews 5	Ezekiel 7-8	Proverbs 23:13-23
6	Hebrews 6	Ezekiel 9-10	Proverbs 23:24-35
7	Hebrews 7	Ezekiel 11-12	Proverbs 24:1-9
8	Hebrews 8	Ezekiel 13-15	Proverbs 24:10-18
9	Hebrews 9	Ezekiel 16	Proverbs 24:19-26
10	Hebrews 10:1-18	Ezekiel 17-18	Proverbs 24:27-34
11	Hebrews 10:19-39	Ezekiel 19-20	Proverbs 25:1-7
12	Hebrews 11:1-20	Ezekiel 21-22	Proverbs 25:8-14
13	Hebrews 11:21-40	Ezekiel 23	Proverbs 25:15-20
14	Hebrews 12	Ezekiel 24-25	Proverbs 25:21-28
15	Hebrews 13	Ezekiel 26-27	Proverbs 26:1-7
16	James 1	Ezekiel 28-29	Proverbs 26:8-12
17	James 2	Ezekiel 30-31	Proverbs 26:13-19
18	James 3	Ezekiel 32-33	Proverbs 26:20-28
19	James 4	Ezekiel 34-35	Proverbs 27:1-7
20	James 5	Ezekiel 36-37	Proverbs 27:8-14
21	I Peter 1	Ezekiel 38-39	Proverbs 27:15-21
22	I Peter 2	Ezekiel 40	Proverbs 27:22-27
23	I Peter 3	Ezekiel 41-42	Proverbs 28:1-7
24	I Peter 4	Ezekiel 43-44	Proverbs 28:8-14
25	I Peter 5	Ezekiel 45-46	Proverbs 28:15-21
26	II Peter 1	Ezekiel 47-48	Proverbs 28:22-28
27	II Peter 2	Daniel 1	Proverbs 29:1-7
28	II Peter 3	Daniel 2	Proverbs 29:8-14
29	I John 1	Daniel 3	Proverbs 29:15-21
30	I John 2:1-14	Daniel 4	Proverbs 29:22-27

DAILY BIBLE READING SCHEDULE

		DECEMBER	
DAY	NEW TESTAMENT	OLD TESTAMENT (A.M.)	OLD TESTAMENT (P.M.)
1	I John 2:15-29	Daniel 5-6	Proverbs 30:1-9
2	I John 3	Daniel 7-8	Proverbs 30:10-16
3	I John 4	Daniel 9-10	Proverbs 30:17-23
4	I John 5	Daniel 11-12	Proverbs 30:24-33
5	II John	Hosea 1-2	Proverbs 31:1-9
6	III John	Hosea 3-5	Proverbs 31:10-16
7	Jude	Hosea 6-8	Proverbs 31:17-23
8	Revelation 1	Hosea 9-11	Proverbs 31:24-31
9	Revelation 2:1-17	Hosea 12-14	Ecclesiastes 1
10	Revelation 2:18-29	Joel 1-2	Ecclesiastes 2:1-11
11	Revelation 3	Joel 3	Ecclesiastes 2:12-26
12	Revelation 4	Amos 1-3	Ecclesiastes 3:1-11
13	Revelation 5	Amos 4-6	Ecclesiastes 3:12-22
14	Revelation 6	Amos 7-9	Ecclesiastes 4
15	Revelation 7	Obadiah	Ecclesiastes 5
16	Revelation 8	Jonah 1-4	Ecclesiastes 6
17	Revelation 9	Micah 1-3	Ecclesiastes 7:1-15
18	Revelation 10	Micah 4-5	Ecclesiastes 7:16-29
19	Revelation 11	Micah 6-7	Ecclesiastes 8
20	Revelation 12	Nahum 1-3	Ecclesiastes 9
21	Revelation 13	Habakkuk 1-3	Ecclesiastes 10
22	Revelation 14	Zephaniah 1-3	Ecclesiastes 11
23	Revelation 15	Haggai 1-2	Ecclesiastes 12
24	Revelation 16	Zechariah 1-2	Song of Solomon 1
25	Matthew 1, Luke 2	Zechariah 3-5	Song of Solomon 2
26	Revelation 17	Zechariah 6-8	Song of Solomon 3
27	Revelation 18	Zechariah 9-10	Song of Solomon 4
28	Revelation 19	Zechariah 11-12	Song of Solomon 5
29	Revelation 20	Zechariah 13-14	Song of Solomon 6
30	Revelation 21	Malachi 1-2	Song of Solomon 7
31	Revelation 22	Malachi 3-4	Song of Solomon 8

ABOUT THE AUTHOR

 Since entering the ministry in 1993, Dave Olson has served the Lord in many capacities. After heading up a Christian school, teaching in Bible college, and serving as a pastor, God called Dave into missions. He and his family faithfully served the Lord as missionaries to Zambia, Africa for ten years until a series of ongoing health problems and life-threatening illnesses led to their return in 2012.

In early 2013, the Lord led Dave to focus on a writing ministry, and his books are now used at home and abroad. Dave's experience as an educator and preacher has uniquely equipped him to communicate God's truths to people from every walk of life. In addition to his writing ministry, Dave preaches in revivals, missions conferences, and special meetings across the country.

Visit www.help4Upublications.com for more titles.

Consider Another Devotional by Dave Olson:

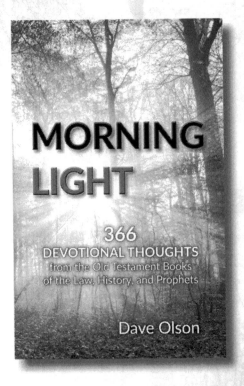

Get ready to take a journey through many of the Old Testament books. *Morning Light* starts in Genesis and includes the books of the Law, History, and Prophets. A practical thought from an assigned daily Scripture reading will challenge you each day. Whether you choose to use *Morning Light* for personal or family devotions, you will develop a better understanding of the Bible and find practical insight for daily living. (206 pages)

62036459R00115

Made in the USA
Middletown, DE
18 January 2018